The

CG CAHPS
Handbook

A Guide to Improve Patient
Experience and Clinical Outcomes

By
Jeff Morris, MD, MBA, FACS
Barbara Hotko, RN, MPA
Matthew Bates, MPH

Published by:
Fire Starter Publishing
350 W. Cedar Street
Pensacola, FL 32502
Phone: 866-354-3473
Fax: 850-332-5117
www.firestarterpublishing.com

ISBN: 978-1-622-18007-3

Library of Congress Control Number: 2015932028

Printed in the United States of America

This book is dedicated to the providers who share their endless passion and commitment with the patients and communities that trust them for their care.

TABLE OF CONTENTS

- Fundamental Tactic: Key Words at Key Times
- Fundamental Tactic: Individualized Patient Care (IPC)
- Fundamental Tactic: AIDET® (the Five Fundamentals of Communication)
- Fundamental Tactic: Managing Up
- Fundamental Tactic: Service Recovery/CARE℠
- Fundamental Tactic: Rounding
- Fundamental Tactic: Employee/Provider Selection

SECTION ONE: ACCESS TO CARE: PROVIDING APPOINTMENTS, CARE, AND INFORMATION

    Questions Covered in Chapter:
        - When you phoned this provider's office to get an appointment for care you needed right away, how often did you get an appointment as soon as you needed?
        - When you made an appointment for a check-up or routine care with this provider, how often did you get an appointment as soon as you needed?

Key Tactics:
- Tactic 1: Keep Patient-Centric Hours
- Tactic 2: Use Care Templates to Standardize Scheduling
- Tactic 3: Move to Open Access Scheduling

Questions Covered in Chapter:
- When you phoned this provider's office during regular office hours, how often did you get an answer to your medical question that same day?
- When you phoned this provider's office after regular hours, how often did you get an answer to your medical question as soon as you needed?

Key Tactics:
- Tactic 1: Track Calls to Find Where Process Improvements Are Needed
- Tactic 2: Implement AIDET® in Answering Medical Questions
- Tactic 3: Centralize Your Phone System
- Tactic 4: Equip After-Hours Call Team to Quickly Respond to Patient Questions

Question Covered in Chapter:
- How often did you see this provider within 15 minutes of your appointment time?

Key Tactics:
- Tactic 1: Daily Huddles
- Tactic 2: Implement Visit Status Boards
- Tactic 3: Use Reception Area Updates and Room and Round℠ to Manage Waits and Delays
- Tactic 4: Care Coordination and Handovers

SECTION TWO: PRACTICING GOOD PROVIDER/PATIENT COMMUNICATION

Question Covered in Chapter:
- How often did this provider explain things in a way that was easy to understand?

Key Tactics:
- Tactic 1: Provide Written Information for the Patient
- Tactic 2: Create a Shared Care Plan
- Tactic 3: Teach Back Method
- Tactic 4: Focus on "E" in AIDET®

Question Covered in Chapter:
- How often did this provider listen carefully to you?

Key Tactics:
- Tactic 1: Follow the Two-Minute Rule
- Tactic 2: Focus on the "A" in AIDET®
- Tactic 3: Use Key Words at Key Times to Demonstrate Careful Listening

Question Covered in Chapter:
- How often did this provider give you easy-to-understand information about health questions or concerns?

Key Tactics:
- Tactic 1: Focus on the "E" in AIDET®
- Tactic 2: Use the Teach Back Method When Answering Patient Questions

A WORD FROM
THE AUTHORS

All three of us are patients. We go to a care provider for annual check-ups, make appointments for minor illnesses, follow up after medical tests. We take our children and our elderly parents to the doctor. We accompany friends who need support. Because we've "been there" we know: The experience we have at the provider's office makes a difference. It makes a difference in how we feel about the provider, our confidence level in being a partner in our own care, and, yes, in our clinical outcomes.

Because we are patients, we are advocates for patients. And because we are healthcare professionals too, we know that the well-being of patients is intertwined with the well-being of the physicians, nurse practitioners, physician assistants, nurses, and staff who care for them. That's why we wrote this book: to better serve those who serve the patient. Our mission is to make healthcare better for care providers to practice medicine and for patients to receive the care they deserve—the same care you want to receive when you visit your provider and the care you most certainly want your family members to receive.

Look at the cover of *The CG CAHPS Handbook* and you'll see it's coauthored by Jeff Morris, Barbara Hotko, and Matthew Bates. While it is true that the three of us put the book together (along with several more contributors, editors, and other helpful souls), many talented and hardworking people deserve to share the credit.

We are only the distillers and reporters of the content in this book. The hard work—the *real* work—was done by the following two groups who have our eternal gratitude:

a. the organizations we've worked with over the years, along with the 100,000-plus providers who work with these organizations, that provided the fertile field for these tactics to take root and grow

b. the Studer Group® Physician Services Team, who discovered, harvested, and collaborated to share the tactics described in this book

The men and women collectively known as Studer Group have spent years doing intensive research in our national Learning Lab of 1,000-plus healthcare organizations. They are masters at discovering what the people inside these organizations are doing right—mapping it out and taking that message to others in the field to be able to produce quality results.

The knowledge that our coaches refine and share has evolved over time. The tactics in this book will continue to evolve as changes in healthcare and the external environment place ever-increasing demands on organizations.

We believe the organizations we coach are comprised of many of the finest healthcare professionals in the world. It is their dedication, their passion for helping others, and their generosity of spirit that made this book possible. Every day, they work tirelessly to provide better and better care to the patients they serve.

To both these groups we offer our deepest appreciation. This relationship is truly a partnership where both parties are enriched by the work of the other—and the real beneficiaries are the patients, their families, and the communities they serve. May we continue to care for them for many years to come.

Jeff, Barbara, and Matthew

Introduction

"It isn't hard to be good from time to time;
what's tough is being good every day."
—*Willie Mays*

Over the last 15 years, Studer Group® has been privileged to work with more than 1,000 healthcare organizations that, in turn, touch more than 200,000 practicing providers across the U.S. Throughout this journey, we have helped clinicians and groups—from small practices with just a handful of providers to large, system-affiliated groups with well over 1,000 providers—improve their patient experience and achieve high quality while delivering cost-effective care.

During this time, we have studied the impact patient experience has on the delivery of high-quality, cost-effective care. What we realized early on is that patient experience and quality are deeply intertwined—in fact, they are two sides of the same coin. This impression has been substantiated over and over again through the years.

This is why Studer Group has never claimed to be a patient satisfaction company. We've always viewed "experience" through the lens of an organization's ability to deliver high-quality, patient-centered care. Clinician and Group Consumer Assessment of Healthcare Providers and Systems (CG CAHPS) is no exception. And so we approach this book from the standpoint that its results are a metric that represents a patient's perception of *quality* care.

It has been clear to us for a long time that CG CAHPS is about more than just "patient satisfaction surveys"— and that it will play an increasingly important role as transparency is expanded in the public arena and healthcare reforms move forward.

Most of the organizations we coach have also been focusing on the role of CG CAHPS questions within their practices. Even before the survey was adopted by public and private payers, many of the leaders of practices we worked with were asking questions about provider communication, access to timely appointments and information, and courtesy of their office staff—and have been benchmarking their performance against the results.

Through our Learning Lab, which is derived from a network of exceptional organizations, we've been able to test, validate, and harvest "leading practices" for CG CAHPS. During this process, we've paid careful attention not only to which practices improve results but also to their ability to sustain those results over time. What's more, we've worked to identify the best tactics that work across practices, regardless of type or size.

We have been privileged enough to talk with some of the smartest people working in healthcare today, experts known not only for their wisdom but also for their burning commitment to make healthcare better. These "fire starters" represent the most passionate and high-achieving leaders we have met during our journey. These are the leaders who, upon reaching ever-higher levels of achievement on CG CAHPS and other patient-centered outcomes, continue to push their organizations to move from good to great.

What we have learned in this process is that many of those tactics that Studer Group coaches healthcare organizations to adopt and hardwire on the inpatient side can also be leveraged, with minor tweaks, to improve and sustain high CG CAHPS results. We have also developed new tactics in conjunction with hospitals and physician practices that have been tested and honed in the crucible of real-world patient care delivery. And we have reconfirmed, once again, what we already knew: that a strong focus on a) connecting people to the *why* behind changes (the well-being of the patients) and b) holding them accountable for consistently executing outcomes-based tactics are pivotal to success.

Most important, we have learned that often, less is more.

A consistent theme that's emerged from our work has been that selecting just a few tactics and focusing on hardwiring them produces better results than trying to adopt many new practices at once. The mistake of trying to do too much at one time is so common many of our partners have developed a name for it: *flavor of the month.* Most of our highest performing CG CAHPS partners have, in fact, focused on just three or four tactics for years in their own journey.

So how do you know if you have hardwired a tactic in your own group? The test is actually pretty easy: Just ask, "Do patients and their families *always* receive care consistent with our standards and adopted practices?" The difficult part is the word *always.* When we at Studer Group say *always,* we have to ask ourselves whether patients who are seen on Saturday morning, or whose calls get returned at 3:00 a.m., or who talk to a temporary provider covering the phones on a holiday weekend receive the same standard of care that we hold ourselves accountable for at 10:00 a.m. on Monday. And do they recognize the consistent high standard of care and report it as such?

While this book is focused on improving CG CAHPS outcomes, it is critical to remember that these efforts are about far more than a practice's performance on the survey itself. Working toward favorable CG CAHPS outcomes is about meeting the patient's (and family's) *what.* The "what" is that one thing that is foremost in a patient's mind—the most important thing that, if addressed by providers, will make him or her feel listened to, understood, and cared for. In other words, it's about measuring how consistently we deliver on things that matter to our patients—how often we *always* deliver on their expectations.

And here is an interesting point: We have found that practices that receive the highest results on CG CAHPS do so *without* a care provider ordering more tests or prescribing more medications to meet patient demands. Indeed, they are actually lower utilizers of many of these services than their peers. In our experience, the idea that patients are seeking a lot of "extras" is a misconception. The vast majority of patients just want to understand *why* their provider is recommending something or nothing at all.

For example, some patients who enter a provider's office with a common cold will ask for antibiotics. This is a fact. But many providers we work with do not prescribe the antibiotics the patient wants (because a cold is viral)—yet still receive high CG CAHPS results. This is because they have worked to find more effective ways to communicate with their patients so that they leave satisfied that the diagnosis and treatment they received were the right ones.

Of course, getting to this point means hardwiring the best possible communication tactics and behaviors—specifically, the ones we cover in this book. And that, in turn, requires leadership practices that simultaneously engage providers and staff members and instill the sense of accountability that drives the desired behaviors.

Perhaps the biggest challenge in improving CG CAHPS results is making the internal shift to a focus on engagement and accountability that is required to become an *always* culture. *Always* is a high standard to achieve, and the culture required both to develop and sustain this is hard to create. It takes many of our partners years to create an *always* culture and hardwire it for sustainability. *Always* literally requires that every member of the team gets it right with every patient and their family every time.

An *always* culture is challenging to create in any industry, and healthcare is no different. Yet difficulty cannot become our excuse for accepting less—on the contrary, it needs to become our calling to deliver more. Given that our industry's reason for existence is to care for people, can we accept anything less?

At Studer Group we have developed a set of strategic tactics and processes that, together, help organizations create just this kind of culture change. You will learn more about this leadership framework in the following pages. For now, just know that the goal is to help make your practice incredibly agile and responsive—well aligned and motivated to respond to the new demands that come your way (and, of course, in an era of continuous change, there will be *many* such demands) in a fast and effective manner.

At Studer Group, our mission is to make healthcare a better place for employees to work, physicians to practice medicine, and patients to receive care. We know this is a mission that you share.

We trust that you will find this book helpful on your own journey to achieve better patient outcomes and become a high-performing organization. This is *always* the goal. The fact that your efforts improve CG CAHPS results and a strong reputation in the community are simply validation that you're serving your patients well.

CHAPTER ONE:

CG CAHPS 101: WHAT IT IS AND WHY IT MATTERS

"Where the art of medicine is loved,
there is also a love of humanity."

—*Hippocrates*

The *New York Times* recently published an op-ed piece titled "Doctor, Shut Up and Listen," written by Nirmal Joshi, the chief medical officer for Pinnacle Health System. The article makes it clear that there is room for improvement in the listening and communication skills of many physicians. (Indeed, Joshi goes on to discuss the physician-training program he and his colleagues put in place and shares the dramatic improvement in patient satisfaction that resulted.)

Yet, this is far from a bad news piece. Its conclusion is a story that illustrates just how powerful it is when a physician takes the time to truly connect with patients—

and the extent to which he or she can impact outcomes. In Joshi's words, "A good bedside manner is simply good medicine."

A passionate diabetes specialist told me how she sat down with a patient to understand why he was not using his diabetes medications regularly, despite numerous hospital admissions for complications.

"I can't continue to do this anymore," he told her, on the verge of tears. "I've just given up."

She placed a hand on his shoulder and just sat with him. After a pause, she said: "You have a heart that still beats and legs you can still walk on—many of my patients don't have that privilege."

Five years later, recalling this episode, her patient credits her with inspiring him to take better care of himself. The entire encounter took less than five minutes.[1]

Moments like these are why people choose to practice medicine. All physicians, physician assistants, nurse practitioners, and the staff members who work with them want to provide the best possible care to patients. It's not just what they do; it's who they are. They train for years and years to examine, diagnose, and treat patients, and everything they do flows from a sincere desire to put that knowledge to work in a way that provides great clinical outcomes.

And it's not just about facts, data, and metrics. Providers *care* about patients! It's difficult to see people in pain and not want to help them get better, to hear them crying and not want to comfort them, to see them struggling with chronic conditions and not want to help them improve their lives. So they *want* patients to have a good experience—but for a variety of reasons this goal isn't always met.

Now that public reporting for CG CAHPS has begun, it's time to bring providers' good intentions together with practical tools that are proven to create better patient experiences and, simultaneously, better clinical quality. That's why we wrote *The CG CAHPS Handbook*.

Later on in this chapter, we'll go into more detail about the survey, but for right now we'll just hit the high spots. Clinician and Group Consumer Assessment of Healthcare Providers and Systems (CG CAHPS) is a family of surveys, built around common core questions that each serve as a standardized tool to measure patients' perception of care given by physicians and other providers in an office setting.

The Physician Compare website (http://www.medicare.gov/physiciancompare/) reports CG CAHPS results, along with certain quality metrics, for provider offices that see Medicare patients. Much like the Hospital Compare website, Physician Compare is designed to help consumers make informed decisions on where to receive care.

Another public CG CAHPS database available today is hosted by AHRQ. They have posted aggregate data for CG CAHPS surveys, and the data can be found at: https://cahpsdatabase.ahrq.gov/CAHPSIDB/Public/CG/CG_About.aspx.

Many practices are finding that conducting CG CAHPS surveys is becoming required to maximize Medicare, Medicaid, and private payer payments.

We at Studer Group® strongly feel that all provider practices need to focus heavily (sooner rather than later) on the patient experience as measured by CG CAHPS surveys. As we'll discuss shortly, there are strong correlations between a patient's perception of care—i.e., her "experience"—and her clinical outcomes. In other words, when we improve experience, we also improve quality. This, alone, is a compelling reason to prepare for CG CAHPS right now.

Another reason, of course, is financial. We all know that healthcare as an industry is moving toward value-based payment models. We also know that performance isn't measured only by clinical numbers but also by patient experience. Some private payers, Medicare Advantage plans, and Medicaid managed care plans have already linked provider payments to CG CAHPS results. And CMS is moving to requiring CG CAHPS public reporting for all providers who treat Medicare patients over the next couple of years.

Certainly, where a practice falls on the Physician Compare website will have an impact on its reputation and, ultimately, on the number of patients who will frequent it. Also, of course, practices that provide a positive patient experience get more return business, more referrals, and better word of mouth.

Our experience has shown us that practices that are early adopters in conducting CG CAHPS surveys not only achieve better results but sustain higher performance against their peers when reporting becomes mandatory. And the sooner you implement the most impactful evidence-based tools and tactics—in the right order and with the right coaching—the sooner you'll see your results start to trend upward.

Studer Group has been focused on the patient experience since our beginning in 1999. Over the years we have gathered a wealth of evidence from our Learning Lab—made up of over 1,000 healthcare organizations—on which tools and tactics most affect how patients perceive their care. This book presents only the most powerful ones—the idea being to *not* overwhelm readers but to provide the fewest possible tactics that are nonetheless impactful enough to help practices meet their goals.

Not only that, we've developed and refined a framework—Evidence-Based Leadership[SM] (EBL)—that helps organizations reduce variation in their leadership skills and practices to achieve a culture of high performance. This framework aligns organizational goals, behaviors, and processes in a way that moves and sustains results. It provides the structure for hardwiring the tactics described in this book, and it aligns the culture with a strong sense of accountability for executing them.

Once EBL is hardwired into a medical practice or any other organization, leaders have the right skill set to introduce changes—and providers (doctors along with PAs and NPs) and staff have the right mindset to quickly embrace and master them.

We'll talk more about this in Chapter 15. For now, let's explore what makes CG CAHPS such a pivotal part of the future of healthcare.

The Evidence: Why CG CAHPS Matters

The Institute of Medicine's 2001 "Crossing the Quality Chasm" report identified patient-centeredness as a key healthcare quality aim.[2] Since this time, patient-centered care has gained significant recognition across the healthcare industry, and measuring patient experience is becoming a keystone component of both certification and compensation programs.

Now, CG CAHPS is rapidly emerging as the national standard for measuring patient experience in the ambulatory settings for both quality and business reasons. Here's why:

The Quality Case for CG CAHPS

For most healthcare professionals, providing quality care is the reason driving everything we do. There is plenty of research suggesting that patient experience and quality are two sides of the same coin. When you focus on one, the other also improves. Consider the following evidence:

Patient experience and clinical quality process of care are related. While patient experience measures reveal how the patient perceived the care they received, these factors are not independent of clinical quality measures. Patient experience at both the provider and practice levels has been shown to be positively correlated with process of care measures for disease management and prevention.[3]

Patient experience is positively correlated with patient engagement and adherence.[4,5] It stands to reason that when a patient feels good about his relationship with a provider, he is more likely to pay attention to what the provider has to say and also to conform to the care plan. This is particularly important in treating patients with chronic conditions where patient commitment and action are critical to achieving positive outcomes.

For example, one study found that "adherence rates were 2.6 times higher among primary care patients whose providers had 'whole person' knowledge of them (95th percentile), compared to patients of providers without that familiarity (5th percentile)."[6]

Patient experience is positively correlated with better health outcomes.[7,8] In one study, patient's perception of care was found to be directly linked to improved blood sugar control in diabetic patients.[9] In another study, positive primary care follow-up was found to offset poor hospital experience and outcomes.[10]

Public reporting of patient experience data has been shown to drive provider quality improvement.[11] As CMS, states, and other public and private enterprises publish CG CAHPS data, they are working to create transparency and the improvement in quality that follows.

Patient experience measurement identifies systemic quality issues. For example, at one of Studer Group's partner organizations, it revealed gaps in communicating lab results. Later, it showed that the processes put in place to fix those issues were working. Specifically, communication between members of the care team is correlated with clinical performance measures.[12]

The American Board of Medical Specialties (ABMS) has endorsed the adoption of CG CAHPS questions as part of the Maintenance of Certification (MOC) process for its 24-member boards.[13] Specifically, collection of CG CAHPS survey data will fulfill some of the Part IV Performance Assessment requirements for MOC.[14]

The Business Case for CG CAHPS

Focusing on CG CAHPS and taking action to improve results can help practices directly maximize reimbursement in the future, but can also immediately create an environment that helps maximize efficiency, keeps patients happy and healthy, sparks growth, and reduces the likelihood of litigation. Consider the following facts:

CG CAHPS is tied to financial incentives/value-based purchasing (VBP) with payers.

- **Centers for Medicare and Medicaid Services (CMS)** started collecting baseline data related to CG CAHPS for many programs in 2014 and has proposed starting to link CG CAHPS to specific payments for FY2015. These programs include:

- Medicare Shared Savings Program (MSSP)
- Medicare Pioneer ACO Model
- Physician Quality Reporting Systems (PQRS)
- Comprehensive Primary Care (CPC) Initiative
- Multi-payer Advanced Primary Care Practice (MAPCP)
- Federally Qualified Health Centers (FQHC) Advanced Primary Care Practice Demonstration

- **Medicaid and Children's Health Insurance Programs (CHIP)** in many states are leveraging the CG CAHPS surveys instrument in either pilot or full adoption models. In many of these states, this is being done as part of Patient Certified Medical Home (PCMH) programs.

- **Some private payers** are using survey results to determine reimbursements. For example, Blue Cross Blue Shield of Massachusetts has created an Alternative Quality Contract compensation model that ties a portion of payment to CG CAHPS survey results.[15] Similarly, the Integrated Healthcare Association in California, which ran the largest non-government pay-for-performance (P4P) program in the United States in 2014, uses the survey results in its performance calculations.[16]

Measuring and improving patient experience contributes to a high-quality culture. According to one study, "a quality-centered culture and outside reporting of results are the strongest predictors of high-performing medical practices."[17] By measuring and reporting patient experience, you will help achieve both of these conditions. Additionally, patients and staff are perceptive of clinician attitude, and a negative attitude will not only be reflected in lower patient experience scores but also in higher employee turnover and lower staff productivity.[18]

Patient experience drives patient retention and growth. It just makes sense that patients will stay with providers with whom they have had positive experiences and leave when they have negative experiences. One study found that "patients who have poor-quality relationships with their providers are three times more likely to voluntarily leave the practice vs. those with high-quality relationships."[19] Another showed that "treatment with respect, the rating of care received, and the helpfulness of the person at the front desk are the strongest predictors of patient satisfaction...patient satisfaction is highly correlated with intent to return and intent to recommend services."[20]

Patient experience is correlated with lower malpractice risk.[21,22,23] In one study, researchers found that 46 percent of malpractice risk was linked to physician-specific characteristics, including patient experience.[24]

The Measure Applications Partnership (MAP) has advised the Department of Health and Hu-

man Services (HHS) to consider CG CAHPS
across all clinician performance measurement
programs. The MAP was created under the Afford-
able Care Act and addressed CG CAHPS in their initial
report, "Coordination Strategy for Clinical Performance
Measurement" in 2011. The report states, "The addition
of Clinician-Group CAHPS…would greatly enhance
the measure set."[25]

National Committee for Quality Assurance
(NCQA) and Utilization Review Accreditation
Commission (URAC) require Patient-Centered
Medical Homes (PCMHs) they recognize to con-
duct patient experience surveys. Certification by
NCQA and/or URAC is, in turn, critical to a provider's
ability to participate in many emerging ACO and PCMH
plans with both private and public payers.

A Brief Introduction to CG CAHPS

Now let's talk about CG CAHPS itself. The Clinician
and Group Consumer Assessment of Healthcare Providers and Systems is a family of surveys that measure patient experience with healthcare in a provider practice
setting. There are separate CAHPS surveys designed
to address patient experience in other care delivery settings, including the hospital (HCAHPS), the Emergency
Department (ED CAHPS/ED PECS), Surgical Care
(S CAHPS), Home Health (HH CAHPS), and Nursing
Homes (LTC CAHPS).

CAHPS surveys provide feedback for those areas in which patients (that is, healthcare consumers) are the best or only source of information. The surveys were developed and released into the public domain by the Agency for Healthcare Research and Quality (AHRQ). The acronym "CAHPS®" is a registered trademark of AHRQ.

To be clear, CAHPS surveys are not patient satisfaction surveys. Rather, they focus on the patient experience by measuring how often the care providers demonstrated behaviors that result in quality patient care and service.

What We've Learned from HCAHPS

For the past few years, we at Studer Group have worked with healthcare organizations seeking to hardwire the tools and tactics that improve HCAHPS results. Here are some of the lessons we've learned:

- Of all the components in the value-based purchasing initiative (which also includes process of care, outcomes, and efficiency measures), patient experience is the toughest to move.

- If an organization isn't improving, it's falling behind. Government and patient expectations create a "downward-moving escalator" effect: There is no way to stand still and maintain great results.

- Patient experience results correlate with quality results. For example, when we at Studer Group compare hospitals that patients rated in the top quartile for the HCAHPS responsiveness question, we found they experienced the lowest number of pressure ulcers. This also holds true for infections and manifestations of poor glycemic control.

- A great operating system is needed to drive accountability and thus consistent results. At least in part because of our Evidence-Based Leadership framework, organizations coached by Studer Group outperform the nation on HCAHPS measures by an average of 23 percentile points, outpace it in improvements at a speed of nearly 50 percent faster, and also beat the national average in every core measure.

The survey results from CG CAHPS can be used broadly to address two strategic needs:

1. To improve the quality of care provided by individual providers, sites of care, medical groups, or provider networks

2. To provide information to healthcare consumers and payers to help them choose physicians and other healthcare providers, physician practices, or medical groups

"Clinicians and Groups" can be a confusing label for this set of CAHPS surveys. We often get questions as to whose performance these surveys are really meant to measure. The answer is "providers," which could be a doctor, nurse practitioner, or physician assistant. The surveys work for a wide range of doctors, including Doctors of Medicine, Doctors of Osteopathy, Doctors of Podiatric Medicine, and Doctors of Chiropractic.

CG CAHPS History

Today's CG CAHPS survey has its roots in work that was begun in the 1990s to develop a CAHPS survey for group practices via several initiatives.[26,27] Around this same time, the CAHPS Consortium, working with the California HealthCare Foundation, developed a preliminary survey instrument known as the CAHPS Group Practices Survey (G-CAHPS), which was published in 1999.

The CAHPS Consortium, supported by the AHRQ, continued to evolve the instrument in the 2000s (as part of the CAHPS II grant) at which time it became known as the Ambulatory Care CAHPS (A-CAHPS) survey.[28,29,30,31,32] The evolution was guided by the A-CAHPS Advisory Group, whose members participated in the development process on an ongoing basis by providing input into both content issues (e.g., composites, topics within composites, item content, and response scales) as well as survey administration issues (e.g., telephone versus mail, sample sizes, frequency of surveys). The A-CAHPS Advisory Group included members from the American Board of

Medical Specialties, the American Board of Internal Medicine, the American Medical Group Association, and the Medical Group Management Association among others.

On August 18, 2004, AHRQ issued notice in the Federal Register that the A-CAHPS survey was ready for field testing. More than a dozen physician groups participated.[33]

In March of 2006, AHRQ formally launched the 1.0 version of the Clinician & Group CAHPS instrument into the public domain. In July 2007, the National Quality Forum (NQF) endorsed the 1.0 version of the Clinician & Group Survey as a measure of patient experience with ambulatory care.

AHRQ has continued to work with stakeholders to study and evolve the CG CAHPS instruments [34,35,36] and released version 2.0 of the surveys in October 2011. Important to the release of version 2.0 was the clarification of Core Questions & Supplemental Questions, along with the use of the word *provider* (in place of *doctor*). While all CG CAHPS surveys should incorporate the core questions, the supplemental questions allow flexibility to meet the needs of various stakeholders and address areas such as culture competency, health information technology, health literacy, and patient-centered medical homes.

AHRQ has also helped develop and release two more ambulatory/CG CAHPS-related surveys in recent years: the CAHPS Patient-Centered Medical

Home (PCMH CAHPS) survey[37] and the CAHPS Surgical Care Survey (S CAHPS).[38,39] In addition, the Health Plan CAHPS surveys for commercial, Medicaid, and Medicare Advantage insured also share several questions with CG CAHPS.

As we look forward, AHRQ is working on CG CAHPS version 3.0 with a wide range of stakeholders. Proposed changes for version 3.0 include a couple adjustments to the core questions, reducing the length of the surveys, and changing all the longitudinal surveys to six months. They are currently planning to release version 3.0 sometime in late 2015.

Understanding the CG CAHPS Family

CG CAHPS is best viewed as a family of surveys designed to evaluate patient experience in an ambulatory clinical setting. There are multiple surveys in the family, and it is important that we become familiar with them so we pick the right tool for our needs. This is critically important: Different payer organizations and clinical needs may require different CG CAHPS surveys for the patients in your practice.

There are several major variations of the CG CAHPS surveys:

- Longitudinal (6 or 12 months) *or* Episodic (Single Visit)

- Adult (18+) *or* Child (<18)

- Core Questions *or* Core + Supplemental Questions

Here, we'll discuss each one.

Longitudinal *or* Single Visit?

One set of the CG CAHPS surveys is designed to measure patient experience longitudinally (i.e., over a period of time), and one set is designed to measure a single clinic visit. In practice, most everyone is using the surveys designed to measure over a longitudinal time period.

In addition, every CG CAHPS-related payer initiative in which Studer Group partners are participating requires the longitudinal surveys. Therefore, we will focus on the "longitudinal" surveys throughout this book and strongly recommend you do as well. However, almost everything we will discuss can be applied to the single visit surveys should you use them.

Adult *or* Child?

The adult survey is designed for individuals who are 18 or older. It has been adjusted to support use with children (under 18 years of age) by expanding the provider communication composite, adding two more composites and phrasing questions to the parents instead of the patient (i.e., the child).

The expanded Provider Communication composite has four additional *never, sometimes, usually,* and *always* questions.

The new composites are Provider's Attention to Your Child's Growth and Development, consisting of six yes/no questions, and Provider's Advice on Keeping Your Child Safe and Healthy, consisting of five yes/no questions. We have not covered these 11 questions in this book as we believe they primarily represent a checklist of 11 items for a provider to discuss with a child's parent or guardian.

If you are implementing CG CAHPS in a practice that includes pediatrics, we suggest you review these questions and ensure that they are covered in your checklist of standard questions that providers discuss with their patients. The core questions and survey can be found in the Appendix of this book.

Core Questions *or* Core + Supplemental Questions?

One critical concept to understand about CG CAHPS is that there are two sets of questions: "core questions" designed to be asked as part of every CG CAHPS survey and supplemental questions designed to be utilized based on specific needs (e.g., Patient-Centered Medical Homes).

Figure 1.1 Formula for CG CAHPS Survey

Every CG CAHPS survey should contain the core questions. This across-the-board consistency makes it possible to compare results between providers and across different versions of the surveys.

There are 34 total core questions in the 12-month CG CAHPS version 2.0 survey for adults. Only 15 of these questions are the critical questions that are normally reported as measures of patient experience rolled up into five overall composites: Access to Care/Information, Provider Communication, Office Staff Courtesy/Helpfulness, Lab Results Follow-up, and Overall Rating of Provider.

Getting Timely Appointments, Care, and Information (Access)
• Getting appointments for urgent care
• Getting appointments for routine care or check-ups
• Getting an answer to a medical question during regular office hours
• Getting an answer to a medical question after regular office hours
• Wait time for appointment to start
Courteous and Helpful Office Staff
• Clerks and receptionists are helpful
• Clerks and receptionists treat you with courtesy and respect
Provider (Doctor) –Patient Communication
• Provider explanations easy to understand
• Provider listens carefully
• Provider gives easy-to-understand information
• Provider knows important information about medical history
• Provider shows respect for what you have to say
• Provider spends enough time with you
Test Results
• Follow-up on test results
Rating of the Provider (Doctor)
• Overall rating of your provider

Figure 1.2 CG CAHPS Core Questions and Composites

The remaining questions are focused on demographics and survey navigation. A copy of the complete 12-month Adult Core Questions 2.0 survey can be found in the Appendix.

There are several AHRQ-published supplemental question sets available to use in creating customized CG CAHPS surveys. These supplemental questions may be added either individually or in composites, depending on the survey designer's needs. The supplemental question sets include:

- Cultural Competence Item Set (10 questions in 2 composites)

- Health Information Technology Item Set (9 questions in 3 composites)

- Health Literacy Item Set (4 questions in 1 composite)

- Patient-Centered Medical Home Item Set (see below)

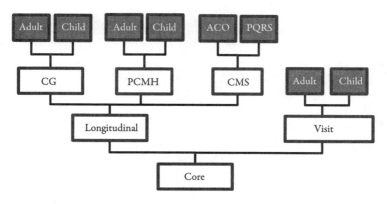

Figure 1.3 Survey Family Tree

The decision regarding which survey to use is primarily driven by the patient's payer; it's quite likely that a given practice may need to use multiple versions of CG CAHPS to address patients who have different payers.

Survey	Who is driving use
CG CAHPS 12-Month Adult	AHRQ, State/Private Payers
CG CAHPS 12-Month Child	AHRQ, State/Private Programs
PCMH 12-Month Adult	NCQA & URAC for State/Private Payers
PCMH 12-Month Child	NCQA & URAC for State/Private Payers
ACO 6-Month Adult	CMS *(pilot in 2014)*
PQRS 6-Month Adult	CMS *(pilot in 2014)*
CG CAHPS Visit Adult	AHRQ
CG CAHPS Visit Child	AHRQ

Figure 1.4 The Eight Surveys in the CG CAHPS Family Tree

Three Special Versions of the CG CAHPS Survey

Because we are focused on the CG CAHPS core questions in this book, we will not be discussing the following three unique CG CAHPS surveys in detail. However, we thought it might be useful to give a quick overview of each one.

Keep in mind that all of these surveys include the CG CAHPS core questions that we are discussing in this book, plus supplemental questions. You can find out more about tactics we recommend to address these surveys and their supplemental questions on our website at www.studergroup.com/CGCAHPS.

CMS ACO CAHPS and CAHPS for PQRS Surveys

CMS has created versions of CG CAHPS surveys for their ACO and PQRS programs. These surveys include all the CG CAHPS core questions plus additional supplemental questions.

They were used by CMS to start publicly reporting patient experience information regarding provider groups in 2015. CMS plans to continue to evolve these surveys and increase the number of practices that they publicly report data for over the next several years. Ultimately their plan is to report CG CAHPS patient experience data at both the practice and individual provider levels.

The CAHPS Patient-Centered Medical Home (PCMH) Survey

The CAHPS PCMH survey represents an expanded version of the CG CAHPS survey designed for providers and groups participating in patient-centered medical homes and/or accountable care organizations. It includes all the CG CAHPS core questions and then adds supplemental PCMH questions to the survey. There are both adult and child versions.

This survey is required for use by patient-centered medical homes seeking recognition under NCQA's "Distinction in Patient Experience Reporting" program. It is also recommended to organizations seeking recognition under URAC's PCMH accreditation program.

Evaluating CG CAHPS Results and Reporting on Them

CG CAHPS measures are designed to be aggregated into composites for public reporting. Think of these composites as bundles consisting of either one question or multiple related questions. The 15 scored core questions in the CG CAHPS 12-month adult version 2.0 survey are mapped to five composites as indicated in the following table:

Composite/Item	Questions	Response Choices
Access to Care (5)	• When you phoned this provider's office to get an appointment for care you needed right away, how often did you get an appointment as soon as you needed? • When you made an appointment for a check-up or routine care with this provider, how often did you get an appointment as soon as you needed? •When you phoned this provider's office during regular office hours, how often did you get an answer to your medical question that same day? •When you phoned this provider's office after regular office hours, how often did you get an answer to your medical question as soon as you needed? •Wait time includes time spent in the waiting room and exam room. How often did you see this provider within 15 minutes of your appointment time?	Never, Sometimes, Usually, Always
Provider Communication (6)	• How often did this provider explain things in a way that was easy to understand? • How often did this provider listen carefully to you? • How often did this provider give you easy-to-understand information about these health questions or concerns? • How often did this provider seem to know the important information about your medical history? • How often did this provider spend enough time with you? • How often did this provider show respect for what you had to say?	Never, Sometimes, Usually, Always
Lab Results (1)	• When this provider ordered a blood test, x-ray, or other test for you, how often did someone from this provider's office follow up to give you those results?	Never, Sometimes, Usually, Always
Office Staff (2)	• How often were clerks and receptionists at this provider's office as helpful as you thought they should be? • How often did clerks and receptionists at this provider's office treat you with courtesy and respect?	Never, Sometimes, Usually, Always
Overall Provider Rating (1)	• Using any number from 0 to 10, where 0 is the worst provider possible and 10 is the best provider possible, what number would you use to rate this provider?	0 to 10

Figure 1.5 The 12-Month Adult Survey Questions Mapped by Composite

Most CAHPS questions have been standardized to four response options, and CG CAHPS has adopted this standard in version 2.0 of the surveys. The four response options are: *never, sometimes, usually,* and *always.* The overall rating of provider question in the CG CAHPS core questions is measured on an 11-point scale from 0 to 10. There are several common ways to examine and report CG CAHPS scores based on these responses.

The method that CMS uses for public reporting is called "Top Box." Top Box scoring is the number of respondents who provided an "always" response divided by the total number of respondents who gave a response at all. (In the case of the overall provider rating, it's the number of individuals who rated the provider a 9 or 10.)

So, for example, let's assume 100 patients each answered the question, "How often did this provider listen carefully to you?" for two different providers. The data for our example is shown here:

Clinic	Never	Sometimes	Usually	Always	Top Box
Clinic A	0	5	40	55	55%
Clinic B	15	15	20	55	55%

Figure 1.6 Sample CG CAHPS Results for Studer Clinic

In looking at the Top Box results (which is what most public reporting focuses on), you likely noticed both Clinic A and Clinic B received the same Top Box score of 55 percent, despite having a different distribution of other responses. This is because both of them received 55 responses with "always" indicated (i.e., Top Box = Percent Always).

As you perform CG CAHPS surveys, it is common to want to understand how you rank compared with others. As we at Studer Group work with organizations across the country, we've found a valuable way to perform this comparison is using "national percentile ranking."

National percentile rankings are published by most of the CG CAHPS vendors and by AHRQ. *(It is important to note that different vendors may produce different results based on their survey population.)* The national percentile rankings tell you how you place relative to others on a given question or composite. So for example, you may have a Top Box result of 70 percent on Access to Care (i.e., 70 percent of the patients you surveyed answered "always") but score in the 82 percent on a national percentile ranking. This means your results are better than 82 percent of the other providers and only 18 percent scored higher than your results.

Here are Top Box national percentiles at the 25 percent, 50 percent, and 75 percent level for reference. This data was published by AHRQ in August 2014 and represents more than 200,000 surveys related to 12-month adult 2.0 survey core questions conducted in 2013. One thing to notice right away is that the 50 percent national percentile maps to a different Top Box result for each composite. Overall, the Access to Care composite was the lowest scoring nationally, and the Provider Communication composite was the highest scoring nationally in 2013.

Composite	Response Counted	25th Percentile	50th Percentile	75th Percentile
Access to Care	Always	58%	65%	72%
Provider Communication	Always	82%	86%	90%
Lab Results	Always	67%	74%	81%
Office Staff	Always	74%	80%	86%
Overall Provider Rating	9 or 10	76%	81%	86%

Figure 1.7 Sample CG CAHPS Results for Studer Clinic

AHRQ recommends another way to analyze CG CAHPS results to improve your practice by using average scores. In general, average scores are *not recommended for public reporting*, but we at Studer Group find that they can be valuable in helping a clinician and/or group work on improvement.

An average score is based on assigning weights to each response and then measuring the average. AHRQ recommends using weights based on a 1-to-4 scale mapped to the four responses as follows: Always = 4, Usually = 3, Sometimes = 2, and Never = 1. To calculate the average score, you take the number of responses times the weighted point value and add that total together. Then divide that number by the total number of customers. If we review our example using average scoring, we will find different results for our providers as follows:

Clinic	Never (1 pt)	Sometimes (2 pts)	Usually (3 pts)	Always (4 pts)	Top Box	Average Score
Clinic A	0	5	40	55	55%	3.5
Clinic B	15	15	20	55	55%	3.1

Figure 1.8 Sample CG CAHPS Results for Studer Clinic

If we were the leader over both Clinic A and Clinic B, this graphic would tell us a lot. In looking at the average score, it is now clear that Clinic A is performing better on this question than Clinic B. If our goal is to improve the results on this question, Clinic B will need more work and support to achieve an improvement than Clinic A will.

When your organization reviews its results, be sure to look at them in various ways so that you can identify those areas that truly need work. In our work with organizations across the country, we have found that those are the areas that should be addressed first. We urge you to follow this principle, using the tactics you'll find in the upcoming chapters.

To jump ahead for just a moment, please be aware that Chapters 15 and 16 will give you more information on EBL and how it works (as mentioned earlier), as well as on how to tackle the important task of goal setting and CG CAHPS improvement. We urge you to read it carefully—perhaps even before you read the tactical chapters. This will give you the context for thinking about the changes you need to make and how they fit into the bigger picture.

Finally, remember that like healthcare itself, your practice is a work in progress. It will take time to get things right, and you will likely never achieve 100 percent perfection—but that is no reason not to strive for it. By working tirelessly to achieve the best possible clinical quality and the best possible patient experience, your practice lives up to its highest sense of purpose. What an incredible gift—not just for the patients you serve, but for every provider and staff member who has chosen to follow this calling.

CHAPTER TWO:

FUNDAMENTAL TACTICS FOR IMPROVING CG CAHPS OUTCOMES

The CG CAHPS Handbook is filled with tactics designed to help practices hardwire a culture of excellence and improve the patient's perception of care. As you read through it, you'll notice that certain key behaviors come up again and again. These are the *fundamentals*—evidence-based tactics that have significant impact on the metrics associated with various CG CAHPS composites. Master these tactics and you'll be able to customize them to impact results in the composite you're focused on.

Every staff member needs to be proficient and skilled in these tactics in order to improve the patient experience—which will then be reflected in CG CAHPS results. Consistency is the key: Excellence involves every employee, every patient, every interaction.

You may be wondering how we determined which tactics deserve to be labeled as "fundamentals." The answer is simple: endless testing, observation, measuring, tweaking, re-testing, and more observation and measuring. Over the past decade and a half, Studer Group® has explored the effectiveness of dozens of tactics in healthcare organizations ranging from huge, multi-hospital systems to small private medical practices. While most of them have proven valuable in specific situations, certain ones stand out as consistently yielding the best results.

This chapter provides a brief overview of each fundamental tactic. It may be helpful to refer back to it as you read through the rest of the book.

The following self-test is designed to assist you in determining how you are doing on the fundamentals. We recommend asking a cross-section of your team (leaders, clinicians, and staff) to participate and compare your results. You may also find it valuable to repeat this self-test a year from now to evaluate your improvement in these areas.

Note: We have adopted the four-response standard of CG CAHPS for the self-test. Using this standard is a great way to build your own competency and experience in what it takes to consistently achieve an "always" response.

Question	Never	Sometimes	Usually	Always
1. How often do all members of our team use the same key words to discuss things with patients and families? (For example, do we all say, "For your privacy..."?)				
2. How often do all members of our team consistently manage up other members of the team?				
3. How often do all members of our team introduce themselves to patients and families in a consistent manner?				
4. How often do we knock and wait for acknowledgment before entering patient exam rooms?				
5. When partnering with the patient on his or her care plan, how often do we know the priorities and preferences of the patient?				
6. How often do we work with the patient to truly understand his or her "what"?				
7. When something goes wrong, how often do we apologize, using a consistent framework?				
8. How often are all of our staff empowered to provide service recovery and understand their authority level to do so?				
9. How often do we track our service recoveries and work to improve them over time?				
10. How often does staff check in on the patient in the reception room and exam room?				
11. When we hire staff, how often do we look for both technical competency and cultural fit?				
12. How often do we involve peers in the interview process?				

Figure 2.1 Fundamentals Self-Test

Self-Test Scoring

If you are like 99.9 percent of medical practices, you have likely identified a couple areas to improve. Please don't try to implement all of the tactics in this section at once. Instead, select the one or two most important to improving your practice and start by hardwiring them first.

Here is a crosswalk between the questions and fundamental tactics to help you get started:

Question	Fundamental Tactic
1. How often do all members of our team use the same key words to discuss things with patients and families? (For example, do we all say, "For your privacy..."?)	Key Words at Key Times
2. How often do all members of our team consistently manage up other members of the team?	Key Words at Key Times
3. How often do all members of our team introduce themselves to patients and families in a consistent manner?	AIDET*
4. How often do we knock and wait for acknowledgment before entering patient exam rooms?	AIDET*
5. When partnering with the patient on his or her care plan, how often do we know the priorities and preferences of the patient?	Individualized Patient Care
6. How often do we work with the patient to truly understand his or her "what"?	Individualized Patient Care
7. When something goes wrong, how often do we apologize, using a consistent framework?	Service Recovery
8. How often are all of our staff empowered to provide service recovery and understand their authority level to do so?	Service Recovery
9. How often do we track our service recoveries and work to improve them over time?	Service Recovery
10. How often does staff check in on the patient in the reception room and exam room?	Rounding
11. When we hire staff, how often do we look for both technical competency and cultural fit?	Employee Selection
12. How often do we involve peers in the interview process?	Employee Selection

Figure 2.2 Fundamentals Self-Test Questions and Tactic Guide

Fundamental Tactic: Key Words at Key Times

It's amazing how much what we're told affects how we feel. When care providers communicate clearly and effectively with patients, patients are more likely to feel positive about the interaction and be more engaged in their treatment. Thus, it's not surprising that survey questions related to communication tend to most strongly correlate to patients' ratings of their overall experience.

You'll see that nearly every chapter in this book includes a tactic related to communication. And while some tactics tackle certain composites more precisely than others, they're all interrelated. Key Words at Key Times is the "wellspring" tactic from which others like AIDET®, Managing Up, and Service Recovery branch off.

Key Words at Key Times refers to carefully chosen words healthcare professionals use to "connect the dots" with patients, families, and visitors. By using key words instead of confusing medical jargon, we can help patients better understand what we as providers are doing during the visit and, most importantly, *why.*

Being mindful of key words helps care providers see opportunities to reassure patients, manage up the practice, and otherwise create positive patient experiences. Studies show that the human brain is highly reactive to positive informational statements as compared to neutral statements.[1, 2] Of course, even without the research, it's obvious why we need to make an effort to be positive as we communicate with patients and family members. People who visit us for care have a lot on their minds. They may be in pain, distracted, frightened, or anxious about family members they are here to support.

Here are just a few examples of key words that we can use when speaking to patients and family members:

- *"Good morning.* **How can we assist you** *today?"*

- *"Dr. Smith is running a few minutes behind because a patient required a little extra time from him, but be assured that* **he will spend as much time as you need** *in your appointment today."*

- *"I* **want to ensure that I capture all of your information correctly** *so you do not experience any problems with your medical record or your billing process."*

- *"I* **care** *about how you do after you get home…"*

- *"I know we discussed this earlier, Mike, but* **I want to go over this again because I know we have covered a lot of information** *during your visit today."*

- *"So this is your first time seeing Dr. Jones! Her patients just love her—***she really listens and cares** *so much about each one of her patients."*

- *"I* **listened carefully** *to your concerns about your increasing pain…"*

- *"***For your comfort…***"*

- *"***To protect your privacy…***"*

- *"I want to keep you* **informed…***"*

- *"I want to be* **respectful** *of your time…"*

- *"Let me* **clearly explain** *why…"*

- *"What questions* **do you have for me?***"*

Key words ensure that the message we are trying to convey is actually heard. They help the patient understand his care better, they reduce anxiety and build trust, and they align the behavior of the staff to the needs of the patient. When we talk about key words, we are really talking about building a relationship with our patients and their families that creates trust and establishes us as longstanding partners in their care.

When introducing key words to staff, don't introduce too many at once; rather, let staff be part of the process of choosing three or four sets of key words that focus on improving patient safety or patient experience.[3]

Also, be sure to emphasize to staff that hardwiring key words is not "scripting"—a hot-button issue that often invites resistance from healthcare professionals. These phrases are helpful tools that in no way detract from a care provider's unique personality. The idea is to build in some proven key phrases (as opposed to robotic word-for-word recitations) to her already caring persona.

Fundamental Tactic: Individualized Patient Care (IPC)

The term "patient-centered care" is pervasive in healthcare today. It is used to describe everything from care models to broad philosophies. No one would argue that healthcare in general needs to be more patient-centered in its approach to care delivery—research suggests that when we accomplish this, not only does quality improve but so does the patients' and families' perception of their care.

Our relationships can span a good portion of a patient's life or they can be brief. Regardless, each patient wants us to care for him as a person and to feel that we care about what is important to him.

Because of this focus on the patient as an individual, we have operationalized a process that has been successful in ensuring that the patient's preferences and priorities are known and acted upon: Individualized Patient Care (IPC).

The only one who can tell us what is truly important to the patient *is* the patient (and/or his family). IPC helps us ask him (and/or his family) and then act on the answers. We take the technical/clinical aspects of care and link them to the individual patient via standardized communication with him. As a result, clinical outcomes and patient perception of care improve. More importantly, this provides a mechanism for our staff to get to know the patient as a person.

IPC allows us to gather a patient's thoughts on what is important to him and to incorporate them into our interactions with that person. It also allows us to use this information to better connect with the patient and to "humanize" care.

Let's say a teenage boy is under our care for a broken collarbone. If we learn that hockey is the most important thing in that boy's life, we can incorporate it into our care. It will make the patient feel we took the time to know him, and it may make him more compliant.

Specifically, we might let the boy know that he can get on the ice faster if he wears his sling and avoids using his left arm till it has healed adequately. Then, during his check-up, we can ask how his hockey team is doing. This builds a relationship that enhances the patient's experience.

Also, IPC prevents us from coming across as if we're simply going through the motions when we assess patients. It helps alleviate that "robotic" effect. We recommend standardization and consistency in asking relevant questions, but those have to be balanced with what should be an honest desire to know what is really important to that individual patient, to make a positive difference in his view of the care he receives.

In fact, it's really about learning the patient's "what" and addressing it. What *is* the *what*? It's that one thing the patient finds most important at the moment—the one overarching need that, if met, will leave him feeling well cared for and understood. The *what* may be pain relief, an adequate diagnosis, or simply finishing with an appointment in time to get back to work.

Knowing a patient's *what* allows providers to better partner with patients to ensure that they can provide the best possible care. By asking patients to tell us what is most important to them, we can avoid or immediately address situations that may create unnecessary anxiety and detract from the healing process.

IPC not only boosts patient perception of care, it improves communication between the patient and care providers and encourages teamwork and efficiency.

The only way we can truly deliver care that is important to the patient is to first understand what *is* important.

Throughout this book are tips and tactics for communicating with patients and learning about their *what* so it can be incorporated into their care. Tracking this in the patient's electronic medical record (EMR) will allow all providers to build on what matters to the patient.

Identifying and capturing a patient's *what* is as much an art as it is a science. All care providers—nurses, physicians, and everyone else who comes in contact with the patient—can be on the lookout for the *what* and record it in the EMR. If necessary, a simple question can work wonders: *"As we care for you, could you share what you feel is most important for us to know as we work to personalize your care?"*

Fundamental Tactic: AIDET® (the Five Fundamentals of Communication)

Of course, as powerful as key words can be, just giving care providers a list of them to pull from isn't always enough. We need a good way to put them into a meaningful context. AIDET®—a communication framework for applying key words and remembering the steps that create a positive patient interaction—is the solution.

AIDET is an acronym that stands for:

A	Acknowledge
I	Introduce
D	Duration
E	Explanation
T	Thank You

Figure 2.3 Acronym for AIDET*

This framework, also known as the Five Fundamentals of Communication, can be used by providers, nurses, practice managers, and virtually anyone who interacts with patients and family members. In fact, AIDET should be used for each new interaction. (At the very least, "A" and "I" should be used each time a new staff member comes on the scene—so that the patient can keep track of everyone's name and the role they play in the care process.)

Let's break it down letter by letter:

- **Acknowledge**—Make eye contact; make the patient and family feel that you expected her. (Research shows that most patients want the physician to shake their hands and use their name—but while physicians usually shake hands upon entering the exam room, more than half do not use the patient's name at all.[4])

- **Introduce**—Introduce yourself—including your skill set, experience, and certification—as well as introducing the other care providers who will interact with the patient during her visit.

- **Duration**—Include specific times and proactively answer questions such as: How long before the test, procedure, visit, or admission takes place? How long will the test, procedure, or appointment actually take? How long will the patient need to wait before she can go home? How long until the results are available?

- **Explanation**—Explain why you are doing what you are doing. Include specifics such as: What will happen and what the patient should expect. Periodically ask if the patient has any questions so far. Ensure that the patient understands her treatment plan. Explain the medication side effects and use the Teach Back method to ensure understanding. End with asking: What questions do you have?

- **Thank You**—Thank her for choosing your organization/clinic/practice. Include specific information, including if she had to wait, and always thank her for being a good patient.

AIDET is not a checklist and it is not necessary to implement all five letters at once, or to do so in any specific order, to begin seeing results. However, the more thorough we can be the better.

In general, AIDET has been proven to:

- Improve patient perception of care or the service they receive

- Help reduce anxiety (thus improving outcomes)

- Build patient loyalty

- Ensure that all service providers are delivering consistent measures of empathy, concern, and appreciation[5]

Figure 2.4 Advantages of AIDET*

When specifically applied to CG CAHPS, AIDET has significant impact on the results of multiple composites. In fact, by emphasizing certain letters in the framework, a practice can increase the likelihood of improving results in specific CG CAHPS composites. The following table illustrates.

CG CAHPS Composites	A	I	D	E	T
Access to Care	●	●	●	●	
Provider Communication	●	●	●	●	●
Test Results			●	●	
Office Staff Courtesy	●	●	●	●	●
Overall Provider Rating	●	●	●	●	●

Figure 2.5 Composites Impacted with AIDET®

For example, if a clinic is focusing on communication regarding test results, remind the providers and staff to focus on the "E" for explanation of why the test has been ordered. As for "D," providers and staff should share when the patient will hear back on the test results. (Always cushion this slightly in case there is a delay.) When we don't explain the duration of the wait for results then the patient will worry.

So, how to get started? Here is an example of using Key Words at Key Times and AIDET with a new patient:

- **A**—"Good morning, *Mrs. Smith.*"

- **I**—"I'm Dr. Williams *and I'll be providing care for you today. I've been in practice for over 20 years and specialize in pain management, which I understand is the reason for your visit today. You are in very good hands with our team.*"

- **D**—"*I'm going to take about* five minutes *to review your medical history with you and discuss your symptoms. I really want to hear from you. The entire visit should take only about 30 minutes. Shall we get started?*"

- **E**—*"First, we are going to review your medical history. Can you tell me more about the accident you had last year that is the cause for your chronic pain? Next we will… (explain the steps of the exam, procedure, etc.).* What questions do you have for me?"

- **T**—*"We're all finished.* Thank you so much *for your thoroughness in providing details today. With this treatment plan, I feel you will find a great deal of relief. Do you have any other questions for me or is there anything I can do for you before you leave?"*

These graphics show how one Studer Group partner was able to make swift and significant improvements to patient experience by using Key Words at Key Times and AIDET.

In the first one, you'll notice that as the team used these two tactics, fewer and fewer patients left due to the demeanor of the staff. (Imagine the negative impact those leaving for this reason would have on recommendations.)

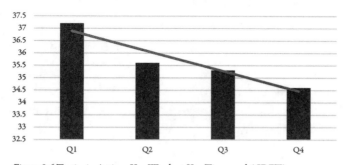

% of Patients Who Left Due to Attitude/Demeanor Post-AIDET*

Figure 2.6 Tactics in Action: Key Words at Key Times and AIDET*

At the same time, as the following graphic shows, the patients' overall rating was dramatically increasing. (Imagine the positive impact of these patients recommending others to visit here.)

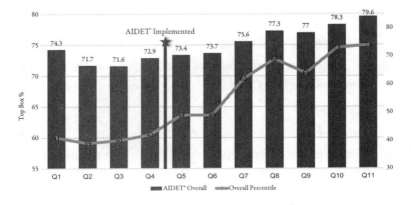

Figure 2.7 The Power of AIDET® to Overall Rating

It's important to remember that every patient encounter matters, regardless of its brevity or the role of the team member. When AIDET is hardwired and we hold people accountable for using the tactic in a genuine and sincere manner, it will impact the overall perception of the patient experience in a very positive way.

When seeking to implement AIDET, start by explaining to providers and leaders *why* this tactic is so important. Yes, it's important to build a strong business case for positive patient experiences, including issues like reimbursement, liability risk, and reputation, but focus more on how AIDET benefits the staff and the patient. When people understand the *why* behind what they're being asked to do, they are far more likely to do it.

Finally, remember that AIDET applies to everyone in the medical practice/office. Regardless of the length of the encounter or role he or she plays, any person who interacts with the patient should be trained and comfortable using AIDET. It's about building trust and engaging the patient to become a part of her care plan. Being part of the team is just that. Each person impacts the total patient experience and any one of those interactions and encounters at any level can bring either negative or positive reactions to the whole patient experience.

Fundamental Tactic: Managing Up

Throughout the following chapters, we will note opportunities for staff to "manage up." To manage up is to use words that position ourselves, the next caregiver, another department, or anyone else in a positive light. This technique helps patients and their family members feel safe and confident that they and their loved ones are in the hands of competent and caring individuals who trust each other.

In other words, managing up is simply making a statement that will help the patient feel more positive about who and what he is about to experience.

Here are some examples of managing up statements to use when speaking to patients:

"My name is Barbara and I have been a nurse for 14 years. I know this test is uncomfortable, but I have a lot of experience *in getting it done as quickly and painlessly as possible."*

"I know you got some difficult news yesterday. My whole purpose today will be to help you adjust to that news as I have helped many others *in similar circumstances."*

"Dr. Smith is so worth the wait. He's the best. He is absolutely who I would go to see if it were me or my family.*"*

"Our lab department is wonderful. You can trust *they will be very accurate and work to get you your results as quickly as possible."*

"Dr. Clark doesn't have any appointments available today, but did you know we have a nurse practitioner on staff? She can order that strep test and write you a prescription if you need one, and Dr. Clark thinks she's great.*"*

Each of these examples is designed to make the patient feel better upon hearing it. We must, of course, be genuine. There is almost always something you can say that you wholeheartedly believe and that will make a patient feel confident and comforted. The challenge is to find that one thing.

Each and every member of your practice needs to get comfortable with managing up. When rolling out this tactic, first emphasize the *why*. The goal is to make patients feel good about the choice of care they made. Managing up helps reduce their anxiety and makes the experience better for the patient.

As with many other tactics, managing up is both a science and an art. Consider giving staff members a list of occasions to use managing up phrases—when they book an appointment, check in a patient, or introduce a patient to the physician—but also encourage them to look for other opportunities.

What's more, you can develop a list of "approved" words and phrases to use, but you can also encourage people to tweak them until the language feels natural. (Just make sure all statements are truthful!)

Fundamental Tactic: Service Recovery/CARE[SM]

Patients place a great deal of trust in their care providers—more so than with nearly any other service. They usually start off with some level of trust, and depending on whether their experience with the care and service they receive is positive or negative, the trust level rises or falls.[6]

Not surprisingly, when a patient has a negative experience with a clinical group, her confidence in the practice may be shaken. This is why service recovery is of critical importance. Its fundamental objective is to restore the patient's trust and confidence. High-performing organizations recognize that effective service recovery is vital to the patient experience.

In fact, patients who have a bad experience, but then encounter a staff member or team who go out of their way to fix the situation, tend to remain loyal—often even more loyal than those who have never had a bad experience at all. In business, this has become known as the "service recovery paradox."[7]

According to one study, for every complaining customer who contacts you, there are 26 others who remain silent. However, the study also found that 70 percent of complaining customers will continue to do business with you if you resolve their complaint. Ninety-five percent will return if you resolve the problem *immediately*.[8]

Effective service recovery enables an organization to accomplish three main goals:

1) Resolve the problem and restore the patient's or family's confidence in the service

2) Address vulnerabilities in the system to improve overall quality

3) Relieve anxiety of the patient, thus increase compliance in their plan of care

In defining service recovery, the word "service" is not about the providers' or staff's expectations or definition of success, but the patient's. If the patient or family has unmet expectations, we must provide guidelines for staff to recover that failure by determining what the patient's expectations are and, whenever possible, meeting or exceeding them.

We can assume that our patients are impressed when we apologize, acknowledge their inconvenience or discomfort, try to solve the problem, provide alternatives and keep our promises, and do so in a timely and courteous manner.

Recommended Service Recovery Processes— CARE^{SM}

The majority of patients who seem difficult are not choosing to be that way; they are frustrated or angry. Our job, as representatives of the practice, is to turn those tense situations into marketing opportunities. Our job is to become so skilled at service recovery that the patient who started out saying he or she would never come back becomes one who says he or she would never go anywhere else. How do we accomplish such a seemingly impossible mission? We CARE.

CARE^{SM} is an acronym for the actions we take when we are confronted with an unhappy patient or customer. When we are the ones who are approached, we are responsible. When we hear it, we own it. The actions are:

	What?	How?	Why?
C	C for Connect	We introduce ourselves. We make eye contact. We say, "What is the problem and how can I help make it better for you?"	This step of the service recovery process puts a face to the solution and allows time for the customer to vent.
A	A for Apologize	Be careful not to stray into excuses or placing blame. Even if the situation is unavoidable or we feel the customer is unreasonable, apologize that the customer is unhappy.	We acknowledge that whatever happened is not up to our usual standard of customer care. If the customer has come to us, we own the problem.
R	R for Repair	Determine what it would take to make the customer happy. If we don't know, we ask. Sometimes the customer just wants acknowledgment. We say, "What can I do to make it better for you?"	Some situations are not in our power to change, but we can apologize and, if possible, offer information (not an excuse!) that will help the patient understand the rationale behind what occurred.
E	E for Exceed	Attempt to go above and beyond the customer's expectations.	Service recovery isn't just a "band-aid" solution. We want to bring that patient back and re-earn his trust.

Figure 2.8 CARE[SM] Service Recovery Model

Poor service recovery compounds the original problem, perhaps damaging the patients' trust for good. However, excellent service recovery can increase patients' confidence in a provider, sometimes to an even higher level than if no problem had occurred at all. A clinical group's willingness to go the extra mile to restore a patient relationship says a lot.

First, identify common problems your practice faces and create service recovery protocols around them. You can visit www.studergroup.com for some helpful tools and resources on service recovery. If after accessing these materials you are still uncertain about how to implement service recovery, don't hesitate to seek professional training. This is just too important an aspect of your service to let it go unaddressed.

Fundamental Tactic: Rounding

We all know about medical rounding, where hospital providers visit patient rooms on a regular and frequent schedule to check patients' status. Similarly, clinic providers and staff can round on patients as a means to manage waits and delays and gather information to use in the diagnosis and treatment process.

Both clinic staff and leaders should make a habit of rounding on patients in the reception room and in the exam rooms at least every 15-30 minutes when there are delays. These interactions serve a number of purposes:

- They can help manage the delay by reassuring patients that you know their time is valuable and that staff are doing their best to expedite their appointments.

- They can make the wait more tolerable if staff offers comfort items, such as water or reading material.

- They can help identify a patient who is distressed or struggling and who needs help faster than others. Regularly assessing the patient's demeanor improves outcomes and also alleviates potential service recovery situations.

- They can serve as opportunities to manage up the provider: *"There was an earlier patient who needed more time than we had anticipated, but you can be sure that we will take the same level of time and care with your appointment too."*

Additionally, when leaders round on patients in the exam rooms and reception areas, it's an opportunity to gather information on staff and ensure that they are demonstrating those behaviors that enhance the patient experience. For example:

- *"I'm sorry that the doctor is delayed. Has someone been in to let you know how much longer the wait will be?"*
- *"Did anyone offer you something to drink?"*
- *"Did the reception staff give you the option to reschedule your appointment?"*

It's important to round with all of these outcomes in mind. Don't round just to round—the goal is to elicit actionable information.

All of this input doesn't do any good if you don't look for trends and act upon the information gleaned. That's why it's important to keep a log of your rounds. For a log template you can use to capture details that will help you identify areas for improvement, as well as note positives to recognize those staff members, please visit www.studergroup.com/CGCAHPS.

When hardwiring this tactic, identify a staff member who is efficient and detail oriented and who will see that the rounds happen every day. Here, as with other changes, it's important to make sure someone "owns" the new tactic. If not, it almost certainly won't happen.

Delays are sometimes inevitable, but frequent communication with patients can make all the difference in how they experience those delays.

This graph shows how one Studer Group partner was able to make swift and significant improvements to patient experience by using Key Words at Key Times and rounding.

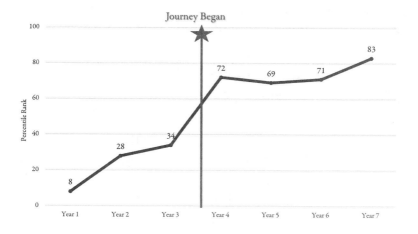

Figure 2.9 Tactics in Action: Key Words at Key Times and Rounding

Fundamental Tactic: Employee/Provider Selection

An organization's biggest expenditure and asset is its human capital. When working to create or sustain a culture of high performance, people are an integral force. It's important to a) hire the right people and b) make sure they stay.

Hiring well is the first step to retention. Not all candidates are right for your organization or department/area, even if they possess the skill set required to do the job. They also must fit within the organization's desired culture. According to the *2012 Physician Retention Survey* by Cejka Search, cultural fit is the top controllable cause of physicians leaving the organization voluntarily.[9]

The next chart shows how physician turnover decreased significantly for one Studer Group partner as they implemented fundamental tactics, including the ones in this chapter. The reason is simple: Together, these tactics create well-run practices, and physicians want to be affiliated with well-run practices. Not only are they more profitable, they result in better clinical outcomes—which is what physicians really care about.

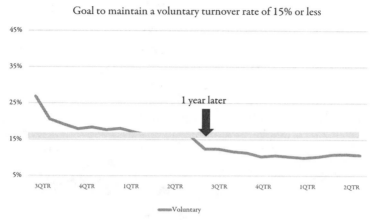

Figure 2.10 Voluntary Physician Turnover Rate Decreases After Implementing Fundamental Tactics

Likewise, when physicians are aligned, engaged, and loyal to an organization, it is more stable. That's good for everyone. So decreased physician turnover isn't just good for the organization's bottom line—it provides patients with consistency of care.

Of course, physicians are only part of the care provider team. It is also crucial that we select and retain the right staff members (those who are a good cultural fit) in all departments and at all levels of the organization.

Hiring well is a critical step to providing higher quality care at lower costs. At a minimum turnover represents a loss of 5 percent or more of an organization's total annual operating budget.[10]

Selecting talent involves three key steps, each of which utilizes behavioral-based interviewing techniques. According to Quint Studer, "Behavioral-based interviewing techniques screen and select individuals who provide a 'best match' for the organization."

The three steps to selecting talent are:

Figure 2.11 Three Steps to Selecting the Right Talent

STEP ONE: The Screening Process: This part of the process (managed by the Human Resources department) involves finding candidates; pre-screening them for proper certifications, licensures, and minimum job requirements; and conducting background and reference checks. Studer Group recommends holding a preliminary interview that assesses a candidate's organizational fit by asking questions based on values and Standards of Behavior.

- **Standards of Behavior:** Have candidates read and sign your organization's Standards of Behavior before completing an application in order to establish clear expectations for behavior.

STEP TWO: The Leader Interview: During this step, the leader interviews those candidates who have passed the Human Resources screening process.

This interview focuses on finding the right person for the job. The leader uses behavioral-based questions to identify experience related to specific job competencies as well as questions to determine an applicant's fit within the relevant department/area.

Behavioral-based questions should be open-ended and candidates must respond with a specific example or story.

Also, behavioral-based questions should not be hypothetical. Use words such as "tell me about a time when..." in place of "what would you do if..." They require that the candidate recount real-life situations and describe how they behaved.

Behavioral-Based Questions for Providers

Dr. Richard Rubin, a coach for Studer Group, has written extensively on the subject of behavioral-based interviews, including an article for *Physician Executive Journal* as well as an article published on the Studer Group website. Following, taken from these sources, are some examples of behavioral-based questions to use when interviewing providers. Questions should cover clinical skills, culture and collaboration, and engagement:[11, 12]

Clinical (should relate to specialty):

- *"How would you work up a patient with pneumonia?"* (Or right-upper quadrant pain, or depression, etc.)

- *"What questions do you ask in taking a history on a patient with chronic headaches? What are some answers or findings that would lead you to obtain an imaging study?"*

Culture and Collaboration:

- *"Do you write or dictate your notes? Why did you choose this option, if it is an option?"*

- *"Do you work with advanced practice professionals (APPs)? If so, how closely or in what way do you monitor their work?"*

- *"Currently, how is your schedule templated?"* (Or, *"How many patients do you see in a day?"*)

- *"If you could customize your schedule in any way you desired, how would it look?"*

Engagement:

- *"How can you tell if a patient understands what you are telling her?"*

- *"How do you calm a patient's fears?"*

- *"Under what circumstances do you feel it is okay to terminate a relationship with a patient? How often have you done so, and what was the procedure you followed?"*

> • *"A mammogram returns with a 1 cm lesion highly suggestive of malignancy. Please tell us how you would start a conversation."*

STEP THREE: The Peer Interview: If the leader interview goes well and the leader is willing to hire them, candidates then meet with colleagues trained as certified peer interviewers. This is an important step, because when peers are included in the selection of a new team member, they are more likely to feel ownership for his success.

Employees engaged as peer interviewers are empowered to support the goals of the organization. By enabling employees to participate in this way, a leader shows respect for their experience and skill. Employees, in turn, feel a sense of ownership in the organization and also in the success of the person recommended for hire. Employees who serve on the peer interview team must commit to:

- Remain on the team as long as the position is open
- Be prepared for interviews (review résumé, leader interview matrix, meet early to decide on questions and flow of meeting, bring a pen to record answers, etc.)
- Interview, evaluate, and take notes
- Maintain confidentiality

- Debrief with HR and leader as necessary

- Evaluate process

- Be a role model/mentor to the candidate who is hired

It's important that each leader conducting interviews is trained to use behavioral-based interviewing techniques. The questions will be similar to those used in the leader interviews, but more focused on issues around how strong the cultural fit is with the team.

Here are just a few examples (of course, in an actual interview, there will be many more questions):

Work Environment Preferences:

- *"What kind of environment have you most enjoyed working in? Please describe what you liked about it."*

- *"Tell me about a work situation that irritated you. How did you handle it?"*

- *"Tell me about the best boss you ever had. Why did you like working for him or her?"*

Communication Skills/Relationships:

- *"What experience have you had with miscommunication with a coworker, patient, or physician, and how did you solve the problem?"*

- *"Describe a time when you had a disagreement with your supervisor. How did you handle it?"*

- *"Describe a time when you had to present a difficult change or new idea to a person or group that was not anticipated to be well received and how you delivered the message."*

Teamwork:

- *"What kinds of people would you rather not work with? How have you dealt with people like this in the past?"*

- *"Tell me about a time you worked on a team that accomplished excellent results. What were the main factors in the team's success?"*

Coping Skills:

- *"Have you heard the expression 'roll with the punches'? What would be a situation in the past in which you had to do that?"*

- *"What methods or processes have you used when you were facing a transitional change in your job responsibilities to ensure a positive outcome for you and the organization?"*

- *"When is the last time you were criticized and how did you deal with it?"*

Diligence:

- *"Tell me about a time when you had to work on a project that did not work out the way it should have. What did you do?"*

- *"When you have had to do a job that was particularly uninteresting, how did you deal with it?"*

Integrity/Honesty/Trustworthiness:

- *"Have you ever experienced a loss for doing what is right? What happened?"*

- *"When was the last time you 'broke the rules' because it was the right thing to do?"*

Remember, sometimes the best decision is not to hire. We have found that one strong objection (from any mem-

Top Ten Tips for Peer Interviewing

1. Select questions in advance.
2. Use the same questions for each candidate.
3. Be prepared and prompt!
4. Establish rapport.
5. Listen for specific examples that include the Event, Action, and Result (EAR).
6. Probe for the EAR.
7. Take notes.
8. Listen 80 percent; talk 20 percent.
9. Allow for silence.
10. Submit feedback to HR within 24 hours.

ber of the interview team) is one too many.

Members of peer interview teams must be trained to follow a standardized process. The same steps need to happen with every candidate, every time. Studer Group recommends that our partner organizations' Human Resources departments train and validate all members of the peer interviewing team to ensure alignment, accountability, and consistency. This training is also important to ensure the peer interviewers are aware of legal restrictions on the kinds of questions they can ask.

Studer Group offers an online toolkit with a variety of resources to help you build a strong peer interviewing process. We also provide an interview matrix template—which should be customized around the organization's specific needs and include behavioral-based questions—and a decision matrix template. You can find all of these tools at www.studergroup.com/CGCAHPS.

These fundamentals will help your organization improve all aspects of the patient experience to some degree, with the added benefit of improving your CG CAHPS scores. Ensure that your practice's staff is skilled in these tactics, and implementing the rest will go more smoothly. As you go through the rest of the tactics detailed in the following chapters, you may use this chapter as a reference, so that you can ensure that these are used by every employee, every time, in every interaction.

Tools & Resources

Studer Group® offers a variety of tools and resources that support the tactics discussed in this chapter. To access the most up-to-date offerings, as well as to see what's new in healthcare, please visit www.studergroup.com/CGCAHPS.

Access to Care: Providing Appointments, Care, and Information

W hen human beings are sick, they want to see a provider *soon*. This is not just a matter of facilitating physical recovery. It's also deeply psychological. The longer people must wait for treatment, whether it's for a minor virus or a life threatening illness like cancer, the longer they feel uncertain and anxious.

Physicians and other care providers who work with them are fully aware of the need to see patients quickly. We care deeply about our patients and want to be as responsive as possible. And yet, for a variety of reasons, access to care is not as efficient as we want it to be.

Research released in January 2014 by Merritt Hawkins, a physician search and consulting firm, shows that the average wait time to get a provider appointment in all metro areas was almost 19 days. In larger cities like Boston, the average new patient appointment occurred 45 days after first attempt to schedule.[1]

In addition, the average time patients wait to be seen after arriving in the actual provider's office is 22 minutes. While this may not seem like an excessive amount of time, the Access to Care question within the CG CAHPS survey specifically asks, "How often did you see this provider within 15 minutes of your appointment time?" With that in mind, 22 minutes becomes 7 minutes too long.

The longer patients are forced to wait, the more their perception of quality care declines.[2] In the future, as reimbursement will be tied to CG CAHPS surveys, this becomes even more important.

Gaining access to care matters to everyone involved in providing healthcare, including the provider, the staff, and of course, the patient.

From a patient perspective, access is more than just confirming an appointment with a provider. It also includes access to key individuals within the practice, such as making the appointment with front desk staff, getting answers to questions from nurses, or gaining imaging/lab results from other providers. It includes access to other members in the same physician practice or the health system as well.

For instance, if a patient needs a referral to another provider within the same practice, is the patient able to get a timely appointment? Were both providers able to effectively hand over patient information? What was the patient's perception about the new, referred provider's knowledge of their medical history and care plan?

From a clinical perspective, it's important that timely care can be provided to patients for both safety and quality purposes. The sooner providers can diagnose diseases and illnesses, initiate treatment, and identify complications from earlier procedures, the better the outcomes will be. This, in turn, impacts patients' perception of care, and ultimately, it will determine a good deal of how practices are reimbursed.

There's also an emotional component to accessing care. Patients want to feel valued, respected, and connected to their provider on a personal level. Getting in to see that provider when it works for the patient (and having office staff that is empathetic and understanding during that process) is a key aspect of this emotional standpoint.

The Survey Questions

This aspect of the CG CAHPS survey asks patients how accessible their provider was in terms of getting appointments and answers to healthcare questions when needed. Answers are given in frequency scale: *never, sometimes, usually*, or *always*. The percent of patients who responded *always* is publicly reported on a growing number of state and private payer websites and is starting to appear on the CMS Provider Compare website located at www.medicare.gov/physiciancompare.

The questions are as follows:

1. **When you phoned this provider's office to get an appointment for care you needed right away, how often did you get an appointment as soon as you needed?**

2. **When you made an appointment for a check-up or routine care with this provider, how often did you get an appointment as soon as you needed?**

3. **When you phoned this provider's office during regular office hours, how often did you get an answer to your medical question that same day?**

4. **When you phoned this provider's office after regular office hours, how often did you get an answer to your medical question as soon as you needed?**

5. **Wait time includes time spent in the waiting room and exam room. How often did you see this provider within 15 minutes of your appointment time?**

The following self-test is designed to assist you in determining how you are doing on the basics of access. We recommend you ask all your staff and providers to participate in this self-test and compare your results to determine where to focus first. You may also find it valuable to repeat this self-test a year from now to evaluate your improvement in these areas.

Note: We have adopted the four-response standard of CG CAHPS for the self-test. Using this standard is a great way to build your own competency and experience in what it takes to consistently achieve an "always" response.

Access Self-Test

Question	Never	Sometimes	Usually	Always
1. How often did patients who called with questions/requests today receive a call back today that resolved their question/request?				
2. How often did everyone who called this morning asking for an appointment today have the opportunity to be seen by a relevant clinician?				
3. How often are patients who call for routine visits able to get appointments with their primary provider within 48 hours?				
4. How often can our patients get timely appointments that do not require them to miss work/school?				
5. When I have tried calling our office after hours, how often have I received a call back within 15 minutes?				
6. How often do we track every phone call, including how long it takes to answer the phone, complete the call, and if the caller hangs up before we complete the call (abandonment rate)?				
7. How often do our patients see their provider within 15 minutes of their scheduled appointment times?				
8. How often can patients use our web portal to schedule appointments, request prescription refills, access their medical chart, and ask our clinicians questions?				
9. When we leave a patient waiting in the reception area or an exam room for more than 15 minutes, does someone check on them?				
10. How often is our no-show rate for appointments under 5%?				

Figure i.1 Access Self-Test

Access Self-Test Scoring

If you are like 99.9 percent of medical practices, you have likely identified a couple areas you can improve. Don't try to implement all of the tactics in this section at once. Select the one or two most important to improving your practice and start by hardwiring them first.

Following is a chart that crosswalks the statements you evaluated your practice's performance against with the CG CAHPS question(s) it aligns with and/or impacts. If you score well on the self-test questions, you should see similar results from patients on the related CG CAHPS questions. This crosswalk can help you ensure that you have the right tactical focus—just periodically match your results up to CG CAHPS results to validate that the right behaviors are happening effectively and always.

Self-Test Question	CG CAHPS Question(s)
1. How often did patients who called with questions/requests today receive a call back today that resolved their question/request?	• When you phoned this provider's office during regular office hours, how often did you get an answer to your medical question that same day?
2. How often did everyone who called this morning asking for an appointment today have the opportunity to be seen by a relevant clinician?	• When you phoned this provider's office to get an appointment for care you needed right away, how often did you get an appointment as soon as you needed?
3. How often are patients who call for routine visits able to get appointments with their primary provider within 48 hours?	• When you made an appointment for a check-up or routine care with this provider, how often did you get an appointment as soon as you needed?
4. How often can our patients get timely appointments that do not require them to miss work/school?	• When you phoned this provider's office to get an appointment for care you needed right away, how often did you get an appointment as soon as you needed? • When you made an appointment for a check-up or routine care with this provider, how often did you get an appointment as soon as you needed?
5. When I have tried calling our office after hours, how often have I received a call back within 15 minutes?	• When you phoned this provider's office after regular office hours, how often did you get an answer to your medical question as soon as you needed?
6. How often do we track every phone call, including how long it takes to answer the phone, complete the call, and if the caller hangs up before we complete the call (abandonment rate)?	• When you phoned this provider's office during regular office hours, how often did you get an answer to your medical question that same day?
7. How often do our patients see their provider within 15 minutes of their scheduled appointment times?	• Wait time includes time spent in the waiting room and exam room. How often did you see this provider within 15 minutes of your appointment time?
8. How often can patients use our web portal to schedule appointments, request prescription refills, access their medical chart, and ask our clinicians questions?	• When you phoned this provider's office during regular office hours, how often did you get an answer to your medical question that same day? • When you phoned this provider's office after regular office hours, how often did you get an answer to your medical question as soon as you needed?
9. When we leave a patient waiting in the reception area or an exam room for more than 15 minutes, does someone check on them?	• Wait time includes time spent in the waiting room and exam room. How often did you see this provider within 15 minutes of your appointment time?
10. How often is our no-show rate for appointments under 5%?	• When you phoned this provider's office to get an appointment for care you needed right away, how often did you get an appointment as soon as you needed?

Figure i.2 Access Self-Test and Composite Questions Guide

Now, here is a crosswalk between the CG CAHPS questions and tactics in this section. You'll notice that most of the tactics impact multiple CG CAHPS questions. In other words, there is no need to add a different tactic for every question; rather, you simply maximize what you're already doing and perhaps add a few new tactics to cover any gaps in your performance.

CG CAHPS Question	Key Tactics
When you phoned this provider's office to get an appointment for care you needed right away, how often did you get an appointment as soon as you needed?	• Open-Access Scheduling • Patient-Centric Hours • Scheduling Templates
When you made an appointment for a check-up or routine care with this provider, how often did you get an appointment as soon as you needed?	• Open-Access Scheduling • Patient-Centric Hours • Scheduling Templates
When you phoned this provider's office during regular office hours, how often did you get an answer to your medical question that same day?	• Fundamental Tactic: AIDET˙ and Key Words at Key Times • Call Tracking • Centralized Phones
When you phoned this provider's office after regular office hours, how often did you get an answer to your medical question as soon as you needed?	• Fundamental Tactic: AIDET˙ and Key Words at Key Times • Call Tracking • Managing After-Hours Calls
Wait time includes time spent in the waiting room and exam room. How often did you see this provider within 15 minutes of your appointment time?	• Manage Waits and Delays: Room and Round℠ • Visit Status Boards • Daily Huddles • Streamlined Patient Flow

Figure i.3 Access Composite Questions and Tactics Guide

Incidentally, you should not attempt to implement all of the tactics at once. It's best to key in on one or two of them to start with and concentrate on doing them well. Once you begin to see consistent results, you can add more.

In the chapters that follow, we will share the top few tactics for each Access to Care composite question that positively impacts the likelihood that patients will answer *always* to the related survey questions. In this section and throughout the book, sometimes a question will get its own chapter, while other times two or more questions will "share" a chapter. This is because there are times when the tactics do "double (or triple) duty" in terms of improving question responses.

These chapters aren't meant to contain a laundry list of all possible effective tactics. Rather, they zero in on a few carefully targeted specific actions you can take to immediately impact patient perception of how well your practice and providers manage the core aspects of Access to Care featured in them.

CHAPTER THREE:

PATIENT ACCESS TO TIMELY APPOINTMENTS

"I must govern the clock, not be governed by it."
—*Golda Meir*

THE CG CAHPS SURVEY QUESTIONS:

- **When you phoned this provider's office to get an appointment for care you needed right away, how often did you get an appointment as soon as you needed?**

- **When you made an appointment for a check-up or routine care with this provider, how often did you get an appointment as soon as you needed?**

Access involves more than patients being able to make a timely appointment. It's also about office staff and providers setting realistic expectations and keeping patients informed throughout the patient visit, starting at the time of making the appointment. As indicated earlier, some patients have to wait weeks to see a provider. This can immediately impact patient perception of their appointment in a negative way.

You may be thinking, *Well, having to wait is having to wait. Isn't it the wait time for the appointment itself that's upsetting?* Not necessarily. How your office frames the "message" about the wait time will go a long way toward determining how a patient views her experience. That's why providing proper training in this area can improve patient perception of care from the first phone call.

Picture this scenario: You try to get an appointment with your regular physician, who is in high demand, and find out she is booked solid for three weeks. Here is the response you hear from the front desk staff:

"Unfortunately, Dr. Clark is not available to see any patients for the next three weeks. Her next availability is…"

Patients immediately become frustrated with the lack of access and may feel that their provider doesn't care about them. On the other hand, if the staff has been trained to provide certain key words, the scenario could go more like this:

"Hello, Mrs. Williams. As you know, Dr. Clark is a great internist and, as you can imagine, is very busy. We'd be happy to schedule your appointment at her earliest availability, which right now is running about three weeks out. I know you're eager to see Dr. Clark, so I'm happy to call you if we receive a cancellation and get you in sooner. However, the other internists in our practice are

excellent as well, and Dr. Clark would be happy to refer you to one of them if you would like to see someone sooner than three weeks from now."

Chances are we can all agree the second scenario will provide a better impression of caring. What's more, it wasn't time consuming or complicated. It took the staff person making the appointment less than a minute to positively impact the patient's experience and leave a lasting impression by providing options, as well as managing up the other providers in the practice.

We urge you to review the Key Words "Fundamental Tactics" in Chapter 2 for more guidance on how to develop engaging, reassuring ways to address issues around appointment times. And keep reading to learn some other changes you can make to positively impact the appointment-focused questions that are part of the Access composite.

...And the Tactics That Make "Always" Responses More Likely

Tactic 1: Keep Patient-Centric Hours

It is important that provider offices be open at times that fit patient schedules. In general, workday shifts across industries range from 7:30 a.m.-5:30 p.m., with lunch hours ranging from 11:00 a.m.-1:00 p.m. Thus, if a provider's office hours are 8:00 a.m.-5:00 p.m. and they are closed during lunch, the majority of patients will be unable to make an appointment—or at least will have to take time off from work to do so.

It makes sense, then, for offices to be open before and after normal working or school hours. And in many practices, patients are increasingly interested in weekend hours. The blunt truth is, when one practice can't meet patients' needs, they will find another care provider who can.[1] In fact, the rapid rise in "retail clinics" is frequently attributed to their ability to provide better patient-centric access.

Currently, there is a definite trend toward being more accommodating to patient schedules. With the advent of CG CAHPS, this trend will only increase. Yes, there may be some initial resistance among staff members and providers when expanded hours are introduced. If so, help them "connect the dots" regarding the better service you're providing and the better outcomes you'll see.

Becoming patient-centric does not have to affect all providers at all times. Rather, we recommend starting with staggered scheduling for providers. A schedule for an office with five providers might look like this:

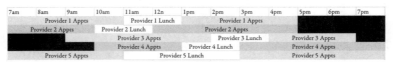

Figure 3.1 Sample Provider Schedule

As you can see from Figure 3.1, at any given time throughout the day, three providers are generally available to see patients. Adjusting your practice's schedule to "flex" to your patients' availability will allow for easier scheduling and fewer cancellations due to work and school conflicts.

When beginning with expanded hours, we recommend the following scheduling procedures:

- Start by analyzing your practice to identify the hours your patient population desires:

    ○ Look at the demographics of your practice's patients and their families. If most of your practice is made up of independently mobile retirees, for example, then a 9-to-5 schedule may work for them. Most practices, however, will have a significant number of patients who work or attend school or whose family members do. Most of these patients require early and late appointments and weekend options.

    ○ Ask your scheduling staff to spend a week tracking what the most commonly requested schedule times are. Also, ask them to track requests for appointments they are unable to accommodate. For specialty practices, tracking referral sources is also critical.

    ○ Study your patients' transportation usage. Do your patients drive their own cars or take mass-transit options? In one of Studer Group's partner practices, they had a significant no-show rate before 10:00 a.m. that was traceable to bus schedule challenges.

- ○ Pay special attention to holidays. Does your practice have significant demand right before and/or after holidays?

- ○ Consider the alternative options patients in your community have. If your practice has patients who have received care elsewhere, take the time to understand why. Then either expand your hours to meet these needs OR form a partnership with an urgent care/retail clinic that will agree to share medical records with you and send your patients back to you for follow-up.

- Determine what hours your practice needs to be open to see patients at times that are most convenient for your patient population. We have found this goes best if you set the hours *before* figuring out the staffing plan. This allows a practice to set weekday and weekend options that meet the patients' needs first and then focus on the clinicians and staff.

- Never tell a patient to call back at another time for an appointment. Develop a structure to assist patients who call and need an appointment at a later time (as many might need to, in order to get time off from work or school). Then, provide her with an appointment time that is convenient for her. Consider this patient's experience:

Maggie had a productive cough and called her provider at 3:00 p.m. for an appointment. She was told that there were appointments available the next day, but she would have to call the following morning to get one. Instead of doing that, she called the retail clinic at a nearby drugstore and was told that they could see her immediately. The patient arrived at the clinic at 3:30 p.m. and was on her way out by 4:00 p.m., having seen a provider and had her prescription filled during that time.

What do you think Maggie will do the next time she has an acute care need?

- Work on staffing your new hours. In some cases, you may need to accommodate some interim overtime as you work with staff to accommodate the hours. Three tips:

  ○ Communicate the new practice hours to your team and give them the chance to volunteer to adjust their schedules. We are constantly surprised at the number of individuals who volunteer for early or late shifts to better support their work-life balance. There are also individuals who will agree to work weekends in exchange for guaranteed days off during the week.

  ○ Be creative with your team. No one ever said lunch has to always be an hour long at noon.

  ○ New staff members are often willing to work hours that existing staff are not able or willing to. Leverage openings to secure staff that supports staffing your newly expanded patient-centric hours.

Tactic 2: Use Care Templates to Standardize Scheduling

Standardizing scheduling for your practice via care templates not only increases access but also increases patient experience and practice efficiency. Care templates are standardized schedules, formatted by time increments, and are typically managed by a clinic "air traffic controller" or flow coordinator. Chapter 5 provides more detail on flow coordinators.

When every care provider and office affiliated with a practice uses different time templates and visit types, scheduling an appointment is a confusing and overwhelming task. Adopting a common care template with standardized appointment timeframes and visit types—all agreed upon by everyone—makes scheduling far easier and more efficient. It also increases everyone's ability to work together smoothly.

Here are the three key steps to migrate to standardized care templates:

1. **Gain provider buy-in up front.** Standardized care templates ideally require an entire practice to adopt them, but you can start office-wide or specialty-wide if needed. The key is to reach agreement with all the providers involved. Without the support of the providers, care template implementation will fail. The key to gaining provider buy-in is to involve the providers in template creation.

2. **Make all appointment blocks the same length.** Regardless of the type of appointment, try making them all for the same length of time, say 15 or 20 minutes. If you know more time will be required based on patient history or complexity of needs, two consecutive appointment time slots can be scheduled for the visit. If you are struggling to determine how long appointment slots should be for your practice, study how long your top 5-10 visit types take from start to finish and use this to guide your decision.

3. **Minimize the number of visit types.** Many top performing practices operate with just a couple of visit types. This leads to increased efficiency in both scheduling and patient visit flow. A key to making minimal office visit types work is a scheduling system that can support both the visit type and the reason for the visit. (This may be a computer program that tracks both or an agreed-upon standard way to track both.) An example of a visit type might be "existing patient visit," with the visit reason being "a diabetic check-up." When defining standardized visit types, start with two or three types and support more types only if required. Even in large multi-specialty practices, we have found that having 10 or fewer standardized visit types is possible.

Gynecological Practice

Schedule Template

Rule of Thumb: Every 2-3 hours leave one appointment slot open as a buffer/break.

	Monday	Tuesday	Wednesday	Thursday	Friday
7:00		HUDDLE		HUDDLE	HUDDLE
7:20		Prepare		Prepare	Prepare
7:40					
8:00					
8:20					
8:40					
9:00					
9:20	SURGERY				
9:40					
10:00					BREAK
10:20					
10:40					
11:00				LUNCH/BREAK	
11:20					
11:40					
12:00			DAY OFF		
12:20		LUNCH/BREAK			
12:40					
1:00					
1:20	HOLD/				
1:40	LUNCH				
2:00					
2:20					
2:40					
3:00					
3:20					
3:40					
4:00					
4:20					
4:40					

Max Visits	6 (6 appt slots)	20 (23 appt slots)	0	20 (22 appt slots)	17 (17 appt slots)
				Max Total Visits	63

Type of Visits (TOV)	Allocated Time	Actual Time
Office Visit (OV)	20	10
New Patient (NP)	40	40
Long Procedure (LP)	60	60

Figure 3.2 Practice Scheduling Template

We at Studer Group® have seen some large multi-specialty practices with upwards of 600 templates. Obviously, in such cases, scheduling and rescheduling appointments can be frustrating and time-consuming. The staff member must hang up with the patient, call another office, and then call the patient back with a potential appointment time—which may or may not be acceptable. If not, the process starts all over again.

When common templates are in use, the appointment can be scheduled during the initial patient call. Thus, the goal is to reduce the number of templates to fewer than 10 for large multi-specialty offices and as low as two for smaller offices.

The following is from a practicing physician:

As a cardiothoracic surgeon, I'm frequently called into surgery, making it difficult to always keep patient appointments. Because my practice uses a common care template, I'm able to call another provider and give him or her a list of symptoms, a possible diagnosis, and share the care plan I've already outlined. This allows my patient to be seen, which ensures great access to care even when I am pulled into an unscheduled surgery.

In other words, when the cardiothoracic surgeon is called into surgery, the scheduler simply needs to type in, say, "3:00 p.m." and any open 3:00 p.m. slot with a colleague will pop up. Without it, the appointment would simply be canceled, forcing the patient to reschedule and perhaps endure a long wait for another one.

Plus, thanks to the template, vital patient information is at the new provider's fingertips. This prevents the need for additional phone calls to track down all the details.

Difficulty and delays in setting up appointments affects a patient's perception before he even walks through your doors. It sets the stage, making the patient feel as though the practice is inefficient and the provider doesn't have time for him. When your practice makes appointments in an easy, convenient, and timely manner, you start off that patient encounter on the best possible foot.

Tactic 3: Move to Open Access Scheduling

The open access method of scheduling (sometimes referred to as *advanced access* and *same-day scheduling*) refers to patients' ability to obtain an appointment with their provider's practice when they call to request one. While ideally this visit would be with a patient's preferred provider, in many cases he will benefit by seeing another qualified provider in the practice the day he calls. Here is a mantra it may be helpful to adopt in migrating to open access: "If they call today, don't turn them away."

Traditionally, providers' schedules are booked weeks or even months in advance. The open access model leaves a good portion of the provider's day, sometimes as much as half, open for same-day appointments. The remainder of her day can then be spent with no-show, rescheduled, or follow-up visits.

There are several benefits of this approach:

- **It removes delays.** Open access enables practices to reduce or eliminate delays in patients receiving care from their provider. This not only increases patient perception of access and care, but also increases satisfaction for both the provider and the patient.

- **Scheduling demand decreases.** The open access format of scheduling allows for the viewing of multiple providers' schedules across a practice. This flexibility helps decrease the volume of calls to a practice because a patient can, in a single phone call, make an appointment with a different provider should their provider not have availability that day. Further, because open access generally allows for scheduling appointments in the near future (usually day of or within one or two days), the need for re-scheduling and confirmation phone calls decreases.

- **It decreases no-show rates.** If patients are able to get an appointment within a day or two, it stands to reason that they are far less likely to forget about them. Many organizations have seen their no-show rate cut by half or more with open access scheduling.[2]

- **Cost and efficiency savings are realized.** This method does not require adding more resources, which helps with cost and efficiency savings. Providers are able to use their clinical time more effectively, patients' wait times are reduced (and they are more likely to show up for scheduled appointments), and staff can better manage flow and backlog of patients. One organization found that costs per visit decreased by 22 percent when they switched to open access.[3]

Implementing open access requires a significant organizational commitment. One of the most important factors to address is the belief that providers will be overwhelmed by demand or, conversely, will have significant idle time.

Here are some tips on how to implement the open access method:

- **Measure demand for commonly requested appointment times.** Track the following areas:
  - Average next-available appointment times
  - No-show rates (including day and time of the no-shows)
  - Bumps (the number of patients with scheduled appointments that need to be rescheduled as the provider was unable to see them at their scheduled time)
  - Appointment requests (including the day/time even if it falls outside the hours you are normally open)
  - Average number of walk-ins and urgent care appointment requests per day

  Start by analyzing a week of patient visits from start to finish. Track the visit length from when the patient walks in the front door until she completes her visit by day of the week and time. (It's best to do this with every patient, but if you can't, a random sample is better than nothing.) The idea is to match up the average visit length to type and time and use the information to map out the open access schedule.

- **Assess the state of access in your practice.** Once you have the amount of time to cycle the day's patients through, you will take that total and divide by the number of patients seen during that time. This will give you the average cycle time for

the open access schedule and will also allow you to see areas where flow or processes can be improved.

It is important to compare the average wait times for patients to get appointments between various offices and specialties. This will allow you to identify those providers who are doing well (so you can offer reward & recognition) and those who may be struggling (so you can address problems with access). While some providers will argue that long wait times are an indicator of how good they are, in reality they show how much volume is being lost to another provider across town.

- **Review patient survey and CG CAHPS scores.** Any patient survey tools, like CG CAHPS, that have specific questions regarding access should be reviewed and monitored. Depending on the patient's experience and those scores, we can better assess how our access is perceived. Start with the locations/providers that have the biggest gaps in terms of access metrics. Also look at those that are key from the health system's standpoint, those with the largest volumes and those in areas where you have the most competition.

- **Get rid of the backlog.** To open up the schedule, you'll need to have care providers and office staff put in some extra hours to get through the days or weeks that have already been filled with appointments, as well as those being booked during that time. It may take several weeks to move through the patients, but once those are complete, office staff and providers can set a date when pre-scheduled visits will no longer make up the majority of each day.

- **Consider "carve-outs."** Many practices, instead of going completely to open-access scheduling, break up the days into open-access and non-open access hours. While this may make scheduling more complicated, it works as long as everyone agrees that the "open access" schedule slots cannot be released until the morning in which they occur. Another option some practices have adopted is to have one or more providers reserve their entire schedules as open access while their colleagues'/partners' days are pre-scheduled appointments. The key is to figure out what makes sense for your patients.

- **Schedule referrals when you make them.** Open scheduling often means a primary care office can schedule their patient with the specialist and/or ancillary service in their organization at the time they make the referral. A patient who is able to schedule his referral visits during check-out will have a great patient experience—and the practice will benefit from the increased in-network capture rates this generates.

- **Develop a backup plan.** On days when patient demand outweighs the availability of providers, a backup or contingency plan can identify substitutes for providers. More and more, physicians are working with nurse practitioners and physician assistants. These individuals should have schedule templates as well, and the provider should indicate the criteria and processes for when the patient can see these individuals. This further opens up access and availability to see more patients and provide better access to care.

The "appointment" experience is a vital one. When patients are able to quickly and painlessly schedule a visit with you, they feel reassured that their concerns are being taken seriously and are on their way to being addressed.

There is so much anxiety tied up in reaching out to a care provider, especially when you don't know what is wrong with you or even if your health issue can be "fixed" at all. Being on the receiving end of that call is a privilege. When we take steps to make the appointment process easier and more pleasant for patients, we show them we recognize and appreciate the trust they are placing in us.

Tools & Resources

Studer Group® offers a variety of tools and resources that support the tactics discussed in this chapter. To access the up-to-date information, please visit www.studer-group.com/CGCAHPS.

CHAPTER FOUR

PROMPTNESS IN ANSWERING PATIENT CALLS ABOUT MEDICAL QUESTIONS

"Don't keep a man guessing too long—he's sure to find the answer somewhere else."

—Mae West

THE CG CAHPS SURVEY QUESTIONS:

- **When you phoned this provider's office during regular office hours, how often did you get an answer to your medical question that same day?**

- **When you phoned this provider's office after regular hours, how often did you get an answer to your medical question as soon as you needed?**

To understand why it's so important to manage patient calls, we need to put ourselves in their place.

For example, imagine that your elderly father, a widower, is experiencing worrisome symptoms. When you called to check on him yesterday evening, he was coughing, hoarse, and listless. After a night of tossing and turning, you woke up early and called him first thing. He sounded worse, so you made the decision to take the morning off work and see about your dad.

You took him to the doctor's office the minute it opened to have lab work done, then brought him back home to rest and wait for the results. But you didn't know the wait would be quite this long. With every minute that ticks by, your father gets more and more anxious. His temperature reaches 101 degrees. His breathing gets more labored.

You've called the doctor and left a message about your father's worsening symptoms, urging them to please call back about the lab results. At this point you're pacing the floor. *Should I take Dad to the ER?* you wonder. *Or should I go on to work and ask the practice to call me there? Maybe I could get at least a little bit of my work done while I wait. If only the phone would ring!*

Can you imagine how frustrating and upsetting this scenario would be? The phone is, quite literally, a lifeline for patients and their families. This is why it's so important to put systems in place that enable your office to get answers to patients and their families quickly and efficiently. Not only will it reduce their anxiety, it will almost certainly improve clinical outcomes and may even save lives.

Plus, being able to manage phone calls efficiently is critical for the well-being of your practice. If yours is like most practices, phone calls account for a significant volume of work. It is not uncommon to find that for every six hours that a provider sees patients in the clinic, the practice may spend six hours of staff and provider time answering and responding to phone calls.

Too often, though, practices leave patients like the worried daughter and her sick dad in the previous scenario waiting far too long for answers to their questions. Why? There are various reasons. Often, there's no one assigned to these calls so staff members "fit them in" around other work or appointments. Or different team members use different systems and codes to track patient information, creating significant variation in responding to calls. Or staff members aren't properly trained in how to triage callbacks, so there is a chance a call could get missed and a sick patient could end up waiting too long.

Here are some of the most common reasons that we have found that patients call medical practices:

- Inquiring about test results
- Anxious about patient symptoms and seeking solutions/reassurance
- Need an appointment made/changed
- Need prescriptions refilled
- Have a question about their treatment plan or the treatment plan for their family member

- Have a question regarding a claim/bill

- Need assistance with a provider referral

What we have learned about this list of common patient call reasons is that, while it is unlikely any one person in your practice can handle all of these call issues, it is highly likely that there is someone in your practice who is best suited to handle each of these. The challenge is to create a well-thought-out system that blends the smart use of technology with the presence of caring, helpful, and above all, accessible human beings.

What's more, by making a deliberate effort to give patients all the information they need up front (regarding lab results and insurance claims, for example) and to proactively set better expectations, you can reduce unnecessary calls.

...And the Tactics That Make "Always" Responses More Likely

Following are some tactics you can use to make sure patients can easily get the service they need and keep your practice running more efficiently.

Tactic 1: Track Calls to Find Where Process Improvements Are Needed

The first tactic is to track your phone calls from patients. If you don't track your calls, then you can't manage and improve them. Tracking your calls allows you to adjust your staffing levels to accommodate peak times, change your call routing and hold processes, and determine if you need to support call hours that may stretch outside your standard practice hours.

Sometimes a practice leader may tell us they can't measure phone calls, but we beg to differ. At a minimum, every practice can manually track the minimum metrics we outline here. Often by working with your information technology and/or facilities team, it is possible to automate the collection of some of these metrics.

Here is a minimum set of key metrics to track to get you started:

- Date and time call was received.

- Length of call.

- General reason for call (use categories like appointment, prescription refill, clinical question, etc.).

- Resolved on first call or did we have to call them back?

- Call completed or abandoned?

- Call placed on hold?

- Call sent to voice mail?

- Call sent to after-hours answering service?

- Call required transfer to another team member?

Figure 4.1 shows a sample call tracking log that a practice can use to capture this data.

We suggest you give this log to everyone who answers patient calls. Appoint one person to tally the results. If possible, tally them at the end of each day to spot trends. Then do so again at the end of the week. By looking at the trends, you can adjust your processes and put in place appropriate staff for higher volume times.

Call Tracking Log

Date: _____

Time rec'd	Total length	Reason for call	Placed on hold	Sent to voicemail	Sent to after-hours answering service	Transferred to team member	Completed	Abandoned	Issue resolved	Call back needed

Reasons for Call:
NA: New appointment
AR: Reschedule
AQ: Question about appointment (date/time/items and prep needed)
PR: Prescription refill
CQ: Clinical question
TQ: Question about treatment
RH: Referral help
BQ: Question re: claim/bill

Figure 4.1 Call Tracking Log Sample

Once you've tracked these calls for a period of time—perhaps a week, or perhaps more if you wish—you'll have a good picture of not just your total call volume but also the trends that flow through it. For example, you'll be able to see the heaviest call periods by month, day of week, and time of day; what most calls are about; how quickly most issues are resolved; and so forth. This knowledge can then be used to create systems to better manage the calls and improve patient perception.

For example, you might find there's a high number of calls requesting updates on lab results four hours or so after tests have been performed. After a bit of digging, you might then find that the lab techs are telling patients they'll hear from you in a few hours. The solution might be to work with techs and let them know patients have been told they will receive results in 24 hours. This will not only prevent unnecessary calls, it will help patients worry less.

Tactic 2: Implement AIDET® in Answering Medical Questions

Ensuring that AIDET® continues to be used with phone interactions will increase patient understanding and compliance. Specifically, the "A" for Acknowledge, "I" for Introduce, "D" for Duration (how long it will take for someone to get back to the caller with an answer), and "E" for Explanation can be particularly helpful. When patients call with questions, AIDET can help to ensure that we are clearly communicating with them.

For example, here is how a nurse might use AIDET when returning a call to a patient who called in with a medical question.

- **Acknowledge:** Always greet the patient by name. *"Hello, Mr. Bell. I understand you have a question for Dr. Yang."*

- **Introduce:** Introduce yourself by name and your role: *"I am Karen, Dr. Yang's nurse. I have been working with Dr. Yang for 10 years and will make sure that I get your question answered."*

- **Duration:** *"Dr. Yang is in surgery but I should be able to connect with him and get back to you within the next two hours."*

- **Explanation:** *"I am going to repeat back to you the question and information you gave me to make sure it is correct, so I can pass it on to Dr. Yang."*

- **Thank you:** At the close of the interaction, thank the patient for their time, patience, or for having all the necessary information or paperwork at hand. *"Thank you so much for calling. I am glad you are checking in with Dr. Yang regarding what you are seeing."*

Providers can also manage up staff and use key words to emphasize the fact that they are focused on service to patients:

"Mr. Bell, this is Karen again, Dr. Yang's nurse. I want to share that Dr. Yang was glad that you called. He wanted to make certain that your question was answered as early as possible so he asked me to call you back. He shared that the swelling is common, and to alleviate it you should elevate your foot above your heart. I also wanted to check on your pain medication. Can you tell me the last time you took it? What dose?"

Can You Spot the AIDET?

If you're worried that AIDET seems too rigid or scripted, the following sample conversations may ease your mind. They show how this framework functions as an organic, almost invisible structure for conversations with patients. As you read these conversations with Amanda and Barbara, see if you can identify each letter in AIDET:

Patient Call Representative: *"Good morning! This is Studer Medical Center; my name is Amanda. How may I assist you today?"*

Patient: *"Hello, Amanda. This is Jenny Smith. I am Dr. McDonald's patient and I am calling to see whether I need to continue with the antibiotics that she prescribed."*

Patient Call Representative: *"Hi, Ms. Smith. I know this is important to you and I am happy to help you get the answers you need. Dr. McDonald is not in at the moment but her nurse, Barbara, is here, and, as you know, they have worked together for many years and she is an excellent nurse. She is at her desk so let me transfer you over to her—if she is on another line and unable to pick up within the next few minutes, I will reconnect with you and make arrangements for her to call you back within the next half-hour. Does that work for you?"*

Patient: *"That would be fine. Thank you."*

Patient Call Representative: *"Great. Thank you for your patience, Ms. Smith."*

****

Nurse Barbara: *"Good morning, Jenny. This is Barbara, Dr. McDonald's nurse. How are you today?"*

Patient: *"Hi, Barbara. I am doing quite well—quite a bit better than when I was last in and Dr. McDonald put me on those antibiotics."*

Nurse Barbara: *"That is good to hear. So now, about your antibiotics...I have been expecting your call because Dr. McDonald had noted on the chart that she had asked you to call today or tomorrow to let us know how you were doing. In fact, she asked me to call you if we had not heard from you by tomorrow. So are you still experiencing any 'burning' when passing urine?"*

Patient: *"No, none at all."*

Nurse Barbara: *"Excellent. In that case, we would like you to stop the Keflex but continue on the Macrodantin that we also prescribed. Do you still have some of that?"*

Patient: *"Yes, I do. And there is also a refill on the prescription that I can get, if needed."*

Nurse Barbara: *"Very good. So this is the plan...stop the Keflex and continue on the Macrodantin, just taking one capsule at bedtime each night. Then, sometime in the next 7 to 10 days, we would like you to come in so that we can get a new urine culture to make sure the infection is all gone. Would that work for you?"*

Patient: *"Yes."*

Nurse Barbara: *"Great, Jenny. So, as it is important for your health that we are all on the same page and work together on this, would you explain to me what you understand to be the next steps going forward?”*

Patient: *“Sure. I will stop the Keflex and continue on the Macrodantin, one capsule at bedtime each night. And you want me to come in in 7 to 10 days for a urine culture.”*

Nurse Barbara: *“Exactly! So before I set up the follow-up appointment for you, what questions do you have for me?”*

Patient: *“None. I think I got it.”*

Nurse Barbara: *“Very good, Jenny. I am looking at the schedule for next week. Can you make a 7:30 a.m. appointment on Tuesday morning? It is just for a urine specimen and you will not need to see Dr. McDonald at that time, so you should be out of here by 8:00 a.m. at the latest. Would that work for you?”*

Patient: *“Yes, that would be fine. I will be able to be at work by 8:30 a.m. then.”*

Nurse Barbara: *“Excellent. Thanks, Jenny. You will also get an email from me reminding you of this appointment. And if for some reason you need to change this appointment, please don’t hesitate to call me.”*

Patient: *“It should be fine.”*

Nurse Barbara: *“Well, thanks for calling in today. We appreciate your being so diligent about your follow-up. What else can we do for you today?”*

Patient: *“Nothing—all is good. Thanks.”*

Nurse Barbara: *“Well, thank you and have a wonderful week.”*

Patient: *"Thanks. You too. Bye."*

Nurse Barbara: *"Bye."*

Tactic 3: Centralize Your Phone System

Studer Group® has found that it's best to centralize the phone systems at large practices or office groups. Doing so makes standardizing processes, procedures, and key words much easier and more efficient.

Large practices should seek to centralize their phone system to the extent it makes sense. In some cases, centralizing by practice area or by office location may make more sense than a single centralized call center. Care templates, as discussed in the previous chapter, can help simplify this process by making it easier for *any* staff member charged with answering the phone (even if he or she is not at the same physical location that the patient is calling) and, in this age of electronic medical records, to access the care plan and help get a medical question answered.

By making sure the phone is always covered by staff members qualified to address patient and family questions—and of course providing staff with the information and tools they need to do the job—callers will experience a much higher level of service. The people tending the phone will be able to:

- Answer the phone with a helpful and friendly tone
- Focus on the person on the other end of the line
- Execute phone call communication frameworks
- Reduce hold time
- Schedule/reschedule appointments according to clinic practice
- Conduct pre- and post-visit calls
- Help callers with referrals
- Answer questions about the bill
- Get prescriptions refilled

By reducing inbound phone calls at the front desk or check-out area, this tactic leads to higher service and quality for the patients who are there for appointments. Why? Because front desk and check-out personnel can then devote their full attention to the patient/family and provide them with an excellent experience. They will be able to:

- Greet patients
- Process check-in information, including:
  - Insurance information and copays
  - Medication reconciliation
  - Distribution of materials that help establish patients' *what*. Examples are shared care agenda, patient visit guide, reception card, or IPC card
- Track reception room times and better manage patient waits

- Monitor reception area

- Process checkouts more efficiently

Of course, we also know that centralizing the phone system is not feasible for all practices. In those cases, we recommend designating a staff member, other than those tending the front desk, to attend to patients and families who call in with questions.

Make Use of Patient Portals

An emerging technology solution that many providers have found success with is the patient portal. Basically, this is an online resource that allows patients to log in to schedule appointments, check on claim payment status, request pharmacy refills, and even ask clinical treatment questions.

The patient portal is a helpful tool, not a replacement for a caring human being. It's critical to designate a staff person who can assist patients with their portal questions. Also, make sure the portal provides clear information on how to call the practice to get questions answered.

Tactic 4: Equip After-Hours Call Team to Quickly Respond to Patient Questions

While medical practices are not required to answer patient calls after hours, patients do expect responsiveness—not just someone who picks up the phone—and that their question be answered. How after-hours calls are handled can be as important to patients as getting timely appointments and having their care transitioned effectively. This is especially true for patients who may be in pain because of a recent procedure and need to ask questions.

In fact, after-hours calls can be the most important interaction patients have with your practice and the entire care system. If patients don't have a good experience in this arena, you can be sure it will negatively impact their perception of the quality of care and access.

It is important to note that this specific CG CAHPS question is about getting your question answered—not about talking to someone after hours. If the after-hours answer is always "go to the ED" it will impact your patient experience (and not in a good way). Patients have an expectation that some of their questions should be answered without a visit—especially when they consider all of the information available at the touch of a fingertip.

For example, what happens if a patient calls after hours saying that she stepped on a rusty nail? Well, if you have licensed medical staff answering after-hours calls and they have access to patients' medical records, they should be able to provide complete and correct medical information to the caller. They'll be able to ask the appropriate questions to determine the extent of the injury and see whether the patient has recently had a tetanus shot.

On the other hand, if the physician or nurse does not have access to patient files, that patient will likely be directed to the emergency department for a tetanus shot—whether or not she truly needs one. This may turn out to be a waste of time and money.

Here's the point: Just answering or returning an after-hours call is not the win. The win is answering the call *and* having all of the patient information needed to be able to truly help the caller and answer her question.

There are several ways to provide after-hours support. The ideal model has a human being answering the phone who can resolve most questions. Another model has a human being answering the phone who can set expectations for provider call backs by someone who can answer the question. And the least ideal model involves after-hours callers being greeted by a message identifying the practice and providing clear instructions on how to access after-hours support.

Key Words for Answering After-Hours Calls

Be aware that the leading practice is to not provide a lot of administrative info as part of the message—like fax number, address, or driving directions—since very few after-hours callers are seeking this kind of info. Instead, the majority of after-hours calls are from patients asking the same kinds of questions they ask during regular business hours.

Whether the patient call is answered by recorded message (Example 1) or an after-hours call service (Example 2), think carefully about what is best to include. The key is to have an efficient process that enables those who *do* have an urgent need to get their questions answered quickly. Below are some examples of how best to use key words in these scenarios.

Example 1 (voice mail)

- *"Thank you for calling the Studer Medical Clinic."*

- *"Our offices are now closed. Our regular office hours are from 7:00 a.m.-6:00 p.m. M-F and 9:00 a.m.-2:00 p.m. on Saturday."*

- *"If your question can wait, please leave us a message after the beep and we will call you back during our regular office hours. Our goal is to return calls within the first hour of business."*

- *"If your matter is urgent and cannot wait for our regular office hours, please push 1 to be put in touch with our on-call provider. The provider will return your call within 30 minutes."*

- *"Thank you for calling the Studer Medical Clinic."*

Example 2 (on-call service answering the phone)

- *"Thank you for calling the Studer Medical Clinic."*

- *"The office is now closed. The regular office hours are from 7:00 a.m.-6:00 p.m. M-F and 9:00 a.m.-2:00 p.m. on Saturday."*

- *"I can take a message to pass on to the practice for you. If your matter is urgent, I can ask the on-call provider to call you back within 30 minutes; otherwise they will return your call during regular office hours."*

- *"Do you have a need for me to contact the on-call provider for you?"*

- *"What is your name and phone number? What is your call concerning?"*

- *"Thank you, Mrs. Jones, for calling the Studer Medical Clinic."*

If a patient calls after hours for an urgent medical question, it is critical to manage her expectations for a return call. Your automated answering message should provide instructions for the patient on how to reach a physician or nurse on call and set clear expectations on when the patient will receive a call back—which should be in 30 minutes or less.

Ideally, this returned call should not only meet or exceed the time expectation but the caregiver on call should also have access to the up-to-date patient's chart so he or she can provide medically appropriate information. (This underlines the importance of completing patient charting each day.)

Here are some common examples of after-hours medical questions your process should be able to address in a timely manner (preferably within 30 minutes):

- *"I recently got a procedure from Dr. Franklin and am in a lot of pain. Can you call in a stronger pain prescription for me?"*

- *"I stepped on a rusty nail. Do I need a tetanus shot?"*

- *"I lost my emergency inhaler for my asthma. Can you call in a prescription / send an e-prescription to a 24-hour pharmacy near me?"*

As you are setting up your after-hours call process and identifying/training the people who will staff it, be sure to think through all possible scenarios. For example, ask yourself:

- What are your options for directing patients to a facility other than the ED? Does your delivery network staff an urgent care clinic, or do you have an agreement with a retail clinic to share medical records?

- Do the providers who make these return calls have the ability to answer at least 80 percent of the questions? People answering after-hours calls should have the necessary medical and practice knowledge, as well as access to the EMR, to be able to answer the patient's question within that call.

- Do you have a backup? What happens if the primary provider on call is busy handling another patient issue or gets called into an emergency? How would you know if that primary person wasn't able to answer calls during his assigned on-call time?

It is also a good idea to contact patients the next day to follow up on their after-hours call, "closing the loop" on the patient. This creates a lot of good will and demonstrates that you really care that they got the care that they needed.

One More Tip

Here is another tip to consider as you are hardwiring the previous tactics.

Tip: Validate the Patient Calling Experience with Mystery Calls

Practice leaders and providers should occasionally call their practices to experience how effective their call process is. It is critical to call on the main practice number so you can experience the phone tree and hold/

transfer process as your patients do. As part of this process, check on the processes for the key reasons patients call, including:

- Need an appointment made or changed

- Need prescriptions refilled

- Have a question about their treatment plan or the treatment plan for their family member

- Have a question regarding a claim/bill

- Need assistance with a provider referral

More on validating your processes to ensure that they are truly improving the patient experience can be found in the last chapter in this book.

Few things are more frustrating and anxiety producing than waiting by a phone that won't ring. If you have ever waited on a call (okay, a text, for younger readers) from a new love interest, or a teenager who was supposed to be in touch two hours ago, or a potential new employer with news about your dream job, you know this truth all too well. Waiting isn't fun.

When a patient has a question about her health or that of someone she loves, or is having scary symptoms or pain, waiting is even worse. As healthcare professionals, we owe it to our patients to help them avoid that kind of anxiety. Let's do all that we can to optimize our phone systems. The fact that we may receive better CG CAHPS results is a nice side effect—but the real benefit is improving the well-being of our patients.

Tools & Resources

Studer Group® offers a variety of tools and resources that support the tactics discussed in this chapter. To access the up-to-date information, please visit www.studergroup.com/CGCAHPS.

CHAPTER FIVE:

TIMELINESS IN KEEPING PATIENT APPOINTMENTS

"Unfaithfulness in the keeping of an appointment is an act of clear dishonesty.

You may as well borrow a person's money as his time."

—Horace Mann

THE CG CAHPS QUESTION: How often did you see this provider within 15 minutes of your appointment time?

It's happened to all of us: You show up for your provider's appointment 15 minutes early, as instructed. You fill out your paperwork and are ready to go at your appointment time. And then you wait. And wait. And wait. At 20 minutes past your appointment time, you return to the reception desk only to be told, "The doctor is running a little behind. He'll see you as soon as he can."

So you return to your uncomfortable chair—and while you wait even longer, you realize that given the amount of time you've waited, the doctor was probably already behind schedule when you first spoke with the receptionist. In fact, he was probably behind schedule before you'd even left your house.

Scenarios like this one create negative patient experiences. When a patient's appointment is delayed, especially when there's little or no explanation, he most likely feels disrespected and unvalued before he ever even sees the care provider. In fact, one study found that patients' ratings of providers decreased by 0.3 rating points for each 10-minute increase in waiting time.[1]

Consider this story from a patient we'll call Frank:

I had an appointment to see a well-regarded otolaryngologist, so I took the day off work and arrived before 10:00 a.m., which was my appointment time. The waiting room was packed. The receptionist explained that the provider had to perform an early morning emergency surgery, and was about an hour behind. But she didn't know how long the wait would be, because he was still in surgery, and all of those people in the waiting room had appointments scheduled before mine! So at best, I was looking at a two-hour wait. I asked why no one had called me so I could have the option to just reschedule, and she said that wasn't their policy. I canceled my appointment that day and made a new appointment—with a different practice.

Preventing long patient waits is often a matter of improving efficiency or changing the scheduling process. However, sometimes delays are unavoidable, caused by a medical emergency or a patient who simply required more time from the care provider. In those cases, however, you don't have to frustrate patients to the point that they, like Frank, leave for greener pastures. There are ways to either a) find an alternative to the patient having to wait for a long time or b) make sure that the patient understands the reason for the delay and feels valued and respected.

...And the Tactics That Make "Always" Responses More Likely

Tactic 1: Daily Huddles

Daily huddles are exactly what they sound like—brief meetings at the start of each day in which all care providers and some or all staff members review the schedule, appointments recognition, flow, or any other specific issues affecting the day and develop a plan to alleviate or minimize any potential problems. While this tactic can help ensure that patient flow is smooth and efficient, it can also be valuable in improving results for many other CG CAHPS questions as well.

The daily huddle allows discussion around any emergency procedures that have come up and provides an opportunity to agree on a plan for addressing patients who might be impacted by them. It facilitates a review of appointments scheduled to pinpoint any areas in the schedule that could lead to delays. It enables the team to get on the same page so they might feel proactive in managing the day. This "we've got it all together" feeling truly can affect staff behavior. Thus, when patients check in, they can often feel whether or not a plan is in place.

Who should be included in daily huddles? The answer may vary based on practice size; however, the providers, the nurses, the medical assistants, the flow coordinator, and anyone with the ability to help triage patients should always be involved. Including the front office receptionist and office manager is a good best practice. Smaller offices or those with significant access issues should include all staff members when possible.

Why is a daily huddle important? There are several good reasons.

- **It facilitates inter-staff communication.** Provider offices can get extremely busy throughout the day, and the daily huddles may be the only time that all staff can communicate with each other.

- **You can address issues from the previous day.** Daily huddles allow staff and providers to talk about what worked well and identify opportunities for improvement from the previous day.

- **It allows staff to proactively plan for the day.** This time is critical to view the day's schedule, identify double-bookings, rearrange the schedule as needed, and so on. This allows everyone in the office to know what the day looks like.

- **You can recognize providers and staff members who deserve special mention.** Public praise not only feels good—it gives others a chance to know the behaviors that are worthy of recognition (and that you want repeated).

Here's how to implement daily huddles:

- **Meet prior to the first patient's appointment.** Every morning, the provider(s) and staff huddle together to review availability for the day (remember, most physicians will have a portion of their schedule open that day). Huddles allow all staff to review what the day looks like, develop a plan or even a backup plan should appointments run behind, and perhaps even tentatively plan for a midday huddle in the event that the team needs to reassess the day.

- **Discuss patient flow.** Daily huddles become very important for quick communication about patient flow. They allow the opportunity to decide where patients can be moved (either rescheduled or handed over to someone else) if a provider's schedule is full. Identifying a flow coordinator can help with this process.

- **Use an agenda to keep huddles on track.** Figure 5.1 shows a sample huddle agenda worksheet.

1. WINS/CONNECT TO PURPOSE LETTER/STORY	
2. CLINIC UPDATE – PROCESS CHANGES	
3. DAILY DASHBOARD REVIEW	
Number of Appointments	
Average Wait Time	
Number of No-Shows	
4. PATIENT EXPERIENCE TRENDS	
Leader Rounding on Patients	
Post-Visit Calls	
IPC/Patient Reception Card Comments	
Other:	
5. STAFF RECOGNITION	
Introduction of New Staff	
Birthdays	
Recognition from Rounding on Patients	
6. OTHER	
(Include other brief information that the staff needs to give great care and have a great day.)	

Figure 5.1 Huddle Agenda Sample

Remember Frank, our disgruntled patient from earlier in this chapter? If the practice in this example had implemented a huddle first thing that morning, they could have come up with a plan the minute they found out about the doctor's emergency surgery. They could have called and rescheduled Frank right away (or perhaps rescheduled the patient before him), and the day would have been much smoother for everyone. In fact, there's a good chance that huddle could have averted the loss of a patient from the practice.

Tactic 2: Implement Visit Status Boards

A status board shows patients whether their physician is on time or running behind, so they know what the wait will be as soon as they check in. This gives them the opportunity to alter plans for transportation or childcare if necessary, or even reschedule if they must. In other words, it gives patients the power NOT to wait more than 15 minutes to see a physician—or, if they do choose to wait, it allows them to make an informed decision.

The status board is typically a "physical" board, not just a schedule on a computer screen (though depending on how high-tech your practice is, you might also update your website at the same time). You can purchase a board or you can make your own. It can be as sophisticated or as simple as you like; even a chalkboard on a stand can work just fine. Just make sure it's in a highly visible spot—preferably near the front desk—and that it's updated regularly.

Status	
Provider A	On Time
Provider B	30-Min. Delay
Provider C	1-Hr. Delay
Provider D	15-Min. Delay
Provider E	On Time
Provider F	45-Min. Delay

Figure 5.2 Status Board Sample

The "status" part of the board is typically expressed in increments of 15 minutes: on time, 15 minutes behind, 30 minutes behind, etc. Make sure you have a process for reassessing and updating the board. This could happen mid-morning or perhaps at lunch. Again, 15 minutes is the magic number—if a physician's status hasn't improved or worsened by that amount, leave the status "as is."

Keep in mind that the board should not be the sole means of communicating visit status—rather, it should be used to supplement conversation with the patient about delays. Whether a physician is running late, on time, or ahead of schedule, verbally let the patient know as you reference the board. (If the physician is on time or ahead of schedule, this is an opportunity to "manage her up": *"Dr. Faruque is right on schedule today. She really values her patients' time and tries hard to spend the right amount of time with patients to best help them."*)

Of course, should the wait be too long for a patient, you need to be prepared to offer other options:

"Mrs. Smith, I am so sorry Dr. Faruque is running late today. I understand that you need to get to work. Would you like to reschedule? She is available three weeks from now at the same time—or if you can wait 20 minutes or so, you can see Dr. Williams instead. He is one of our best cardiologists—you will really like him."

Tactic 3: Use Reception Area Updates and Room and Round℠ to Manage Waits and Delays

Sometimes delays cannot be prevented. In these cases, communication with patients is key. This is one more place where Key Words at Key Times can be really useful. As we've seen in organizations we coach, patients are far more tolerant about waiting if staff is apologetic and provides frequent updates. That's because the updates make the time seem shorter—even if, in reality, it was more than 15 minutes.

Here's how it works in the reception area. The receptionist or a nurse comes out and addresses the entire room with an overall update. For example:

"Good morning, I'm Dottie, one of the team of nurses who will help care for you today. We feel it is important to keep you updated

on timing, so I wanted to let you know that Dr. Xavier was called into surgery early this morning. We are focused on getting all of her patients seen so they don't have to make a return visit. At this time, each of our doctors is about 20 minutes behind. Our goal is to provide the best care and not make our patients feel rushed. We also don't want anyone to have to wait an unnecessarily long time. We know your time is valuable. Please let us know if you would like to reschedule instead. We appreciate your understanding."

You'll probably want to round about every half-hour or hour, depending on how far behind your providers may be. As you're giving this update, it's important to assess the room. If you notice any patients who seem visibly upset, we recommend that you speak to them personally after the update.

In Chapter 13, the full Rounding in the Reception Area[SM] is shared as a tactic. It has a much more patient-centric focus than the previous example, providing individual updates to those in the reception area every 15 minutes to every half-hour, based on when they checked in. The version you use will depend on the needs of your practice. You may want to start with the version here and progress to the full Rounding in the Reception Area version once your practice is ready to go deeper with this tactic.

Once a patient has been brought to an exam room, Room and Round begins. Nurses or other staff will tell him that the provider will be in within 15 minutes. Should there be a delay, staff will round on the patient at least every 15 minutes, providing updates on the delay and making sure he is comfortable. Key words such as the following let the patient know that he has not been left in the exam room and forgotten:

- *"Hi, Mr. Wallace, I am checking in to see how you are doing while you wait."*

- *"Dr. Mantor is delayed by 15 minutes. I apologize for the delay. If there is further delay, I will keep you well informed."*

- *"May I offer you something to drink while you wait?"*

- *"Thank you, Mr. Wallace, for waiting as we know your time is valuable. Is there anything I can do for you to make you more comfortable while you wait?"*

The following graphic shows some more key word options. The left hand column shares examples of what the nurse or medical assistant should do when the patient is assigned a room. The right hand column includes the action that should happen when the nurse rounds on the exam room every15 minutes. (If the wait is less than 15 minutes, the actions in the right hand column will not take place.)

Upon Room Assignment	As You Round on Exam Rooms (every 15 minutes)
- Narrate your care.	- Address any comfort needs.
- Provide comfort measures.	- "Mr. Jones, Dr. Guy knows you are here ..."
- Before leaving the room, say: "Dr. Guy will be with you within 15 minutes."	- "Mr. Jones, Dr. Guy will be delayed– he will be with you within 15 minutes."
- "Is there anything I can help you with before I leave the room?"	- "Is there anything I can help you with at this time?"
- "I am going to close the door to respect your privacy."	- "Thank you for your patience, Mr. Jones."

Figure 5.3 Rounding for Outcomes: Room and Round^{SM} by Office Staff

Tactic 4: Care Coordination and Handovers

Traditionally, care coordination has been focused on the ability of the patient to schedule appointments with more than one provider. Now, it's becoming much more associated with clinical handovers as well—the idea being to ensure that if a patient must schedule an appointment with a different provider than usual, that person will receive the same level of care.

This situation typically occurs when a primary provider refers a patient to another provider for specialty care, but handovers can also occur when a provider is tied up in a surgery or procedure that is running long. We need to make sure our desire to keep patients from having to wait longer than 15 minutes (driven in part by this CG CAHPS question) doesn't lead us to neglect the free-flow of information between Provider A (the patient's usual physician) and Provider B (the one she is being handed over to).

It is important that when the second provider steps in he has all the appropriate patient information so he isn't starting from scratch. It is a huge relief to patients to feel that their doctors are in coordination regarding their care.

You'll notice we use the term *handover* versus "handoff." "Handoff" implies that you are transitioning patient information, data, history, etc. with the intent of never looking at it or caring about it again. "Handover" implies a sense of caring, determination to ensure quality care, and realization that the patient is still one of your patients at the end of the day. (Not only does Provider A need to share background information with Provider B, but Provider B also needs to make sure to later dialogue back with Provider A.)

Proper handovers directly tie to patient access in the following ways:

- They ensure that patients receive access to healthcare, even if their personal provider cannot see or speak to them that day.

- They remove the delay in receiving information, test results, and so on, when a patient's personal provider is unavailable.

- They align office staff by identifying a common goal. Excellent patient care is about providing access to whatever needs the patient has that day.

Care coordination or care transitioning through handovers can be implemented in several different ways.

- **Contract with a call center.** Call centers are typically used for scheduling initial appointments with primary care groups. However, there are some call centers doing care coordination between primary and specialty care appointments so that the care is expedited.

- **Assign a flow coordinator.** The flow coordinator in this case is used as a liaison between call centers and office scheduling centers, as well as with the provider. In this instance, it's helpful for the flow coordinator to be an RN or have a clinical background so she can appropriately triage patients better and get them in the right appointment slot. (See the tip on this role later in this chapter.)

- **Utilize technology.** The coordination of care and the transference of patient data and their history and information are also expedited through technology with tools like electronic medical records (EMRs). Multiple systems can tap into a patient's record without the physical chart having to be transferred and moved from one office to another, or one location to another.

- **Phone another provider.** Sometimes the old-fashioned way is the best way: A provider or flow coordinator can simply pick up the phone and call another to request that he see a patient that day.

Not only does care coordination take the work off the patient and place it on the office, it also allows a provider a) to ensure that his patients were seen the day they requested, and b) to access the EMRs at the end of the day so he can see what happened. He can also follow up with the provider who offered care to close the loop and discuss any next steps.

Let's discuss some best practices around care transitions.

- **Coordinate with other groups ahead of time.** For example, let's say a primary care physician coordinates with an orthopedic group and that the majority of these referrals stem from five different patient health complaints. The two groups can work together. For example, the orthopedic group can then list what they need from the primary care physician in these top five instances in order to have the information necessary should a patient need to be seen quickly—for example, records, images or other information.

- **Build a template into the EMR.** Computerized templates allow the primary care physician's office to share vital information with the referred physician (and his office) without the need for additional communication with or access to either provider. A template can leverage the technology of the EMR and help ensure that nothing is missed.

- **Review and reassess care templates included in the scheduling system.** Meet with the scheduling staff, the providers, and the clinical staff to understand how the templates currently in use were developed and what they consist of. Then ask what items are most worthwhile, if there are any barriers, and so on. You can then compare the findings with the current template and edit it as necessary.

A Few Additional Tips

Here are a few more tips to consider as you are hardwiring the previous tactics.

Tip: Assign a Flow Coordinator

Flow coordinators, also referred to as "air traffic controllers" and triage coordinators, are staff members who have a good understanding about what type of appointment goes into which time slot once open access scheduling has been implemented.

For instance, if the provider has half of his day open for same-day scheduling and a new patient requests an appointment due to cold symptoms, the flow coordinator can quickly schedule her into an open 20-minute time slot that day. If the patient is complaining of severe back pain that comes and goes and slight tingling in her right leg, the flow coordinator would recognize the need for a longer appointment and would schedule two 20-minute appointments back to back.

The flow coordinator is also in charge of making sure the daily appointments stay on time and patients don't get backlogged. When the backup plan is discussed in the daily huddle, she will know exactly who the backup provider or non-physician provider will be for the day in the event she needs to reassign the patient.

The flow coordinator can also manage up any non-physician providers that patients may need to meet with throughout the day. By using key words, she can ease patient anxiety about seeing someone other than their own provider. For example:

"Ms. Jones, we would be happy to see you today. I know you typically see Dr. Edwards when you visit us; however, his schedule

is completely booked. We can schedule you an appointment with his physician assistant, Sharon, who has worked with Dr. Edwards for more than five years and is an excellent healthcare provider. Would you be willing to see Sharon today or would you like to wait to see Dr. Edwards in a few days?"

If the patient feels urgency to see someone immediately, then you've provided her with a good option to meet with Sharon. You've informed the patient that she will still be getting the same quality care she gets from her personal provider, and you've also managed up the fact that she could receive timely access to care.

If the patient realizes the appointment isn't as urgent as she first thought, it now becomes *her* decision to wait to see her regular provider. Thus, she is less likely to be frustrated or feel she wasn't given access in a timely manner.

Tip: Pagers and/or Text Messages

Some practices have implemented the use of pagers (similar to those used by restaurants when you're waiting for a table) for those patients who are looking at waits of 30 minutes or more. Others take down the patient's mobile phone number so they can text her when she can be seen. Patients have responded very positively to this acknowledgment that their time is valuable. When you can go get a cup of coffee or just take a walk in the fresh air instead of being stuck in the waiting room, that wait doesn't seem as long.

Improving your results for the timeliness question will also improve your results in other composites as well. When patients' appointments occur in a timely manner, they feel respected by staff and care providers and get the message that your practice cares about their needs. As a result, they feel more positive about their experience overall.

Tools & Resources

Studer Group® offers a variety of tools and resources that support the tactics discussed in this chapter. To access the up-to-date information, and to download a worksheet that will help you create a plan to improve patient perception of care in the "Access to Care" arena, please visit www.studergroup.com/CGCAHPS.

Practicing Good Provider/Patient Communication

W e all know communication is a two-way street. As healthcare clinicians, whether we're doctors, nurses, or other clinicians, we have the training and experience to diagnose, prescribe, and treat. Only we can do these things. Yet we are only half of the equation. The other half is the patient, and only she can know all her symptoms, all the facets of her lifestyle, and the entire unique set of circumstances that impacts her physical and psychological health.

Only when we're able to establish a strong, clear, meaningful connection between provider and patient can this vital information be exchanged effectively and efficiently. And communication is the conduit through which that information flows. Both provider and patient play a role—but it's up to us to set the stage, to create the conditions that allow communication to flourish.

Effective communication fosters stronger relationships between care providers and patients and builds a foundation of trust, compliance, and collaboration. As your practice gets better at shoring up your relationships with patients, both perception of care and clinical quality will improve—often dramatically.

The evidence, as well as our coaching experience, tells us that good communication offers many benefits to both the patient and the providers, including:

- Improved clinical quality outcomes, safety, and measures of clinical effectiveness[1]

- Better alignment and adherence to care plans and medication regimens; patients whose physicians communicate poorly have a 19 percent higher risk of non-adherence than patients whose physicians communicate well[2]

- A statistically significant positive impact on clinical outcomes[3]

- Better patient experience of care and experience-based quality measures[4]

In fact, one study clearly shows that clinicians who have a strong awareness of and focus on communication also perform well on CG CAHPS.[5]

The Provider Communication Composite is also highly correlated *(r=0.89 based on the 2013 AHRQ CG CAHPS database)* to a patient's Overall CG CAHPS Experience Rating. That means if you master the tactics in this section, patients will most likely feel good about their entire visit. Strong provider/patient communication is a "silver bullet" of sorts—get it right and you automatically fix many other potential problems.

How well providers communicate with patients is about more than just the information shared. It also encompasses vocal expression, body language, and ability to convey empathy. In fact, Albert Mehrabian's work on effective communication has taught us that our "Total Liking" of a person breaks down to 7 percent Verbal Liking, 38 percent Vocal Liking, and 55 percent Facial Liking.[6,7] Clearly, clinicians must not underestimate the importance of the words we use, the tone we speak in, and our facial expressions.

Non-verbal cues often speak louder than our actual words—for instance, making eye contact, sitting down to talk to the patient, and using posture such as "leaning in" can affect the way the patient experiences what we are saying as much as, or even more than, the spoken words.

Even details such as provider attire can impact communication. This is why some organizations have instituted a dress code—whether business dress or scrubs—to ensure that providers are putting forth a professional image. Patients look for physician appearance to be one that garners trust and assuredness.[8]

Effective communication benefits the provider as well as the patient. Making those connections gets to the core of why most providers went into this profession—it's about doing worthwhile work and making a difference. And perception of care data or results aside, it's the right thing to do for patients and their families.

Enhancing one's communication skills is *not* a long or complicated process. The goal isn't to add more work to a provider's already jam-packed schedule. Rather, the tactics outlined in this section are meant to help providers be more efficient, improve clinical effectiveness, and maximize the impact of work they are already doing.

After all, we want to provide the best possible care to patients, and communication is at the foundation—effective communication is, in fact, a "clinical skill."

Following is a story shared from a patient's perspective of just how much it meant to her to have a provider who listened, showed respect, and worked together with her and her father for his care plan at a difficult time in his life.

In 2007, my father was diagnosed with advanced gallbladder cancer that had already spread to his liver. Dr. Aurora and his staff showed more compassion and communicated more than any physician I had ever met. My father and I knew we had someone in our corner fighting for us.

My father did not always understand everything, and Dr. Aurora would make sure to explain things in an easy-to-grasp way. He would also schedule family meetings so I could ask questions and be there when he was explaining things so I could help my father with his medications and treatments. Phone calls were always returned, and he never rushed me when I had questions.

The last time my father went to the ER, it was extremely obvious that he was nearing the end of his life. Dr. Aurora came to see him and told him that he would make sure his last days were as comfortable as possible and that he would keep his dignity. He then went outside the room with me and let me cry; he hugged me and I swear he shed a few tears himself. He thanked us for letting him be a part of my father's care and said he had learned from the experience.

I was my father's only child, and he was not married. I was his sole care provider other than my 85-year-old grandfather, who had failing health himself. I can't imagine how I would have made it through such a horrible experience without Dr. Aurora and his staff. He truly went above and beyond what he had to do and he truly cared for my father and also for me.

Dr. Aurora held my hand every step of the way and eased my fears as best he could. I will be forever grateful to him.

This is what communication is truly all about. We're not computers sharing information to be plugged into some precise formula to get some exact result. We are human beings connecting with other human beings, and that means we're doing more than exchanging data. We're sharing with our patients the joy and fear and hope and anguish and peace that come along with living, dying, and loving others. This is a monumental responsibility and also an honor. We need to make certain we're worthy of both.

The Survey Questions

This aspect of the CG CAHPS survey asks patients how well their provider communicated, listened, shared important information, and whether he or she spent enough time with them and showed respect. Answers are given in frequency scale: *never, sometimes, usually,* or *always.* The percent of patients who responded *always* is publicly reported on a growing number of state and private payer websites and is starting to appear at the CMS Provider

Compare website located at www.medicare.gov/physiciancompare.

1. **How often did this provider explain things in a way that was easy to understand?**

2. **How often did this provider listen carefully to you?**

3. **How often did this provider give you easy-to-understand information about these health questions or concerns?**

4. **How often did this provider seem to know the important information about your medical history?**

5. **How often did this provider spend enough time with you?**

6. **How often did this provider show respect for what you had to say?**

The self-test on the next page is designed to assist you in determining how you are doing on the basics. We recommend you ask all your clinicians to participate in this self-test and compare your results to determine where to focus first. You may also find it valuable to repeat this self-test a year from now to evaluate your improvement in these areas.

Note: We have adopted the four-response standard of CG CAHPS for the self-test. Using this standard is a great way to build your own competency and experience in what it takes to consistently achieve an "always" response.

Question	Never	Sometimes	Usually	Always
1. How often do I acknowledge what the patient has told other team members about their visit today?				
2. When I enter the exam room, how often do I sit down to talk with my patients at the beginning of the visit?				
3. How often do I show empathy in my non-verbal communication?				
4. How often do I plan my day so I will not be interrupted when I am with patients, and my staff supports me in doing so?				
5. How often do I take the first two minutes of every visit to listen to my patients before I start the diagnostic exam?				
6. How often do I demonstrate personal knowledge/interest in my patients to them? *(for example: "Weren't you getting ready to go on a vacation to Alaska last time I saw you?")*				
7. How often do I employ teach back to ensure that my patients understand what I have shared with them?				
8. Before getting up to leave the room, how often do I ask my patients if they have any questions for me and reassure them that I have time to address them? *(for example: "We have covered a lot of information in your visit today. You must have some questions for me. I have time to answer any questions you have.")*				
9. How often do I acknowledge family members and involve them in the conversation when appropriate, including asking them if they understand their role in the treatment plan?				
10. How often do we have a standardized process to identify each patient's primary reason for visiting and ensuring the entire team knows the patient's *what?*				

Figure ii.1 Provider Communication Self-Test

Provider Communication Self-Test Scoring

If you are like 99.9 percent of medical practices, you will likely have identified a couple of areas that you can improve. Don't try to implement all of the tactics in this section at once. Select the one or two most important to improving your practice and start by hardwiring them first.

Following is a chart that crosswalks the statements you evaluated your practice's performance against with the CG CAHPS question(s) it aligns with and/or impacts.

Self- Test Question	CG CAHPS Question(s)
1. How often do I acknowledge what the patient has told other team members about their visit today?	• How often did the provider seem to know the important information about your medical history? • How often did this provider show respect for what you had to say?
2. When I enter the exam room, how often do I sit down to talk with my patients at the beginning of the visit?	• How often did this provider listen carefully to you? • How often did this provider spend enough time with you?
3. How often do I show empathy in my non-verbal communication?	• How often did this provider show respect for what you had to say? • How often did this provider listen carefully to you?
4. How often do I plan my day so I will not be interrupted when I am with patients, and my staff supports me in doing so?	• How often did this provider listen carefully to you? • How often did this provider spend enough time with you?
5. How often do I take the first two minutes of every visit to listen to my patients before I start the diagnostic exam?	• How often did this provider listen carefully to you? • How often did this provider spend enough time with you?
6. How often do I demonstrate personal knowledge/interest in my patients to them? *(for example: "Weren't you getting ready to go on a vacation to Alaska last time I saw you?")*	• How often did this provider show respect for what you had to say? • How often did this provider spend enough time with you?
7. How often do I employ teach back to ensure that my patients understand what I have shared with them?	• How often did this provider explain things in a way that was easy to understand? • How often did this provider give you easy-to-understand information about these health questions or concerns?
8. Before getting up to leave the room, how often do I ask my patients if they have any questions for me and reassure them that I have time to address them? *(for example: "We have covered a lot of information in your visit today. You must have some questions for me. I have time to answer any questions you have.")*	• How often did this provider show respect for what you had to say? • How often did this provider spend enough time with you?
9. How often do I acknowledge family members and involve them in the conversation when appropriate, including asking them if they understand their role in the treatment plan?	• How often did this provider show respect for what you had to say?

Figure ii.2 Provider Communication Self-Test Questions Guide

Now, here is a crosswalk between the CG CAHPS questions and tactics in this section.

CG CAHPS Question	Key Tactics
• How often did this provider explain things in a way that was easy to understand?	• Provide Written Information for the Patient • Shared Care Agenda • Teach Back Method • Focus on the "E" in AIDET˙
• How often did this provider listen carefully to you?	• Two-Minute Rule • Focus on the "A" in AIDET˙ • Fundamental Tactic: Key Words at Key Times
• How often did this provider give you easy-to-understand information about these health questions or concerns?	• Focus on the "E" in AIDET˙ • Teach Back Method
• How often did this provider seem to know the important information about your medical history?	• Fundamental Tactic: Key Words at Key Times • IPC • Patient Scouting Report
• How often did this provider spend enough time with you?	• Managing Wait Times • Two-Minute Rule • IPC • Sitting Down *(tip)*
• How often did this provider show respect for what you had to say?	• Empathy • Focus on the "A" in AIDET˙ • Shared Care Agenda

Figure ii.3 Provider Communication Questions and Tactics Guide

In the chapters that follow, we will share the top few tactics for each Provider Communication Composite question that positively impact the likelihood that patients will answer *always*.

These chapters don't cover every possible effective tactic. Rather, they zero in on a few carefully targeted specific actions you can take to immediately impact patient perception of how well your practice and providers are communicating.

CHAPTER SIX:

UNDERSTANDABLE PROVIDER EXPLANATIONS

"The more you explain it, the more I don't understand it."
—*Mark Twain*

THE CG CAHPS QUESTION: **How often did this provider explain things in a way that was easy to understand?**

Medical issues can be complicated—sometimes *very* complicated. It's not always easy for patients to grasp the implications of their diagnosis and all the nuances of their prognosis and treatment. When several different medications and treatment options are involved, it can be even more confusing. Absorbing all the details can be overwhelming even to a person who is not facing health challenges. Add in the complex medical terminology that's often used and it's not surprising so many patients have a hard time understanding what they're told.

Especially when dealing with patients who are struggling with pain or fatigue and with family members who are anxious about their loved one, providers need to be certain that their explanations are being heard and processed. That's why AHRQ included the "easy to understand" question in the CG CAHPS survey.

Of course, providers have always cared about effective communication with patients. But with the advent of healthcare reform and the ever-increasing emphasis on the patient experience, their focus has moved beyond the science of diagnoses, test ordering, and examinations to include the art of truly "connecting" with those we serve.

As treatment plans grow increasingly complex, communication becomes an ever-more-essential component in driving clinical quality, safety, and perception of care. Explaining clinical information like diagnosis, treatment, medication, and next steps in a way the patient can understand is just as important as the facts themselves.

Patients who really "get" what their physicians and other providers are saying are more likely to acknowledge and share health risks or concerns, understand their treatment options, adhere to a Shared Care Plan, and follow other instructions appropriately. Yet, all too often, what physicians believe they are saying and what patients say they are hearing can be miles apart.

One study on postherpetic neuralgia showed that the patients, primary care providers, and neurologists surveyed were all in agreement that insufficient treatment options exist for this pain occurring long after a shingles infection has cleared up. However, while almost all physicians felt they shared the cause of this condition, a full 25 percent of patients said that their physician had not done so. Similarly, 25 percent of patients were not aware of the duration of postherpetic neuralgia, the treatment side effects, or what to expect from treatment. Clearly, such communication gaps between physicians and their patients would impact how health conditions are managed.[1]

Another study,[2] illustrated in Figures 6.1 and 6.2, found there are often large discrepancies between what physicians believe they have communicated and what patients understand and remember.

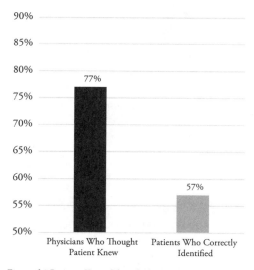

Figure 6.1 Patients Know Their Diagnosis

As you'll see from Figure 6.1, the study shows 77 percent of physicians surveyed thought patients understood their diagnosis, but in reality only 57 percent of the patients who were seen by those same physicians really did understand. The implication is clear: Many physicians need to do a better job of explaining important information to patients and probing to make sure patients really understood what they were told.

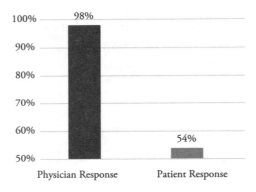

Figure 6.2 Physician Discussed Patient's Fears and Anxieties

What's more, 98 percent of the physicians in the aforementioned study responded that they had discussed patient fears and anxieties. Yet, again, the patients saw it differently. Only 54 percent of them perceived that these same physicians had addressed those topics.

Why is it so important for providers to discuss patient fear and anxiety? We find that tackling these issues head on gets them out of the way so that patients can better focus on and process what the physician is saying. Also, when physicians are willing to discuss these feelings, patients feel more connected to them. This makes patients more likely to listen carefully and, later, to comply with treatment plans.

It seems clear there is a disconnect here. The providers feel they are sending patients home confident that they (the patients) understand their diagnosis and treatment plan, when in reality this is not always true. And when patients don't understand explanations, they can't possibly take proper care of themselves. This hurts clinical outcomes. Lack of clarity also means providers are falling short of the goal to build a relationship of trust and connection—which undermines the entire foundation of the provider/patient partnership.

...And the Tactics That Make "Always" Responses More Likely

Effective explanations involve providing patients with information on diagnosis, treatment, medication, and the next steps in ways they can understand, as well as confirming their understanding. Studer Group® has identified the following tactics to help improve results and achieve a better patient experience through effective provider explanations.

Tactic 1: Provide Written Information for the Patient

While verbal explanations are very important and do the "lion's share" of the work in helping patients understand their diagnosis and treatment, they must also be supplemented by written information. After all, patients may forget details and will need something to refer back to later when they have questions or just need a refresher. And reassuring them, ahead of the explanation, that you will also be providing the information in written format will reduce their anxiety about trying to remember every detail that you are telling them.

The written information should be a quick summary of the diagnosis, treatment plan, patient responsibilities, and any post-care actions the patient may need to take. Figure 6.3 is an example of a Patient Visit Guide card that some of Studer Group's top performing organizations use for this purpose. It allows the provider to make notes and document with the patient what was discussed, treatment plans, medications, and next steps. It will also trigger the provider to ensure that they understand the patient's "what" and discuss it.

Patient Visit Guide

We are committed to providing you with **very good/excellent** healthcare. We work as a **team**, which includes you and your family, as well as our experienced staff and physicians.

You will be an **active participant** in your care. We will discuss all test results with you and your family. **Together** we will decide which treatment options are best for you.

We will **listen** to your healthcare **concerns** in a respectful, courteous, and supportive manner.

Your time is important and we will work to keep you **informed** of waits and minimize delays.

We believe you should have **easy access** to your caregivers. If you have questions or problems, please call _____.

What is the primary reason for your visit today?
_____
_____

☐ I have prescriptions that need to be refilled.
☐ I need a work excuse.
☐ I need forms filled out (*please fill out your portion of the forms prior to the visit*).
☐ I need a referral for _____

What is the one thing we need to focus on to assure your visit is very good/excellent?
_____
_____
_____

Vital Signs

Pulse _____ Blood Pressure _____

Weight _____ Height _____

If we need to call you, what is the best number to call? _____

Provider's Notes
_____
_____
_____
_____

Medication Instructions

☐ I **DID NOT** make changes to your medications today.

☐ I **DID** make changes to your medications today.
_____
_____
_____

Recommendations/Instructions

Before you leave today, please:
☐ Wait for immunizations in the exam room
☐ Schedule a mammogram
☐ Schedule a bone density test
☐ Go to the lab for blood work
☐ Schedule lab services
☐ Go to radiology/x-ray
☐ Schedule radiology/x-ray
☐ Other _____

Follow-up Care

1. Please schedule an appointment with _____ in _____ weeks/months.
   Reason: _____
2. Please schedule an appointment with _____ in _____ weeks/months.
   Reason: _____

Post-Visit Care/Expectations

How will I learn about my test results?
☐ Telephone call
☐ Mail
☐ WILL be notified of normal results
☐ WILL NOT be notified of normal results

If you have not heard from us within two weeks of your testing, please call us at _____

Figure 6.3 Patient Visit Guide Sample

To download a sample Patient Visit Guide card, please visit www.studergroup.com/CGCAHPS.

Make sure that any written information provided is well organized and neat, and uses everyday language that patients will be able to understand. (Keep in mind that the average American adult reads at an 8th-9th grade level; one in five reads at a 5th grade level.)[3]

Also, be sure to avoid medical lingo, regardless of grade level—for example, "push fluids" is a phrase most adults can read, but they may not understand what it really means from a medical standpoint.

Tactic 2: Create a Shared Care Plan

A Shared Care Plan (also commonly referred to as a Shared Care Agenda) is a process that works hand in hand with the other tactics detailed throughout this section. The Shared Care Plan provides cues to ensure that the provider poses questions and frames the conversation to involve patients in decisions, making them active participants in managing their own health rather than passive recipients who "follow orders."

A study published in the *Journal of General Internal Medicine* describes a process similar to what we're discussing here. The "shared decision making model" or SDM is described as "an approach where clinicians and patients share the best available evidence when faced with the task of making decisions, and where patients are supported to consider options, to achieve informed preferences."[4]

The authors write: "Achieving shared decision making depends on building a good relationship in the clinical encounter so that information is shared and patients are supported to deliberate and express their preferences and views during the decision making process. To accomplish these tasks, we propose a model of how to do shared decision making that is based on choice, option and decision talk. The model has three steps: a) introducing choice, b) describing options, often by integrating the use of patient decision support, and c) helping patients explore preferences and make decisions."

The study goes on to say that "SDM is supported by evidence from 86 randomized trials showing knowledge gain by patients, more confidence in decisions, more active patient involvement, and, in many situations, informed patients elect for more conservative treatment options."

The concept of "shared care" is more than merely addressing the patient's "what" (that one thing that's most important to them about their visit). It's about creating a dialogue between the provider and patient, to ensure that both are able to have all of their concerns addressed. The provider and patient should both leave the encounter knowing that they were heard and understood.

After listening to the patient, gathering symptoms, and talking about the reason for their visit, now the provider can actively discuss the items on the Shared Care Plan and engage the patient in diagnostic and treatment decisions.

There are a variety of ways to incorporate the Shared Care Plan process into the patient care process. Some organizations use a form that the provider completes and keeps with the patient's record, as seen in Figure 6.4; others may use a form that is shared and completed with the patient.

Patient Name: _____   Date: _____

Provider Name: _____

- Review the patient's *what* with him/her. Ask if you interpreted it correctly.
- Review your plan for the flow of the appointment.

  "These are the items I wanted to cover. What other issues might we address today?"

  "Does that sound like a good plan to you?"

- Discuss diagnosis and treatment plan.

  "I recommend the following course of treatment/next steps…" (review care plan)

  "Can you tell me what you heard me say and what you understand about your diagnosis and my recommendations?"

  "What are your thoughts about my recommendations?"

  "Do you think they are reasonable?"

  "What concerns do you have?"

- Ask the patient if you have answered all his/her questions and discussed what is of utmost importance to him/her for your time together.

  "Is there anything important to you that we did not discuss?"

- Thank the patient for his/her time.

Provider Signature: _____

Figure 6.4 Shared Care Plan Conversation Starter

The Shared Care Plan may also be noted on a pocket card that providers may simply reference to ensure that they are asking the necessary questions to engage patients in their own care.

When we listen and deliver on what we discuss with patients, they feel respected and cared for. They know that we are listening and keeping their concerns in mind at all times.

Tactic 3: Teach Back Method

Research shows that 40-80 percent of the medical information patients receive is forgotten by the time they leave the provider's office[5, 6] and nearly half of the information that patients retain is incorrect.[7] These are concerning statistics, especially when you consider that a patient's ability to understand and remember what she's told is directly connected to her clinical outcome.

The good news is there is a way to close the communication gap between clinicians and patients. It's called the Teach Back Method, also known as "closing the loop."[8, 9]

The Teach Back Method ensures that the patients fully understand their Shared Care Agenda, including the medications they are taking and why. It provides the opportunity not just to reiterate and express to patients the importance of their care plans, but also to engage patients in their own care.

How does the Teach Back Method work? Essentially, the provider asks patients to repeat what he has said to make sure they fully understand the diagnosis, treatment, and next steps. This will also ensure they understand their medications—patients are more likely to comply when they truly understand the "why" behind the explanation.

Specifically, the provider asks the patient to describe the care plan in her own words (as if the patient were giving the instructions to another person). The provider should use open-ended questions to allow the patient the opportunity to "explain back" what has been said in as much detail as possible. For example:

- *"I just want to make sure we're on the same page, so can you describe the diet requirements that we discussed?"*

- *"The information will be on the prescription bottle, but I want to make sure you know it by heart: Can you tell me how you're supposed to take the medication I'm prescribing?"*

- *"Can you explain what symptoms you're supposed to watch for?"*

Here are a few tips for implementing the Teach Back Method:

- **Ask open-ended questions.** Instead of setting up the patient to answer "yes" or "no," ask her questions that encourage her to open up more. This will provide more data to the provider so he can identify areas that still need to be addressed.

  "Mrs. Adams, we are covering a lot of information today for this visit. I care that you walk away from this informed. You must have some questions for me. I am happy to answer."

- **Pause during explanation for questions.** By pausing during the explanation to the patient, it allows the patient to ask the questions as she thinks of them rather than holding on to them till the end. During this time, she may forget the questions or be so focused on making sure she asks the question she does not fully hear all the information the provider is giving.

"I want to do a good job of explaining everything we are covering today during your visit, so please tell me when something I say isn't clear or if you have any questions."

- **Watch your body language.** In addition to using simple words and providing in-depth information, be mindful of body language. There's been plenty of research showing that providers' facial expressions and the way their body is positioned can greatly affect the quality of communication with patients.

  It's important that providers' body language remains focused on the patient. This sets the tone for the entire encounter. If a provider has one hand on the door and his back to the patient and uses words such as, "Do you have any questions?" the patient will assume that he's not really listening and doesn't have time for questions. She will likely say "no" but may still have doubts in her mind or may leave with a set of questions unanswered.

  When off-putting body language (or anything else) makes the patient feel she isn't being heard, it creates anxiety that will remain with her until it's resolved. This can negatively impact the encounter and the goal for the visit, which is to help the patient understand and feel informed.

- **Check for understanding.** Explain in a way that aligns with a patient's education and intellect. Using Teach Back methodology such as, "I have given you a fair bit of information today. Would you mind telling me what you understand about this illness?" allows the provider to evaluate if the patient has effectively understood what has been shared. If the patient has not, take responsibility for explaining again, perhaps in a new way.

Some of Studer Group's highest performing organizations take this method to the next level by using key words to encourage the patient's engagement. Here are some examples of key words to use during Teach Back:

- *"I want to make sure you understand..."*

- *"I care that you walk away feeling confident about what we discussed..."*

- *"To help me know we did a good job of explaining..."*

- *"Knowing you understand your care is important to me..."*

Tactic 4: Focus on "E" in AIDET®

Being able to offer clear, effective, understandable explanations leads the provider to become more of a trusted advisor rather than just someone the patient visits when sick. The patient-provider relationship is built to foster trust. Trust is important because it's what allows the patient to partner with the provider to determine the best treatment plan and next steps. Thus, the "E" in AIDET® is tremendously important.

As you'll recall from Chapter 2, AIDET is an acronym that represents the framework for effective communication with patients. It has been proven to not only improve the patient experience but also to impact clinical outcomes. Patients are more likely to adhere to the treatment plan and experience less anxiety when the provider follows this communication framework.

Remember, AIDET should not be considered a checklist, but rather an "awareness tool" that can and should be customized for each interaction. It's not necessary to use all the AIDET steps in every encounter. Focus on the steps that will impact the goal you are trying to achieve in the communication with the patient.

Figure 6.5 provides a quick reminder of the "E" in AIDET and how it can be applied for this CG CAHPS survey question.

E: Explanation
• Explain to the patient the diagnosis, treatment—including medications—and any testing involved in appropriate terms, followed up with information they can easily understand.
• Ensure understanding by "teach back" and asking for questions in an open-ended manner.

Figure 6.5 AIDET® for Effective Explanations

AIDET® for Effective Explanations

To download a guide to AIDET for effective explanations, please visit www.studergroup.com/CGCAHPS.

For this particular interaction with the patient, the goal is to provide an effective explanation on a level the patient will easily understand. Therefore, the "E" will be the main focus for these communications. Sometimes, we don't get the impact we think we're getting until we really listen to the words we're using and cue into the goal we're hoping to achieve. As one physician said to a Studer Group coach, "I always thought I did a good job with explanation, but once I began to focus on the 'E' in AIDET, my explanations became excellent."

Here are a few helpful tips:

- **Provide explanations in a clear order.** Provide the information in the following order with clear transitions:

  1. Share the diagnosis OR what you are attempting to clarify or rule out.

  2. Share the recommendations for treatment.

  3. Share the expected clinical course of the condition.

  4. Explain what the patient needs to do.

  5. Address symptom management.

- **Share the name of the diagnosis.** Patients want to know what they have. Let them know the name and write it out for them. Equally important is talking about the serious diseases they *don't* have. Reassure them. Many people tend to anticipate the worst-case scenarios, and if you can alleviate that fear, it is best to do so early on to reduce their anxiety so they will be more open to hearing the rest of the explanation and partner with the provider to determine treatment options.

- **Avoid medical jargon.** When providing information and possible diagnoses, use language the average person can understand. Describe the condition or medication in everyday words, keeping in mind that the *average* American adult reads at an 8th-9th grade level; that level tends to be lower for older people, those not fluent in English, and the economically disadvantaged.[10]

One Studer Group coach observed a provider saying this to a patient: *"This condition is called 'dysphagia' and is usually due to atresia or stenosis. I am going to keep you NPO for now till I can get a GI specialist, but if needed, we will give you an analgesic PRN."* This statement is unintelligible to a layperson and could even be intimidating or frightening to patients. The following would have given the patient information he could understand: *"Your difficulty and pain in swallowing is called 'dysphagia.' It is usually caused by a narrowing in your throat, but I'm going to get a specialist to examine you to be certain so we can decide how to take care of you. In the meantime, I'm going to restrict your food and drink to minimize your pain and prescribe some pain medication."*

A Few Additional Tips

Here are a few more tips to consider as you are hardwiring the previous tactics. They help physicians and providers offer more understandable explanations and gain patient partnership in their care plans.

- **Use analogies and metaphors.** In using a metaphor to explain something to the patient, the provider is taking something that appears to be complex or new to the patient and relating it to that of a familiar experience. This will help to encourage the patient to retain the knowledge being shared and create clarity. It also helps the patient process the emotional aspect of the explanation. This may seem simple, but this is what helps to separate a standard explanation from an effective explanation.

  Example: *"Sarah, the bump you are feeling on the side of your neck is a blocked sweat gland that is nothing to be too concerned about. It happens more frequently to people than you would think. It is basically like a plug on that one gland, so when you sweat it has nowhere to go and it backs up. We can simply and quickly remove it to alleviate your discomfort. You should not need any additional testing or follow-up treatment."*

- **Know the patient's "what" and speak to it.** A key element to remember when explaining clinical information to a patient is what is important to the patient. The provider needs to address his "what" up front. Try asking, *"What is your biggest concern?"* or *"When you leave today, what is the one thing you would really like to have accomplished?"*

- **Share the information several times.** Often a patient will be thinking of a question or digesting what the provider has just shared with him and will miss a portion of the information. This is particularly the case when the patient has received a frightening or confusing diagnosis: As one patient said, "I heard the word 'cancer' and tuned everything else out."

Remember the thesis paper structure that you learned in high school composition class? Begin with the main idea, present your key points, then summarize the main idea again. That same structure works when sharing information with the patient: Give them the main point (the diagnosis and treatment plan), then explain the details (the specifics of care), then reiterate your main point.

Also, if there is a lot to remember, reassure the patient at this time that it will also be provided in written form before he leaves. Share the information with him several times and in multiple ways to ensure a complete understanding and retention of the information. It might even help trigger the patient to ask additional questions that will help him to better understand his care plan and comply. Here's an example:

"I know we discussed this earlier, Mike, but I want to go over this again because we have covered a lot of information during your visit today. The antibiotics I am giving you are to be taken twice daily, with food preferably. You will need to take all the medication until it is gone. It is a 14-day prescription and it is important that you take the entire amount I am prescribing for you, even after you feel better. So to sum up: Take twice a day with food, for the full 14 days. What questions do you have for me about this medication?"

- **Request commitment to adhere to the treatment plan.** Patients need to be partners with their providers, so before they leave your office, ask the patient, *"Are you comfortable with the plan of care we agreed upon? What questions do you have?"* The way the last question is worded is important because it is more open and inviting of questions and will elicit a deeper thought process than some other similar versions such as, *"You don't have any questions, do you?"* or *"Do you have any questions?"* (which may be perceived as more "closed" and inviting only a "yes/no" response).

Patients today desire communication with their providers that garners respect, trust, alignment, and understanding—a truly shared approach to their healthcare needs. Patients are more likely to share symptoms or changes in their health and become more engaged in their treatment plan when they trust that their provider has their best interests in mind. Ultimately, this leads to better clinical outcomes.

By implementing the tactics in this chapter, you create a "win-win": Patients attain better health outcomes and adhere more closely to recommended treatment regimens; providers and staff fulfill our mission of evidence-based, complete care and end each day knowing they maximized their impact in healthcare. In turn, patients will perceive and report on your care more positively, which will then be reflected in your improved CG CAHPS results.

Tools & Resources

Studer Group® offers a variety of tools and resources that support the tactics discussed in this chapter. To access the up-to-date information, please visit www.studergroup.com/CGCAHPS.

CHAPTER SEVEN:

CAREFUL PROVIDER LISTENING

"One of the most sincere forms of respect is actually listening to what another has to say."

—*Bryant H. McGill*

THE CG CAHPS QUESTION: How often did this provider listen carefully to you?

We all care about being listened to. It's a deep-seated human need. And when what we have to say is directly connected to our health and well-being, it's even more critical. Why? Because the extent to which providers listen to their patients is often directly connected to clinical outcomes.

Consider the case of Lucille, a 49-year-old woman who visited her family physician complaining of gastrointestinal problems: constipation alternating with diarrhea, abdominal discomfort, etc. Having read up on her symptoms, which had suddenly appeared after a lifetime of glowing health, Lucille was worried about cancer and actually mentioned this to the doctor. "I just have a feeling that something is really wrong," she said.

The physician asked some questions, took a few notes, acknowledged Lucille's fears, and finally reassured her that what she was worried about was extremely unlikely. "It sounds like you may have a classic case of irritable bowel syndrome," he said. "I'm going to write you a prescription and would like to see you back in a month. Please call me if your symptoms don't start improving."

Two more weeks went by and Lucille called again and said, "I know I have an appointment in two weeks, but if there's any way I can come in sooner, I'd appreciate it," she said. "I'm taking my medicine, but my stomach is still bothering me a lot. I'm really worried."

Concerned, the physician told her he could fit her in the next day. He quickly ordered some diagnostic tests and—sure enough—Lucille did have advanced ovarian cancer. Fortunately, he had listened to his patient's concerns and caught the cancer while it was still treatable. While life has been tough since then, Lucille is still alive and enjoying her family.

Careful listening can detect serious problems and sometimes even save lives. On the other hand, not giving patients our full attention can lead to misdiagnosis, causing them to suffer from illnesses and injuries longer than they have to. At the very least, a failure to carefully listen can cause patients to lose faith and stop sharing information that could be important to their health. And when that happens, we lose the ability to engage them as true partners in their care.

Of course, no care provider *wants* to be a careless listener. No provider wants to miss a crucial detail that leads to a poor diagnosis and ultimately a poor clinical outcome. Yet it does happen.

In the exam room, providers are almost always going through the lists of things they need to accomplish for the patient in front of them. The focus on checking things off the list can detract from hearing some of what the patient is saying or missing non-verbal cues that could aid in their care. If that's the case, they're not providing the best possible care and they may miss cues that would allow them to make better treatment decisions. And even if they really do hear everything the patient says, their focus on "the list" can give the impression they're not truly listening.

It is only through *actively listening* to the patient that providers can build relationships, which allow them to individualize care to achieve the best outcomes. In the provider-patient relationship, communication involves more than the transmission of information; it also involves transmitting feelings, recognizing these feelings, and letting the patient know that her feelings have been recognized.[1]

For example, an obstetrician might be trained to pay close attention to his post-partum patient's tone of voice, body language, and description of how things are going with the new baby. This isn't just small talk—by actively listening, the obstetrician can uncover symptoms of post-partum depression, which, if left untreated, can have a strongly negative effect on the health of the patient and the new baby.

Care providers are balancing many patients' needs, so taking the time to consistently listen and seek patient input—to hardwire this behavior—can be a challenge. Being a good listener requires an intentional effort. It is an essential skill worth mastering, because it creates a sense of partnership that helps the patient feel she is being heard and that she can be part of the process.

Listening to the patient and engaging her in her care will help to build a positive relationship and reduce anxiety. This, in turn, makes it more likely that the patient will follow her treatment plan, which also improves the likelihood of good clinical outcomes. The listening process starts from the minute the provider walks in and sees the patient.

...And the Tactics That Make "Always" Responses More Likely

At Studer Group®, we've analyzed the evidence gathered via research through our Learning Lab and identified the following tactics that assist with this crucial element of provider/patient communication. In this chapter, you will read about the top tactics that will improve patients' responses to the "listen carefully" question.

Tactic 1: Follow the Two-Minute Rule

Listening is a key step in building a lasting relationship with patients. The two-minute rule is an easy reminder to providers to spend the first couple of minutes of the patient encounter actively listening and engaging in conversation with the patient on a topic other than his clinical care. The provider may even be able to use what the patient has said to help develop better treatment plans. The two-minute rule allows the patient time to talk and the provider to understand the patient's "what" to really collaborate with him on his care.

Also, the two-minute rule can be applied after asking open-ended questions to the patient. Providers should allow the patient to speak uninterrupted and maintain eye contact. This may seem difficult to do, and at times the patient may not talk for two minutes, but it lets him know you are listening.

Additionally, allowing the patient time to speak allows time to listen for cues or symptoms that the patient may otherwise not realize are related or even fail to mention. If you actively listen to the patient when he is sharing his symptoms, and you ask some open-ended questions, you may realize that his symptoms are actually sub-symptoms to a bigger problem. A snap diagnosis may not be the correct one.

A well-known study found that providers interrupt their patients within 18 seconds of the start of the conversation.[2] Another found that patients were interrupted an average of 12 seconds after the resident entered the room, and that female patients were interrupted even more frequently than male patients.[3] Practicing the two-minute rule makes it impossible to interrupt—at least early in the conversation. And once you've "set the stage" for listening, you're likely to continue. Plus, the patient has gained trust that you are really listening and care about what he is sharing, which creates an environment conducive to ongoing dialogue.

Consider having another team member join the provider for the first part of a few appointments and time the initial conversation (without the patient knowing—if they know they're being timed, they'll feel like they're being rushed along). Two minutes feels like a long time when someone isn't accustomed to listening for that amount of time—many providers may think they're already doing it and will be surprised by the data.

Patients understand how busy providers are on any given day, but they still want to feel as though their voice and concerns are heard and that the provider has the time to effectively treat them. Listening matters. Through active listening, you can build an engaged relationship with the patient, obtain more and better information about the patient's health concerns, and develop a more comprehensive diagnosis and treatment plan. For these reasons, active listening by providers leads to improved outcomes for patients.

Tactic 2: Focus on the "A" in AIDET®

As you have read in previous chapters, the "A" in AIDET stands for "Acknowledge." Acknowledging a patient includes more than just verbal communication. By focusing on this step of AIDET, the provider is showing the patient he is present in the room with her—and only her—and is engaged and listening to what she has to say.

A: Acknowledge
• Acknowledge the patient's concerns and repeat back to her to reassure her you are listening and care about understanding her concerns to determine the next steps or right treatment.
• Use non-verbal actions to acknowledge to the patient you are listening and engaged in the visit.

Figure 7.1 Acknowledging the Patient's Concerns with the "A" in AIDET®

Following are a few scenarios that show what "acknowledging the patient's concerns" might look like:

"I know that you are a new patient to this practice, Ms. McDonald, and that you were referred by your primary care physician, Dr. Wolfe, for possible carpal tunnel surgery. It is natural for a patient to be a little anxious about meeting a new doctor, particularly when you might need surgery. I want to reassure you that I have seen many of his patients here for this type of surgery. My team and I have an excellent record (here, you might cite number of times you've done this surgery and metrics that show successful outcomes.) *I'll spend as much time as you need explaining what will happen so that you know what to expect. I'll gladly answer any questions and concerns you may have. I want you to know*

you're in good hands and we'll do whatever it takes to get you back to work and feeling normal again."

"Thank you for coming in today to review your mammography findings with Dr. Steele. I know it is really scary when you hear that they saw 'something' of concern and you immediately start to worry about all the possibilities. Dr. Steele is very compassionate and takes wonderful care of many patients with abnormal findings on mammography. He will give you the time you need, will help you better understand what this finding is and what it means for you, and will let you know the treatment options that are available for you to consider, especially knowing that you have young kids at home."

Here are a few tips to help ensure that you're listening to and acknowledging the patient:

- **Note personal information.** Be sure to write down a short note of something of personal importance to the patient in their file and reference it during the next visit. When patients feel providers have truly listened and really care about them as people, they are more likely to connect with the provider and adhere to their care plan.

  Instead of starting with, *"Okay, Bill, let's go over your recent blood count results,"* try starting with: *"So, Bill, last time you were here you were getting ready for a big vacation to Australia. How was your trip? What was your favorite part?"*

- **Practice reflective listening.** Pay close attention to what you are hearing so you can repeat it back to the patient. By paraphrasing what the patient just said, you are creating trust with the patient. She knows she is being heard and understood and that you are engaged in the conversation.

- **Look for ways to demonstrate empathy.**
When a patient believes you "feel her pain," so to speak, she also believes you are hearing her. The two go hand in hand. Demonstrating empathy takes virtually no time and it can make a big difference in the patient's perception of whether you're listening.

  Let's say that a patient who had a big summer trip planned gets sick and finds herself in the doctor's office instead of lounging on the beach. After gathering her history, you might take a moment to acknowledge her personal situation: *"I'm so sorry you are here and not enjoying that fun vacation you planned. I'm sure this must be really, really tough. I promise, we're going to do everything we can to take care of you."* That's empathy and it can be quite powerful.

Remember, it is not always *what* you say. Following are some non-verbal communication tips to keep in mind as well.

- **Sit whenever possible.** Occasionally we tend to stand next to the patient out of convenience or to save time. Sitting takes only a few seconds to position ourselves in proximity of the patient. It brings the provider down to eye level with the patient to create a more comfortable atmosphere for the patient. Sitting while speaking to the patient encourages eye contact, allows providers to listen more effectively, and also helps the patient feel the provider is not in a hurry and has time to listen.

What's more, one study reported in *Patient Education and Counseling* found that when providers sat at their patients' bedside, patients perceived them as being present longer than when the providers stood. What's more, during the "sitting" interactions, patients reported that they experienced "a more positive interaction and a better understanding of their condition."[4]

- **Be mindful of what your body is saying.**
  Body language and facial expressions can impact the quality and perception of the provider/patient encounter. Receptive gestures and posture can often times speak louder than words. Smile or nod (when appropriate, of course) and avoid crossing your arms or using other "defensive" stances.

It's not all what you say. . .

Non-Verbal
- Appearance
- Eye Contact
  - Keeping eye contact with the patient while they talk
- Eye Level
  - Sitting when the patient is talking to be on their level
- Proximity
- Receptive Posture
  - Not crossing your arms and leaning forward to listen
- Receptive Gesture
  - Nodding when patient is speaking

Figure 7.2 Non-Verbal Communication Techniques to Show Engagement

Tactic 3: Use Key Words at Key Times to Demonstrate Careful Listening

Key Words at Key Times help connect the dots for the patient, so he can better understand what the provider is doing and why. For a refresher course on the tactic, you might want to revisit Chapter 2: Fundamental Tactics for Improving CG CAHPS Outcomes. For this aspect of provider/patient communication, key words are used to signal to the patient the provider is carefully listening to what he has to say.

Examples of key words demonstrating careful listening:

- *"I want to make sure I understand I heard you correctly..."*

- *"To ensure I heard you, you are saying..."*

- *"I care about you and your concerns. Let me repeat what I heard you say..."*

- *"So what I am hearing from you is..."*

Here are some tips on using key words to show you are listening:

- **Narrate that you're switching gears from "talking" to "listening."** Show a patient or family member that you are considering what they say as you plan care: *"Mrs. Jones, I've done a lot of the talking; it is my turn to listen to you. How do you feel about the treatment plan I've proposed?"*

- **Explain your note taking.** During a patient visit, it is highly likely you will need to document what he is saying. This is expected; however, the patient may perceive your note taking as a sign you are not listening. Explain, using key words, why you are taking notes.

"Mr. Barnes, as we talk I may look down and take notes to document the points you are making and what is important to you. It is very important to me that you have a say in your care and that I capture that. However, I am still listening to you as I write/enter information into the computer."

- **Balance the personal with the technological.** We live in an electronic age where perceived distractions have become common. Giving patients our undivided attention may seem difficult when using technology like electronic medical records (EMR), which is why it becomes even more important to truly connect the dots and use key words to communicate with them.

  Be mindful of how you multi-task while talking with a patient. If you must enter data, explain what you are doing and why. It can be difficult to simultaneously attend to the screen and the patient, but you can use key words to explain: *"I want to make sure I accurately review your health conditions, recent visits, and medications. Even though I may look at the screen from time to time, please know that I am listening."* This explains why you may not be looking directly at the patient, but lets him know you are still listening, processing, and caring about him as a person.

The "caring" aspect of listening cannot be overemphasized. (In fact, notice that "care" is right there in the phrase "careful listening.") Beyond making it easier to diagnose and treat the patient, careful listening helps providers convey a crucial message: *"I am going to pay attention to you because what you have to say matters. Your health and well-being matter. You matter. You are not 'just' a diagnosis or the recipient of a treatment; you are the reason I practice medicine."*

When we show patients we care, we create a powerful bond with them—and it's that bond that yields the kind of outcomes all providers want to see.

Tools & Resources

Studer Group® offers a variety of tools and resources that support the tactics discussed in this chapter. To access the up-to-date information, please visit www.studergroup.com/CGCAHPS.

CHAPTER EIGHT:

UNDERSTANDABLE INFORMATION ON HEALTH QUESTIONS AND CONCERNS

"The single biggest problem in communication is the illusion that it has taken place."

—George Bernard Shaw

THE CG CAHPS QUESTION: How often did this provider give you easy-to-understand information about health questions or concerns?

Consider the following scenario:

Sixty-one-year-old Alice Ferguson is visiting her physician for a follow-up appointment after some tests had been run. After some initial pleasantries, the patient asks, "So, Dr. Presnell, how did my blood work turn out?"

Looking up from her laptop screen, the doctor replies, "As I review it, we see on the CBC a hemoglobin of 14.8 and platelets of 252,000. Your chemistry shows a sodium of 142, potassium of 4.3, BUN 18, and creatinine 1.1. I am concerned with your cholesterol level of 240 and LDL 150…"

"So what does all of that mean?" asks Mrs. Ferguson.

"Oh, it's kind of complex," says Dr. Presnell. "I think I'm going to start you on an antilipidemic medication and that should fix you right up."

Mrs. Ferguson waits a few more seconds. Then, when it becomes obvious the doctor isn't going to continue, she hesitantly asks, "What do you mean? Were the numbers way off?"

"Just take the medication and you'll be fine," replies Dr. Presnell, patting her patient's hand. "I promise."

In the previous scenario, it's likely that Dr. Presnell has good intentions. In her mind she is reassuring her patient and caring for her by prescribing the medications she needs. Yet from the patient's perspective, the exchange is quite frustrating. She wants to understand what her test results mean, and that's a good thing.

When patients ask medical questions, care providers owe it to them to give clear, understandable answers that are not couched in medical jargon. In fact, knowing that many patients won't even ask the questions, we need to offer these explanations up front. This creates a "discussion" rather than a "report."

Following is one option of how the scenario could have played out:

Mrs. Ferguson: *"So, Doctor, how did my blood work turn out?"*

Dr. Presnell: *"I am so glad that you have an interest. Recall we did a series of blood tests to make sure that you were not anemic or low on blood. Those tests were fine, and the other test that looked at the kidney and liver function was fine.*

"The test that I have more concern over is the lipid profile. We do this one to see how your body is processing fat. It showed that your total and 'bad' cholesterol are a bit high. What does that mean for you? We know that over time, these fatty chemicals floating around in your bloodstream could lead to hardening of the arteries, and that can increase your risk of heart problems or a stroke. Let's talk about what we can do to lower this…"

Mrs. Ferguson: *"Thanks for helping me to understand and, yes, I want to get that under control…"*

It's no mystery why patients need to be able to understand the information physicians and other providers share. To achieve "buy-in" to following "doctor's orders," it is preferable that the patient first understands what these orders are intended to address and how. Patients who don't are less likely to adhere to treatment plans, take medications properly, follow up their visits with needed future appointments, and so forth. Clearly, shortfalls in understanding impact clinical outcomes, and not in a good way.

Plus, a lack of health literacy, which the National Institutes of Health describes as the extent to which patients are able to understand information and services and use them to make appropriate decisions, has serious financial costs.

In fact, the NIH website reports: "A 1992 study at the University of Arizona, Tucson, found that healthcare costs for patients enrolled in Medicare who were identified with low health-literacy skills were more than four times as high as costs for patients with high literacy, roughly $13,000 per year compared to $3,000 per year."

Specifically, the website says that [a lack of] health literacy "is estimated to cost $106-$236 billion annually."[1]

And this statistic is from 1992—imagine what this amount would be in today's costs.

Of course, some patients do have a higher level of understanding than others. In today's high-tech world, people have easy access to a wealth of information from numerous resources, including medical websites, articles, blogs, talk shows, and so forth. More and more patients are researching symptoms before even stepping foot inside a provider's office. Still, having access to information is no panacea: Many sources can be unreliable or difficult to understand for someone without a medical degree or specific healthcare training in the field.

Regardless of health literacy levels, *all* patients need to understand their diagnoses and participate in creating their treatment plans. When they understand the *how* and the *why*, they'll be better able to adhere to their treatment plan and communicate any side effects or symptom changes to their provider.

This is why it is so important that a provider is able to assess the knowledge level of a patient, talk to her in a way she can understand about her diagnosis and care plan, address her concerns and questions, and make sure she is adequately and accurately informed before her appointment is over.

Also, it's important to put patients at ease and establish a healthy dialogue. When a patient feels nervous or uncomfortable around her provider, she is unlikely to ask clarifying questions at all (or at least not as many as she'd like to ask). And of course it stands to reason that when a provider can't draw the patient out and create the kind of comfort level that invites questions, the patient is more likely to leave still feeling confused or uncertain about her health concerns.

...And the Tactics That Make "Always" Responses More Likely

In this chapter, we will show you simple yet effective tactics to hardwire easy-to-understand information for patients in response to their questions and/or concerns.

Tactic 1: Focus on the "E" in AIDET®

If your practice needs to focus on providing easy-to-understand information, then the "E" in AIDET® (Explanation) should get special emphasis—although all of the elements of AIDET can be valuable as well. Just as we zeroed in on the "A" in Chapter 7 in a way that tailored it to the careful listening question, here we'll discuss Explanation as a way to help ensure that patient questions (and those of their family members) are answered in an easy-to-grasp way.

E: Explanation
• Explain the answer to the patient's question or concern in a way he will understand. Repeat the question back to him in your own words to be certain you have accurately interpreted his question. Avoid medical jargon and acronyms.
• Avoid explaining too much at one time. Provide bite-size bits of information for the patient to digest to ensure he understands and is retaining the information.

Figure 8.1 Using the "E" in AIDET® for Easy-to-Understand Explanations

Here are a few tips for providing answers and information regarding questions or concerns:

- **Think of the information as a dialogue, not a monologue.** Use repetition and the Teach Back Method (see Tactic 2) to ensure that patients understand exactly what you're telling them. When they ask questions, provide a complete answer and validate that it is helpful to the patient.

- **Use language the patient understands.** Medical terminology is acceptable but must also be followed by a clear explanation of *what the terms mean*. Use appropriate terms; avoid jargon. See the scenario in the open of this chapter for a good example.

- **Make use of analogies when possible.** This allows the patient to relate to what you are explaining so he understands and is more likely to remember after the visit is completed. Here are a couple of examples:

"Mr. Jones, you might think of hardening of the heart arteries like lime building up inside an old pipe…if it builds up heavily, it can clog up the pipe to the point the water won't flow. It is much more serious in a blood vessel to the heart, though, as the heart can be damaged by lack of blood flow."

"Arthritis is like a door hinge that gets rusty over time and then it won't move as freely as it used to. A hinge inside the body (called a joint) can also develop limited movement and even cause pain."

- **Use pictures or diagrams to enhance an explanation.** A visual representation can support what patients are learning and help them remember all of the information they are hearing. For example, let's say a burn patient is wondering when hair will grow back in the areas where she was burnt. The provider might respond using graphics and hand-drawn images created in "real time." These visuals can then be taken home by the patient to reference later. For example:

"You had deep second- and third-degree burns. The areas that do not have skin grafts were deep second-degree burns and are healing nicely (points to drawing on white board to draw an arrow for level of burns and explain using the diagram). In this type of burn, hair and oil glands can grow back. However, where you have skin grafts, the burn went through all three layers of skin (again draws on image to demonstrate). These are third-degree burns, and here the hair and oil glands are gone. In the areas that you have skin grafts, you will not be able to grow hair. Does that make sense?"

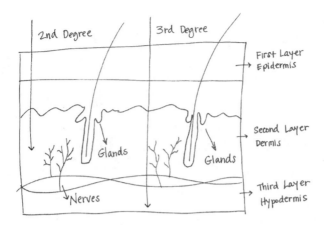

Figure 8.2 Sample Diagram

At one of Studer Group's partner organizations, there is a gynecological oncologist who is a "master" at focusing on the "E" in AIDET. Here is what one of our coaches had to say about him:

"Because of his specialty, Dr. W is nearly always dealing with patients with very high levels of anxiety. It's important that they understand their diagnosis and treatment plan, so when he explains those to the patient, he does so without using complex jargon. Then he asks them to repeat the information back to him.

"He says, 'So I can be sure that you understand what we're dealing with and what our next steps are, can you explain them back to me? I want to be certain that we're on the same page here, because we're a team.'

"Dr. W never asks, 'Do you have any questions?' but instead says, 'We have covered a lot of things and there must be something I can explain better for you—what questions do you have

for me?' This shows patients that he's open to their questions and validates concerns.

"He also calls all of his patients the day before their surgery to answer any last-minute questions, make sure they understand the procedure, and reassure them that the surgical team is fully prepared. By doing these things, Dr. W helps reduce patients' anxiety so they can focus on their treatment and recovery."

Tactic 2: Use the Teach Back Method When Answering Patient Questions

As you read in Chapter 6, the Teach Back Method is a great tactic to help validate the patient's understanding of the explanation for diagnosis, medications, treatment, and next steps. It is also useful when answering her questions or concerns. By avoiding medical jargon and speaking on a level the patient will understand, you will ensure better compliance with care plans and reduce anxiety around her concerns or questions.

You may want to review the tactic in Chapter 6 and also focus on the following tips:

- **Use key words when providing information.** When using the Teach Back Method, start the process with key words. This will help put the patient at ease to ask questions or address any concerns she may have.

  "Now that we have talked about your care plan and next steps, you must have some questions for me. I have the time to answer anything you feel we didn't cover or you are still

concerned about." (The wording here is important because it will elicit a deeper thought process than asking, "You don't have any questions, do you?" or, "Do you have any questions?")

- **After answering, ask about patient understanding.** There is nothing wrong or insulting about asking the patient if she understood what was said when doing so in a caring way. Remember, the goal of the Teach Back Method is to ensure that the patient understands the care plan and gets answers to any questions. Have her repeat back the answer to her question or concern. Here is a good example:

Provider: *"Ms. Kennedy, to be certain that I understand your question, let me rephrase it. You want to understand why we are placing the feeding tube prior to the start of your husband's treatment for esophageal cancer?"*

Patient's spouse: *"Yes, he is clearly able to eat just fine. I don't understand why he has to go through the surgery to have the tube placed when we don't know if he'll need it."*

Provider: *"I understand your concern for Paul to not go through any more than the chemotherapy and radiation treatments he has in front of him. Let me explain why we need to place the tube now. There is a very high likelihood that in several weeks, as he is going through both of these treatments at the same time, his throat will become very sore and he also may feel ill. When that happens, eating becomes challenging. We want to maintain his health as much as possible, and the feeding tube allows us to get nutrients directly to his stomach.*

If we wait, placing it will be harder on his health and him personally. Does that make sense to you?"

Patient's spouse: *"Yes, it does now."*

Provider: *"Can you tell me why you think it is now the best choice to place the feeding tube before his treatments start?"*

Patient's spouse: *"To avoid him having to have it placed when his health is in a weaker state and to make it faster to get nutrients in his system."*

Provider: *"Perfect, I just wanted to make sure we were on the same page. Thank you for asking the question. I want to make sure you and Paul are very comfortable with his treatment plan. Please do not hesitate to ask any questions that come up. What other questions do you have for me? What are you most worried about?"*

- **Get commitment to adhere to the treatment plan.** Patients need to be partners with their providers, and that means making sure they agree to uphold their end of the deal. Before a patient leaves your office, ask, *"Are you comfortable with the plan of care we agreed upon? What questions do you have?"* Then say to the patient, *"Please tell me your understanding of what your treatment plan is."* When human beings promise out loud to do something, we are more likely to actually follow through with it.

Because we in the healthcare field often speak our own language, it is important that we learn to "translate" that language into communication that our patients can understand. Patients deserve to know what their diagnosis is and how it's being treated, and providers have a duty to communicate that. It's all about ensuring the best possible care.

One of our most crucial tasks is establishing a productive dialogue with patients. How else can both parties make sure we understand each other? When we can help them grasp and process the (often complex) information we're sharing—and ensure that they are comfortable asking questions and we are willing to respond with good, thorough answers—we forge the kind of partnerships that lead to great clinical outcomes...and positive patient experiences.

Tools & Resources

Studer Group® offers a variety of tools and resources that support the tactics discussed in this chapter. To access the up-to-date information, please visit www.studergroup.com/CGCAHPS.

CHAPTER NINE:

PROVIDER KNOWLEDGE OF MEDICAL HISTORY

"Fortune favors the prepared mind."

—Louis Pasteur

T**HE CG CAHPS QUESTION: How often did this provider seem to know the important information about your medical history?**

When Dr. Fleishman walks into the exam room to see her new patient, a 73-year-old man named Mr. Dwyer, she feels confident and positive. The reason why is simple: She's prepared. She arrived at work an hour before her first appointment so that she could look over the patients' EMRs for the appointments that day. (She's occasionally been stuck in the "grab the chart just outside the room and skim it in 30 seconds" approach, and it doesn't work well. Besides, it doesn't allow her to provide the best care to her patients, and they can sense that she's distracted.)

In the case of Mr. Dwyer, who is complaining of numbness and pain in his hands and feet, she knows he's struggled with diabetes for years. Besides that, his records indicate ongoing bouts of insomnia and severe anxiety and depression. Indeed, four years ago he ended up in the Emergency Department with a middle-of-the-night panic attack. Dr. Fleishman intends to discuss these issues with her new patient. There's a new treatment regimen that she thinks may help his peripheral neuropathy and she wants to make sure his psychological issues are under control.

Before getting into the medical talk, she plans to ask him how he's adjusting to his recent move into his daughter's home—which she knows about because the nurse gave her a heads-up five minutes earlier during the daily huddle. *I'm so glad our staff and the staff of the referring physician practice are on top of getting all this information to me,* thinks Dr. Fleishman. *The standard care template we use really helps us manage information in a consistent way. The patients and I are really able to make the most of our time together.*

Thorough provider preparation is so important. Not only do we need to make sure we build in enough time to properly review patient information before the appointment, we also need to make the needed updates immediately afterward. This is not just a matter of discipline but also of having the right systems and processes in place. Doing so shows patients that we have a good grasp on their "big picture" and enables us to form productive partnerships with our patients.

Patients and families can sense when providers are prepared and understand their medical history. And, when patients and families are treated as respected partners in their healthcare, they are more likely to adhere to treatment and have better health outcomes.[1, 2, 3] In addition, patients who are involved as partners in their own care have been shown to develop better relationships with those who treat them,[4, 5] are less likely to sue their providers if things go wrong,[6] and are in a stronger position to help prevent errors from occurring in the first place.[7]

Although patients may feel more informed through effective explanations and the additional research they do outside the provider's office, many patients express frustration and dissatisfaction with their care because they do not feel like they have adequate (if any) input into the decisions that providers are making about their health and their lives. They worry that the provider may not have the "full picture" of their health situation.

It's not surprising that when we make sure we do have a good grasp on a patient's medical history, and when we actively involve him in his own care based on a mutual understanding of that history, outcomes are more likely to be positive.

One review of randomized controlled trials on patient-physician communications reported that the quality of communication in the history-taking and management-discussing portions of the interactions influenced patient outcomes in 16 of 21 studies. Outcomes influenced by such communication include emotional health; symptom resolution; function; pain control; and physiologic measures, such as blood pressure level or blood sugar level.[8] Patient anxiety was reduced in patients whose physicians encouraged questions and also encouraged them to share in the decision-making process.[9]

Think back to Dr. Fleishman and all of her preparations for her appointment with Mr. Dwyer. If she uses all of her knowledge about her new patient's background to engage him in conversation, he will become a true partner in his own care—and he is far more likely to follow his treatment plan and enjoy positive clinical outcomes.

Unfortunately, patients often do not know enough about their treatment options to make informed decisions. This is why it is essential that we ensure that we're obtaining the patient's *full* medical history, as well as what the patient feels is most important about this history. We also need to make it known to the patient that we are maintaining this information in his electronic medical record so that all providers he sees now or in the future have access to it and can use it in his care.

...And the Tactics That Make "Always" Responses More Likely

Over the past 10 years, Studer Group® has worked with hundreds of organizations coaching to improve quality and perception of care. In this chapter, you will read about tactics we have identified to truly partner with the patient to share medical information and develop a shared care plan. When a patient is an active partner in determining the best care plan and is engaged in her treatment, she is more likely to provide a more complete medical history, adhere to the care plan, and improve her clinical outcomes.

Tactic 1: Use Individualized Patient Care (IPC)

Each patient's health history and concerns are unique. Combine this truth with the fact that everyone's personality and lifestyle are also unique and you can see why everyone has different healthcare needs. That's what's so powerful about Individualized Patient Care—it allows us to provide each patient with the best care *for her*.

No one would argue against the idea that healthcare in general needs to be more patient-centered in its approach to care delivery—research suggests that when we accomplish this, not only do clinical outcomes improve but so does the patient's perception of her care.

The only one who can tell us what is truly important to the patient is the patient. Through IPC we take the technical/clinical aspects of care and customize them to the individual patient, documenting and communicating these using standardized techniques. It can also be valuable to gather the patient's insights into her own health history. This provides a mechanism for providers to get to know the patient as a person and to use the knowledge we gain to truly customize her care.

Let's say we are meeting with a patient who has to have an MRI. Because we've looked closely at her history and asked probing questions about it, we know she's taken anti-anxiety medications in the past and that this anxiety tends to escalate in medical situations. Thus we are able to say, "I see here you have a history of anxiety. Sometimes people with anxiety don't do well in traditional MRI machines because they feel claustrophobic. Would you prefer that we use the 'open' MRI machine?"

It's easy to come across as just going through the motions when we assess patients, especially when asking questions to build their health history—and IPC helps alleviate that "robotic" effect. We recommend standardization and consistency in asking relevant questions, but those have to be balanced with an honest desire to know what is really important to a particular patient if we're to make a positive difference in her recognition of the "personalized" care she receives.

Here are a few tips for implementing Individualized Patient Care:

- **Determine the patient's *what*.** IPC allows us to gather a patient's information and thoughts on what excellent care means to him or her and to incorporate it into our interactions with that person. It also allows us to use this information to better connect with the patient and to "humanize" our care. Figure 9.1 shows an example of a poster or sign you could hang in the reception area asking the patient for their *what* up front. Chapter 2 of this book on the Fundamentals includes more on learning the patient's *what*.

  Examples of statements and questions that help ascertain what is important to the patient:

○ *"We want to provide excellent care to our patients. Of course, that's a phrase that means different things to different people. Can you tell us what excellent care means to you?"*

○ *"Can you share information that will help me understand how this pain is impacting you? I am aware of your medical history and you have tried Botox to offer relief. How did that work? ...I want to make certain that we consider options that will matter the most to you."*

Figure 9.1 Sample Poster Asking for Patient's *What*

Write the patient's responses on her Individualized Patient Care card as described next. What's important to the patient should be considered and addressed during every interaction.

- **Use an Individualized Patient Care card.** Complete card and note priority items during pre-visit call and/or at check-in. If this is for a new patient, it can be sent with any paperwork you require the patient to fill out ahead of time. Code the card of the patient as "New" to the practice or "Return" so that the staff providing the care can see it and treat the patient accordingly.

INDIVIDUALIZED PATIENT CARE

Our goal is to consistently provide the best quality care possible. To do this, we need to know what this means to you. What can we do to make certain we provide you with the best quality care possible?

_____

_____

_____

_____

_____

Please circle one

New Patient   Returning Patient

Figure 9.2 Sample Individual Patient Care Card

Place the card on the front of the chart so it can be easily located throughout all stages of the office visit. Each staff member who interacts with the patient should review the card from the chart. If using electronic medical records (EMRs), the information should still be noted on a card (or an easily seen IPC card created in the EMR) so that everyone who encounters the patient will have easy access to this information.

Tactic 2: Implement Patient Scouting Report

It stands to reason that patients will be more comfortable and confident in their providers when those providers demonstrate knowledge of key information that the patient has shared. In the days of paper charts, many physicians would write key medical points on the inside cover of the chart and great ones would attach a note in the chart to remind themselves to ask about a patient's key life event.

Thanks to electronic medical records, those days are in the past. Many EMRs provide a summary, but often they are cluttered with tons of data points and don't zero in on the most important points. Additionally, it does the provider little good if she can't get to the summary until a few minutes into the visit.

Our recommendation is simple: Create a short summary and have providers view it *before* knocking on a patient's door. The summary should contain a couple of critical data points to reassure the patient he is in good hands and that nothing is "falling through the cracks." It should also highlight any current or recent non-medical key life events, to enable the provider to "connect" with the patient on a personal level. This information should be referenced early in the encounter, helping the patient to recognize that the provider is informed and on top of things.

Figure 9.3 shows an example of a Patient Scouting Report to use when gathering patient information.

Care team member who helped patient to room/collected vitals:

Patient's Full Name:
Patient's Preferred Name:
Age: **Gender:**
Primary Language:

Who is with the patient today?

Why is the patient here? (chief complaint/referral, etc.)

What is the patient's *what*—the "one thing" they want us to know in order to make this visit the best possible?

History:
•New patient?

•Date and reason for last visit?

•Any active conditions they are being treated for by you or others?

•Any medications you or others have placed them on?

•Any major life events you captured as pending at their last visit?

•Any specific time constraints the patient has shared with the practice?

Figure 9.3 Sample of a Patient Scouting Report

Following is an example of how a provider could use the information from the Patient Scouting Report:

Prior to entering the exam room, the provider reads the scouting report and knocks on the door. *"Mr. Jones, may I come in?"*

Patient: *"Yes, Doctor."*

Provider: *"Mr. Jones, thanks for coming in. And, Mrs. Jones, a pleasure to have you with us as well. Last year when I saw you, you were getting ready for your daughter's wedding. How was the wedding?"*

(Patient responds)

Physician: *"I understand from my medical assistant Bettie that you are here today with some breathing issues. (Pause to confirm the patient's nod) Can you tell me about your breathing issues?"*

(Patient explains symptoms.)

Physician: *"I see here that you were diagnosed with sleep apnea a couple of years ago and are currently using a CPAP machine. Can you tell me how you're sleeping at night and if you're using the machine regularly?"*

Tactic 3: Use Key Words at Key Times to Connect Back to Patient's Medical History

Using Key Words at Key Times can help reassure the patient that the provider has all the information needed to provide the care she needs. It also provides opportunities to manage up the practice's staff and record-keeping system. For example:

- *"It says here that when you saw Dr. Jackson last month, you were concerned about pain in your right hip. How is the physical therapy she recommended working out?"*

- *"The nurse tells me that you've got a sore throat. Can you tell me more about it?"*

- *"While you're describing your symptoms, I'll be entering what you say into your electronic record. This system is terrific, because all the information from this visit will then be available to any other providers in our practice if they need it."*

- *"As you can see here on the computer screen, your son has been consistently in the 45th to 50th percentile for growth over the last three years."*

Note that when asking about the patient's reason for visiting, the provider should acknowledge the information that the patient may have told other team members while giving the opportunity to expand upon it (as in the second preceding example). Sometimes, patients may be more comfortable telling the "whole story" to a physician than another care provider.

A Few Tips:

- **Question the patient about relevant facts deeper in her history.** *"I see a few years back you were treated for acid reflux. I am wondering if that could be affecting your breathing problem. Are you still taking the Protonix?"*

- **Reference family history if applicable**. *"I see that you have a family history of heart disease and your cholesterol level has been increasing. With that in mind, can we talk about your cholesterol level and what you are doing to lower it?"*

- **Ask open-ended questions whenever possible (and let the patient fill in the blanks).** *"Can you tell me about your recurring headaches? What patterns do you see in terms of when they occur, what precedes them, how long they last, and so forth?"*

- **Allow time for the patient to answer.** Resist the temptation to answer for him or to make assumptions. While some providers may feel uncomfortable with silence, it's actually a good thing when patients carefully consider their response. *"Please take all the time you need. It's important that we know exactly when this problem started so I urge you to think carefully about it before you answer."*

- **Get the patient back on track if he starts to wander off course.** You don't want to offend the patient or make him think what he's saying isn't important, but at the same time it's crucial to keep the appointment efficient. *"It's very important to me that we maximize our time together and that I focus on the main reason you are here today. So, for now, let's focus on your digestive issues."*

No illness, injury, or medical condition exists in a vacuum. There's a good chance most of your patients have been sick before. They may have had hospital stays, surgeries, recurring infections, chronic pain, or bouts of life-threatening illness like cancer. They may have had lifelong struggles with anxiety, depression, or other psychological issues.

The past always impacts the present—and knowledge of that past shapes the future. Having a good handle on this medical history plays a crucial rule in helping you diagnose and treat your patients. You owe it to them to do everything possible to make sure you've identified the most important points and to incorporate them into your patients' care.

Tools & Resources

Studer Group® offers a variety of tools and resources that support the tactics discussed in this chapter. To access the up-to-date information, please visit www.studergroup.com/CGCAHPS.

CHAPTER TEN:

PATIENT PERCEPTION OF "ENOUGH" TIME

"No matter how busy you are, you must take time to make the other person feel important."

—Mary Kay Ash

THE CG CAHPS QUESTION: How often did this provider spend enough time with you?

Spending the right amount of time with patients can be tricky. Care providers must take enough time with each patient to maximize outcomes, yet not so much that they deny access to other patients who need them. It's a balance that's sometimes tough to master, and yet we as an industry *must* master it if we're to carry out our mission of providing the best possible care to the patients who trust us with their health and well-being.

It should go without saying that every patient wants to feel that the provider has taken the time to listen, to understand, and to treat her concerns effectively. If a provider rushes through an exam, the patient may feel that he didn't obtain all the information she (the patient) needed to share. Or the patient may feel that the provider doesn't have time to answer any questions, so she won't ask them.

Spending adequate time with each patient is vital to their care as well as their overall experience in your practice. Consider this story:

I used to see a well-respected ophthalmologist—he was "the guy" to see in our area. The problem was that he always had a very full schedule. Every time I went for an appointment, he had a patient waiting for him in every exam room, plus more in the "waiting" room. He practically ran from exam room to exam room and spoke very quickly. Overall, he still provided very good care, but it was stressful to be his patient. I always left the office wondering if he'd really heard what I'd said, or if I'd missed anything important when he was talking so fast.

You'll notice that the survey question asks how often the provider spent "enough" time with the patient. There's no magic number of minutes given. That's because each patient's concept of "enough" is different. In one study, researchers found that those patients who wanted more time with their provider frequently expressed dissatisfaction with the emotional aspects of the interaction and were less likely to adhere to the provider's recommendations.[1]

Therefore, instead of worrying about spending *more* time with each patient, we need to focus on *how* we use that time. If a patient feels listened to and cared for during the time we spend with them, that time will have been "enough."

...And the Tactics That Make "Always" Responses More Likely

Tactic 1: Practice the Two-Minute Rule

Listening is a key step in building a lasting relationship with patients. Unfortunately, statistics show that doctors tend to interrupt patients frequently. Interrupting tells the patient that you don't have time to listen to him.

That's why it's so important to spend the first two minutes of the visit focused entirely on the patient. While natural "give and take" during this time is fine—it's all part of active listening—interrupting is not.

If you'll recall from Chapter 7, this is called the two-minute rule. Two minutes seems to be the "sweet spot." It allows the patient the time she needs to communicate her concerns, and it allows the provider to understand the patient's *what* so that he can develop a shared plan of care.

Especially if the provider sits during this time, the patient is likely to perceive the conversation as an engaged one. As a bonus, it makes the patient feel she has spent a much longer time with the provider.

One study reported in *Patient Education and Counseling* found that when providers sat at their patients' bedside, patients perceived them as being present longer than when the providers stood. What's more, during the "sitting" interactions, patients reported that they experienced "a more positive interaction and a better understanding of their condition."

Results of this study are depicted graphically here:

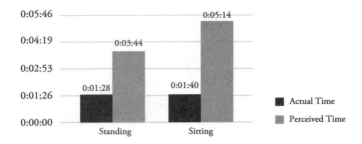

Figure 10.1 Standing vs. Sitting: The Effect on Patient Perceptions of Provider Time Spent with Them

This tactic can also be applied after asking open-ended questions to the patient. Allow the patient to speak uninterrupted and maintain eye contact. This may seem difficult to do, and at times the patient may not talk for two minutes, but it lets her know you are listening.

Tactic 2: Use Individualized Patient Care (IPC) to Make a Real Connection

Research shows that quality communication between providers and patients, particularly during the medical history portion of the exam, can have a powerful effect on a patient's anxiety as well as on his physical health.[2]

Although some of the questions on the history form may be routine, providers should take care to listen closely and not rush through this part of the patient encounter.

It makes sense that when a patient feels you know his background and medical history—and just as important, that you know what is important to him—he will perceive the interaction as "long enough." After all, you are investing meaningful time with him and making a genuine connection—and that connection is what patients want, no matter what the clock says.

To help providers slow down and take the necessary time to get to know the patient's concerns, Studer Group® has developed a process called Individualized Patient Care (IPC). Through a series of questions, IPC takes the technical and clinical elements of healthcare and helps the provider customize them to the individual patient—this helps eliminate the "routine" quality of an exam. It allows the provider to get to know the patient as a person and to create a care plan that the patient is invested in.

More on IPC, including a sample IPC card, can be found in Chapter 9. Following are some examples of IPC questions:

- *"We want to consistently provide excellent care to you. Of course, that means different things to different people. Can you tell me what excellent care means to you?"*

- *"What two or three things do you most want out of this visit?"*

- *"How do you feel about this plan we've developed? Do you think you will be able to stick with it?"*

- *"What fears and worries do you have about your future? Is there anything we can do to help you alleviate some of your concerns?"*

Questions like these demonstrate that you value the patient's input and that you want to make certain you gather as much personal information as possible. Doing so improves the "emotional" aspect of the visit and makes the patient feel you're doing all you can to help—which, in turn, makes him feel the appointment, no matter how long it may actually be, is time well spent.

Tactic 3: Manage Wait Times

If a patient has to spend a long time in the reception area, it can make the time spent in the actual appointment seem shorter. That's why it's so important to make sure patients spend as little time waiting as possible. To learn more about managing wait times, see Chapter 5.

It's also important to provide a warm, welcoming reception area, with comfortable seating; coffee, water, and other refreshments; and up-to-date magazines that are appropriate for your patient mix. Many practices have found that simply referring to the room as the "reception area" rather than "waiting room" can help with patients' perceptions.

Simply by listening to and watching patients you can get a sense for when they start to get unhappy. Track this information and create goals around it. For example, you might realize that in your practice it's important to get patients to an exam room within, say, five minutes.

Managing wait times actually involves a number of tactics that are described throughout this book. Key Words at Key Times and AIDET® (the "D" in particular) are two of the most critical. We urge you to revisit Chapter 2, Chapter 5 (as mentioned earlier), and other appropriate chapters to review these tactics. Here are several other tips that help you manage wait times:

- **Empower staff to take action when wait times are long.** They need to be able to demonstrate caring and apologize, as well as offer options such as rescheduling, an appointment with another provider, or leaving the office and receiving a phone call when the patient can be seen. It is helpful to hold a meeting with reception staff and allow them to offer examples of when patients get upset. Then in small groups they can come up with solutions. This allows the staff to feel empowered and that they have input into how situations are handled. They should also use this strategy for service recovery, if that becomes necessary. See Chapter 5 for some helpful hints.

- **Implement service recovery when needed.** From time to time, patients will have a negative experience with your practice. That's why it's so important to know how to restore their trust and confidence. The CARE℠ method, briefly outlined here, can help you not only do that but also address vulnerabilities in your system and relieve patient anxiety—which, in turn, increases their compliance with their plan of care.

C	C for Connect
A	A for Apologize
R	R for Repair
E	E for Exceed

Figure 10.2 CARE^{SM} Service Recovery Model

To learn more about the CARE method, see Chapter 2. Also, visit www.studergroup.com for some helpful tools and resources on service recovery.

- **Manage the flow of patients to minimize waiting time.** A flow coordinator can help keep patients moving through the practice smoothly. For more on flow coordinators and managing wait times, see Chapter 5.

In these days of high patient volumes and packed schedules, it's easy to get caught up in the rush and hurry through patient exams—at least the less complicated ones. But providing high-quality, individualized care takes time. By slowing down, even just a bit, we can make sure that our patients know that we are listening and we are taking the time we need to give them the best care possible.

Time is the most precious gift anyone can give another person. But that's true only when you're fully engaged. Giving a patient our full attention is no different from, say, a mother comforting her daughter as she cries over a break-up, or a man giving up his Saturday night to sit with a grieving friend. Whatever the setting—and however long the window of time—when we tune into the needs of the man, woman, or child in front of us, we create a space in which change for the better is possible.

Tools & Resources

Studer Group® offers a variety of tools and resources that support the tactics discussed in this chapter. To access the up-to-date information, please visit www.studergroup.com/CGCAHPS.

CHAPTER ELEVEN

PROVIDER RESPECT FOR PATIENT INPUT

*"They won't remember what you did. They won't remember all
that you said, but they will always remember the way that you
made them feel."*

—*Maya Angelou*

T HE CG CAHPS QUESTION: How often did
this provider show respect for what you
had to say?

Dr. Ryan listened carefully as his new patient Margaret hesitantly broached the subject of alternative medicine. The 57-year-old woman had heart disease and high
blood pressure and was clearly worried about what her
new cardiologist might think about such remedies as acupuncture, tai chi, and herbal supplements. "I imagine
this all sounds a bit 'out there' to a doctor like you," Margaret concluded, her downcast gaze and crossed arms

betraying her anxiety. "But I've done a lot of reading on it and I really think it's worth a shot."

While Dr. Ryan's typical treatments ran along the lines of calcium channel blockers, ACE inhibitors, and angioplasty, he was certainly not closed-minded. He knew there were plenty of strong arguments in favor of integrative medicine. Even more important, he knew discounting his patient's point of view would surely have a negative impact on her trust level in him as well as her willingness to comply with the treatment plan.

"I think incorporating these into your care plan is a great idea," he said gently. "There really have been plenty of studies showing that acupuncture can help control blood pressure, and of course, tai chi is a wonderful relaxation technique. Let's explore some herbal supplements to make sure we find one that won't interact with your prescription medications. Thank you for being so proactive with your research. I wish I had more patients like you."

This is respect in action. When Margaret realized Dr. Ryan was not only taking her seriously but actually incorporating her ideas into her treatment plan, she instantly relaxed. Right then and there she stopped being merely a patient and became a true partner. She would remain his patient for the rest of her life—which, because of her faithful compliance, turned out to be a long one.

Virtually all care providers want to show respect to patients. Not only do we feel a human responsibility to do so, we also feel a certain amount of financial pressure. When patients feel they haven't been treated respectfully, they leave. Physician practices have always faced this risk but there's something about the transient, digitally connected nature of today's society that makes it more likely that they'll get the dreaded "please transfer my records" call.

After all, people move around a lot. They change jobs. They change health insurance. And thanks to social media, a disgruntled patient can easily go online, browse patient reviews of various providers, and switch to a practice they feel will treat them with more respect. (And yes, possibly leave a less-than-glowing review of the practice that offended them.)

But here's the question: What, exactly, *is* respect? Merriam-Webster defines it as "a feeling or understanding that someone or something is important, serious, etc., and should be treated in an appropriate way." As a directive, that's pretty vague.

An article published by the *Journal of Medical Ethics* shines a little more light on the subject. "Understanding respect: learning from patients," by N.W. Dickert and N.E. Kass, shares the results of a qualitative study from an academic cardiology clinic. Patients were interviewed with a goal of eliciting their "views on and expressions of respect or disrespect in medical or non-medical contexts…"

The article reported, "The following elements represent the salient themes of patients' views regarding respect: attention to needs, empathy, care, autonomy, recognition of individuality, information provision, and dignity."

Here are just a few quotes gathered during the study (as well as the respect "theme" they were identified with):

"I think doctors and the nurses should be conscious of the speed in which they move and the speed with which they talk and how they pick up things and look at their beeper and all of those machinations because it makes you feel like a cow, one of the minions, and that's not a good thing." *(546)* (EMPATHY)

"He showed concern. He showed that he cared about you as opposed to you being a number or another paycheck, or how you feeling and so on, etc, etc, etc. You know, warmth in the voice, general attitude, body language." *(Husband of a patient, 428)* (CARE)

"I think you would have to think about the wishes of those people and still from your professional standpoint, I think you should be able to explain to them you know the possibilities of what's going on and try to weigh out your opinions with their opinions and come up with a decision." *(916)* (AUTONOMY)

(According to the article, the numbers at the end of each quote are "unique identifier numbers assigned to each patient.")[1]

Of course, by showing respect, providers aren't just trying to create a positive experience for the patient so that she will like them (or even provide a good CG CAHPS rating). They do it in large part because they are seeking to engage the patient as a partner in her own care. When a patient feels like a relationship is a "two-way street" in which the physician respects her input, opinions, and ultimately her decisions, she is far more likely to engage on that level.

She'll be more comfortable and confident in sharing vital information. She won't be embarrassed about sharing personal details. She'll be more forthcoming about "barriers" that might hinder her recovery, rather than withholding information from the provider, so that they can work together to find solutions. And ultimately, she'll be more compliant with the care instructions that will lead to a good clinical outcome.

...And the Tactics That Make "Always" Responses More Likely

Based on research from our Learning Lab, Studer Group® has identified certain tactics that, when applied and customized appropriately, will have the most impact on improving providers' ability to show respect to patients. Here are a few of the most impactful:

Tactic 1: Demonstrate Empathy Using Key Words

Much like respect, empathy can be tough to quantify. In medicine, it's essentially the ability to say, "I understand that you are frightened/anxious/hurting/sad, and while I can't literally 'feel your pain,' I have experienced similar feelings because I'm human…and I do care." And while this tactic is about using key words to demonstrate empathy, words alone can't do it. The intention behind our words, the tone of our voice, the speed at which we move, and the body language we use all play a role.

Yet, empathy is incredibly valuable. A Studer Group *Insight* blog post by Mike Nelson, MD, reports that empathy has been linked to improved clinical outcomes in metabolic complications and improved glucose in LDL-C control in diabetic patients, as well as reduced incidence of malpractice claims. What's more, it improves patient perception of physician communication regarding patient medication adherence.[2]

Empathy also diffuses tension and fear. It opens the door to the patient's comfort in asking the questions needed to help the provider in developing a shared care plan for treatment and in driving compliance. Best of all, while expressing empathy takes virtually no additional time, it makes a huge difference in the patient's perception of care.

Let's say, for example, a patient has a big tryout for the state all-star baseball team and he has come in due to pain in his ankle after a fall during practice. After gathering the patient's history, the provider might acknowledge his situation: "I'm sorry you are experiencing this right before the big tryouts. I am sure you are worried about your ability to play. We are going to do everything we can to take care of you."

Here are a few concrete things you can do to demonstrate your empathy for the patient:

- **Say, "I'm sorry."** You can't always understand exactly what the patient is going through or feeling, but you can always say you are sorry for the situation, the pain the patient feels, or his worry. For example, *"I'm sorry to hear that you're having so much trouble sleeping—let's try to find out why,"* or, *"I'm sorry your shoulder has been so painful—may I take a look at it?"*

- **Use other key words to reinforce your empathetic stance.** Two examples from Dr. Nelson's *Insight* are: *"I can understand your frustration with this challenging illness. We are here for you and will continue to do everything we can to help you through this,"* and, *"I so admire how you have maintained a positive attitude and never given up since the stroke and rehab process."*

- **Be aware of your body language.** Look at the patient while he is speaking and sit rather than stand. Lean forward to demonstrate you are intent on hearing his concerns and questions. These and other body-language cues show the patient that you're paying attention and care about his situation.

- **Try putting yourself in the patient's shoes.** If you are sitting in an office, in pain and describing your symptoms, would you want to hear, *"Mr. Smith, we should be able to treat your pain with some medication today"?* Or would you prefer to hear, *"Mr. Smith, you are in good hands today. I've worked on hundreds of cases throughout my 10-plus years as a physician where patients had a similar type of pain that you are describing, so I have a lot of experience with this. Here is what I would like to propose for your care plan."* Not only have you introduced yourself ("I" in AIDET®) and provided your background, but you've reiterated that you are an expert in your field, helping to reduce the patient's anxiety.

- **Reflect upon what the patient said.** In doing this, you are showing the patient you understand what he said and are demonstrating your concern. For example:
  - ○ *"I heard you say you are still having continuous head-aches. I see this is really upsetting you and causing you pain so I will do everything I can to work with you to determine an appropriate treatment plan to start making you feel better."*
  - ○ *"It sounds like your knee pain is making things difficult for you at your job. I'm going to do my best to find out what's causing it so you can get back to normal."*

Tactic 2: Focus on "A" in AIDET

While all of AIDET is meant to help providers communicate respect, the act of acknowledging—the "A" in AIDET—creates a powerful first impression for the patient. It shows that the provider is engaged and present in the room with her. It helps the provider show empathy and support during a time when the patient may be frightened or in pain.

As you read in the chapter on fundamentals, AIDET is the foundation for meaningful dialogue and should not be thought of as an initiative to be implemented all at once. Key elements can be emphasized first to drive outcomes in the area where the efforts are most needed. (Organizations engaged in coaching agreements with Studer Group can access a suite of tools specifically on the topic of Provider AIDET at www.studergroup.com/resources/learning-lab.com.)

A Few Tips for "A" in AIDET...

- **Knock first.** By knocking before entering the room, you are showing the patient you respect their privacy, taking your time, and are entering when they are ready. It gives the patient a second to prepare for the person to enter the room. It may seem like a minor thing, but when a provider opens a door without knocking and goes straight into the patient-provider encounter, it can leave the patient flustered, feeling you are in a rush and not acknowledging the need for their visit.

- **Shake the patient's hand.** It's a common courtesy that applies in most social and business settings that belongs in our clinic encounters as well.[3] (However, providers must be aware and sensitive to cultural and religious preferences and adjust this custom accordingly.) Patients report a much higher level of satisfaction with their providers when they shake their hands, and high-performing physicians on patient experience report that shaking hands is just as important as introducing themselves.[4] Providers who start by sanitizing, narrate that they are doing this for the patient's safety, then shake their patient's hand also get recognition by patients for good hand hygiene.

- **Make proper introductions for new patients.** Once the patient and family have been acknowledged (the "A" in AIDET), introduce yourself (the "I" in AIDET):

  ○ For new patient: *"Good morning, Mrs. Wilson. My name is Dr. Andrews but feel free to call me 'Barbara.' I will be your provider today. I've been practicing medicine for over 30 years and specialize in chronic gastrointestinal conditions, which my nurse Anne tells me is why you're here today. I am sorry you are having these problems; I know how painful and inconvenient they can be. But I do want you to know I've been able to help many patients with similar symptoms get them under control and I'm optimistic that I can help you, too."*

  ○ For returning patient: *"Good afternoon, Robert. Sorry you are experiencing a sore throat, but it is nice to see you. How did your vacation last month go?"*

  ○ Acknowledge people with the patient: Patients often bring family members, friends, or significant others along to appointments. Introduce yourself to those folks as well as to the patient, and find out what their relationship to the patient is. *"So, Robert, who do you have with you today?"*

- **Remember that AIDET applies to everyone in the medical practice/office.** Regardless of the length of the encounter or role they play, any person the patient encounters should be trained in and comfortable using AIDET. Each person impacts the total patient experience, and any one of those interactions and encounters at any level can bring either negative or positive reactions to the whole patient experience. When a patient feels respected by everyone, she'll be more engaged in her care and more likely to adhere to a treatment plan.

Tactic 3: Use a Shared Care Plan

Implementing AIDET and Key Words at Key Times can help you implement this tactic, in which the provider works with the patient to develop a care plan over which they both have ownership. Key words can provide cues for the provider and patient that ensure that both are sharing necessary information. For example:

"You told the nurse, Patricia, that your biggest concern today is to get some pain relief. Do I have that right?"

"Here is what I recommend we do next."

"What do you think about those recommendations?"

"Do you have anything going on at home or at work that might keep you from being able to follow the plan you and I have developed here?"

"What questions do you have for me?"

For more details on the Shared Care Plan as well as a sample form, see Chapter 6. Ideally, the use of this tactic ensures that provider and patient leave the encounter knowing they were both heard and understood. Being secure in this knowledge is the heart and soul of a mutually respectful relationship.

We'd like to close with a story that illustrates the incredible bond that can develop between patients and care providers.

My Aunt Allison recently passed away after a long struggle with pancreatic cancer. All through her journey, her surgical oncologist, Dr. Kaufman, consistently respected Allison's wishes and took the time to know who and what mattered most to her. For example, she knew how much Allison loved her cat, Mario. She also knew that Allison cared deeply for her parents—her greatest concern was always for them. Dr. Kaufman knew which family members and friends to call at critical moments and thought of them when her patient couldn't. She even drove to be with my aunt as she passed. She cried along with the rest of us. Aunt Allison could not have asked for a better, more caring, more compassionate doctor, and we'll all be eternally grateful for her.

All provider/patient relationships cannot be this intense. Still, the story of Aunt Allison and Dr. Kaufman reminds us of the impact respectful listening, empathy, and genuine care and concern can have on the life of patients and family members.

Tools & Resources

Studer Group® offers a variety of tools and resources that support the tactics discussed in this chapter. To access the up-to-date information, and to download a worksheet that will help you create a plan to improve patient perception of care in the "Provider Communication" arena, please visit www.studergroup.com/CGCAHPS.

SECTION THREE:

FOLLOW-UP ON TEST RESULTS

P rompt communication of test results is so important. When we don't get back to patients quickly enough, we set them up to be unhappy with their experience.

When we don't contact patients in a timely fashion, they will surely contact us. And when a patient has to pick up the phone and check on the results herself, it means one of two things: a) either we haven't managed her expectations regarding when she might hear about her test results, or b) we've simply waited too long to call her (even if it's just to say, "Sorry, no results yet"). By the time she calls us, she will have spent a fair amount of time wondering and fretting over why she hasn't yet heard anything.

Communication of test results is an area that many providers don't focus on—even though their office staff will quickly tell them it generates a large number of pa-tient phone calls. In fact, we've found in many practices, it is one of the top three reasons patients call and ask to speak to their providers. And patient expectations for getting quick results are only increasing.

As the industry progresses with technology, it's becoming more and more common for providers to be able to perform a number of tests (quick strep tests, for example) and obtain the results during the patient's visit. Of course, there are still plenty of tests that require communicating results post-visit—the vast majority of blood work and radiology exams, for instance—but having gotten accustomed to the "instantness" of our society, patients are becoming less and less, well, *patient* overall.

But there is something worse than not getting test results to patients promptly enough—and that's not communicating them clearly enough or sometimes even at all. Both of these missteps happen more often than we'd like to admit. When they do, the consequences are serious.

Evidence shows that failing to clearly communicate test results and their implications has a negative impact on healthcare quality, in addition to creating a negative patient experience. In 2009, a study of 5,434 patients from 23 practices found that, in aggregate, 7 percent of the time, providers failed to notify patients of *clinically significant* outpatient laboratory results.[1]

Further, electronic medical records (EMRs) that contain lab results did not eliminate this issue.[2] In general, however, EMRs may help to close the notification gap when they contain patient portals.[3]

Of course, portals are no panacea. While they can be helpful, they also imply that ownership lies with the patient to access her own test results. The fact is, there are plenty of non-tech-savvy patients who need or at least prefer a phone call from a provider or a nurse. Speaking to a human being allows the patient to ask further questions about the results—otherwise, she must rely on her own interpretation, which may or may not be accurate.

Here's the point: The information may be with the practice, but if there is not a consistent process for communicating and educating patients, there will be gaps. All providers need a plan for letting patients know how we'll communicate test results, how long it will take to communicate them, and what follow-up actions should be taken. Finally, we need to document every step of the process.

Good and timely communication of test results is important not only to improve patient experience, but also to improve patient safety and reduce malpractice risk. Sometimes treatment needs to occur quickly to maximize the patient's likelihood of recovery. Other times a patient may have a communicable disease and needs to know to protect the health of her family members and members of the public who may come into contact with her.

This section focuses on the tactics that will help you ensure that patients get test results quickly, clearly, and accurately—and that *someone from your practice* follows up on them.

The Survey Question

This aspect of the CG CAHPS survey asks patients about communication received from providers. Answers are given in frequency scale: *never, sometimes, usually*, or *always*. The percent of patients who responded *always* is publicly reported on a growing number of state and private payer websites and at www.medicare.gov/physician-compare.

When this provider ordered a blood test, x-ray, or other test for you, how often did someone from this provider's office follow up to give you those results?

The following self-test is designed to assist you in determining how you are doing with key elements of this CG CAHPS composite. We recommend that you ask all your clinicians to participate in this short self-test and compare your results to determine where to focus first. You may also find it valuable to repeat this self-test a year from now to evaluate your improvement in these areas.

Note: We have adopted the four-response standard of CG CAHPS for the self-test. Using this standard is a great way to build your own competency and experience in what it takes to consistently achieve an *always* response.

Question	Never	Sometimes	Usually	Always
1. When a provider in our office promises a patient they will personally call them with their test results, how often do they?				
2. How often do we accommodate our non-English-speaking patients in how we communicate test results?				
3. When a patient requests a unique way to communicate test results with her, how often do we accommodate this request?				
4. How often do patients know how long it takes to get test results and refrain from calling to ask for them before they are available?				
5. How often do we push test results to our patient portal with provider comments when available?				
6. How often do we coordinate patient communication with other offices/labs that perform tests on our patients?				
7. How often are test results communicated with patients, regardless of the findings?				
8. If we don't get a test result back when we should, how often are we aware of that?				
9. How often does our test results communication process meet our patients' expectations?				
10. How often do we avoid telling patients to call us to get their test results?				

Figure iii.1 Test Results and Follow-Up Self-Test

If you are like 99.9 percent of medical practices, you have likely identified a couple areas you can improve. Don't try to implement all of the tactics in this section at once. Select the one or two most important to improving your practice and start by hardwiring them first.

Because there is only one CG CAHPS question that provides the data for this composite, a crosswalk between CG CAHPS question(s) and the self-test statements is not needed. To focus on a specific area of the self-test, please refer to the following chart, which aligns tactics to self-test statements.

Self-Test Question	Key Tactics
1. When a provider in our office promises a patient they will personally call them with their test results, how often do they?	• Test Communication Menu • Focus on the "D" and "E" in AIDET®
2. How often do we accommodate our non-English-speaking patients in how we communicate test results?	• Focus on the "D" and "E" in AIDET®
3. When a patient requests a unique way to communicate test results with her, how often do we accommodate this request?	• Test Communication Menu
4. How often do patients know how long it takes to get test results and refrain from calling to ask for them before they are available?	• Test Communication Menu • Focus on the "D" and "E" in AIDET®
5. How often do we push test results to our patient portal with provider comments when available?	• Add Notes to Electronic Medical Records (tip)
6. How often do we coordinate patient communication with other offices/labs that perform tests on our patients?	• Test Communication Menu
7. How often are test results communicated with patients, regardless of the findings?	• Test Communication Menu • Focus on the "D" and "E" in AIDET®
8. If we don't get a test result back when we should, how often are we aware of that?	• Test Communication Menu
9. How often does our test results communication process meet our patients' expectations?	• Test Communication Menu • Focus on the "D" and "E" in AIDET®
10. How often do we avoid telling patients to call us to get their test results?	• Test Communication Menu • Focus on the "D" and "E" in AIDET®

Figure iii.2 Test Results and Follow-Up Self-Test Questions and Tactics Guide

This section of the book includes one chapter based on the question in the CG CAHPS "Follow-up on Test Results" composite. We will share the tactics, along with a few tips, that will positively impact the likelihood that patients will answer *always* to this question.

While this chapter does not list every tactic that Studer Group® coaches, it provides an excellent place to start for any provider wishing to see quick improvement. To achieve sustained improvements, these tactics will need to be hardwired into every encounter, always.

CHAPTER TWELVE:

COMMUNICATION OF PATIENT TEST RESULTS

"How much of human life is lost in waiting."
—*Ralph Waldo Emerson*

T HE CG CAHPS QUESTION: When this
provider ordered a blood test, x-ray, or
other test for you, how often did someone from
this provider's office follow up to give you those
results?

...And the Tactics That Make "Always" Responses More Likely

For many patients, the wait for test results can be painful. Whether they had a simple blood test or a biopsy, patients want answers to their medical questions as soon as possible. That is why communicating test results is such an important part of the patient experience. When you deliver the news, good or bad, you're showing patients that you care about their peace of mind, that you care about them receiving care as soon as they need it, and that you value them as a part of their own care team.

What's more, not sharing results right away can sometimes worsen a patient's condition. Consider the following story:

Francesca had been experiencing pain and swelling in her right knee for several weeks. She went to see her provider, Dr. Hildebran, who promptly ordered an MRI. He scheduled a follow-up appointment to discuss the results two days later. (So far so good.)

Unfortunately, the day of the MRI, Francesca's elderly mother who lived a few states away came down with a serious case of the flu. Because she had to get on a plane to visit her mother, Francesca was unable to keep the follow-up appointment with Dr. Hildebran. When she called to reschedule, she asked the nurse about her test results. "I'm nervous about hurting my knee even more and need to know how to take care of it," she said. The nurse promised to call when the test results came in—but in the midst of a stressful day, she forgot to do so.

Meanwhile, Francesca was overwhelmed with worry about her mother's fragile health. She and her siblings had to decide who would take care of their mother once she was discharged from the hospital, and Francesca ended up agreeing to do it. Thoughts about her injured knee kept creeping in, but since the nurse hadn't called, she assumed the results had been delayed.

Later, when she finally got the results at her follow-up appointment, Francesca realized all the lifting and walking involved in caring for her mother had aggravated the injury further. Had she known the extent of her knee problem, her sister could have taken on "Mom duty" instead—sparing Francesca a longer, more difficult recovery period.

It's so important not to let a lack of communication on test results create this kind of situation with our patients. First, we need to understand exactly what this CG CAHPS question is asking.

The question for this composite specifically mentions blood tests, x-rays, and other tests. In studying thousands of CG CAHPS responses with patients, we have found that "blood test" means any test in which a blood sample is obtained. "X-ray" means any radiology study, including not only x-rays but also CAT scans, MRIs, and so on. Other tests may refer to, for example, urine cultures.

Note, also, that the question asks about follow-up from "this provider's office." Receiving results from the lab or the radiologist rarely satisfies the patient's need— they want to hear from the provider who ordered the test. The lab can give results, but it is the provider's office that the patient feels a connection with and that will help to determine next steps if needed. The patient also wants to be assured that her provider is aware of the test results as well.

Of course, communication is the key to getting an "always" response to this question: Providers need to communicate with patients when the tests are ordered (that is, setting their expectations for when and how they will receive their results) and ensure that the practice meets those expectations when the results become available.

Following are some tactics you can use to make sure that patients are never left waiting.

Tactic 1: Standardize a Test Communication Menu

As we've worked with medical practices, we've found those with the best outcomes regarding communication of test results have implemented a standardized test communication menu. Basically, providers meet as a group and categorize the types of tests they typically run. They then determine how best to communicate back to the patient regarding each "type" of test and in what timeframe. This creates consistency for the organization (and their patients). It also creates agreed-upon expectations across all providers of what is an appropriate timeframe and response.

Of course, the communication method will depend on the type of test in question and the results. A test for strep that turns out negative could easily be communicated by email or even text. If it's a biopsy for cancer that turns out positive, results will most likely be communicated in person during a follow-up appointment or on a phone call.

Once the communication menu is created, it is included with orders for any test a provider requests. The provider indicates how the results are to be communicated to the patient at the time the test is ordered. This allows her to not only set the right expectation with the patient at the time of ordering but also, critically, lets the entire team know what expectation has been set.

In the following menu example, the providers review the table for the test they have ordered. They place the menu code along with the number of days in the patient's record to indicate the communication method they have told the patient to expect and the timeframe. For instance, the provider might designate a test she orders with the code "N5"; this tells the rest of the team that the patient is expecting to get results from the nurse via a phone call within five days.

Code	Menu Option	Common Test Examples
M	Set expectation with patient that we would **mail** results to them. Results mailed in X days.	Cholesterol Panel, Pap Smear, HgA1c (diabetic), INR (Coumadin therapy)
E	Set expectation with patient that we would securely **email**/share results to them. Results emailed in X days.	Cholesterol Panel, Pap Smear, HgA1c (diabetic), INR (Coumadin therapy)
N	Set expectation with patient that the **nurse** would call them to communicate results. Results by nurse phone call within X days.	Pregnancy, 2-hour Glucose Tolerance, Bilirubin levels for newborn
S	**Schedule** patient for follow-up appointment to review results and discuss options. Schedule within X days.	Genetic testing, HIV, biopsies, CTs, MRIs
C	**Clinical provider** set expectation with the patient they would personally call to follow up with them. Results by provider phone call within X days.	Cholesterol, Thyroid tests, CTs, MRIs
P	Set expectation that patient can access results on the patient **portal**. Results available in X hours/days.	Cholesterol Panel, Pap Smear, HgA1c (diabetic), INR (Coumadin therapy)

Figure 12.1 Menu Example

When discussing this tactic, a provider will often raise a concern of what happens when a test result requires more rapid communication than the menu option indicates. When quicker communication is called for clinically, then a direct call to the patient can be made. In our experience, patients are always okay with getting a phone call from a nurse or provider sooner than the letter or email they were told to expect.

Tactic 2: Focus on the "D" and "E" in AIDET®

As we've discussed throughout this book, AIDET® is a great communication framework. In this case, a focus on the "D" and "E" when communicating about test results can make all the difference. The "D" helps you zero-in on how long the test will take and how long it will be until results come back. The "E" prompts you to explain the test or procedure and set expectations around how the results will be shared.

Do not feel forced into following the order of the "D" and "E." Instead, focus on communicating effectively with the patient. Following are some things to consider as you use AIDET to share test results.

- **Set realistic expectations on timing.** For example, if you know it normally takes two to three business days to get cholesterol levels back on the blood draw, explain to the patient that he can expect results back within five business days. By setting the expectation a little longer than average, you have the opportunity to deliver the results faster than expected, thereby creating a positive patient experience almost every time. You also make an allowance for any delays. It is rare that a patient will complain if you have results to share with him sooner than they expected, but there's a good chance he will be unhappy if it takes longer than you led him to expect.

Be sure to reinforce with the patient that he should contact the provider's office if he has not received his results during the timeframe and via the delivery method outlined.

- **Explain how you will communicate results.** Another critical area to manage with patients is the expectation on how you are going to communicate the results to them. Do you call them with every lab result? Just abnormal readings? Or only when a change in care is indicated?

  A standard practice for expectations setting is to let patients know you will share their lab results via mail (or secure email) if the results indicate that no change in treatment is needed. If the results indicate that a change in treatment plan *is* needed, set the expectation that patients will receive a phone call to discuss next steps. By setting this expectation up front, you greatly reduce patient anxiety and also alert them that returning your phone call is important. Under no conditions should you ever set expectations with a patient that you will not be communicating results back to him at all.

As you are setting expectations for how results will be communicated, take a moment to check on the accuracy of phone numbers, email addresses, portal registration status, and so forth. Also, alert the patient to be on the lookout for them.

We frequently like to give examples of "what right looks like," but it's equally important to mention what "wrong" looks like. Here's a patient story that should serve as an example of what *not* to do.

I had been feeling "off" for a few months so I made an appointment to visit my primary doctor. Over the course of several visits, she determined that I needed to get some blood work done and she would let me know the results. Instead of my doctor calling me, the reception staff called and said my doctor needed me to come in to review the results. I asked if everything was okay, and they said they weren't given a copy of the results and the doctor would have to review them with me. I had to schedule an appointment that was five days away from when I received the call.

Let me tell you, I didn't sleep much for those five days. I was in a constant state of panic and worry about what she had found in my test results. Was it cancer? Was it curable? The day of my appointment, my heart was racing. When my doctor walked through the door, I almost burst into tears and immediately asked what was wrong with me. She simply said, "Nothing. Your blood levels look fine. We will need to run some more tests, but everything looks fine."

Not only did this mean that I just paid for a two-minute visit for my doctor to tell me that I was essentially fine, but I felt like I lost five days of my life worrying that I was dying. Not only that, but now I'd have to schedule another appointment to get additional testing, which could've been handled during that visit if she had looked at my results prior to my appointment. I was infuriated and asked why she didn't review the results sooner and call me to tell me I was alright. She said, "I asked my nurse to do that...did she not?"

After this happened, I lost complete faith in my provider and her office staff. So much so, I ultimately ended up switching to another practice.

- **Manage expectations for follow-up care.** It is important that we clearly communicate what follow-up care and/or changes in care are needed as a result of a test. Nothing frustrates a patient more than to hear they have abnormal test results but need to schedule a follow-up appointment just to get the results and understand what changes are needed. If there is a possibility that you may need the patient to come back in to get the results and discuss their implications, it is critical to set this expectation up front.

Here is an example of how this expectations-setting conversation may go:

"Mr. Matthews, this is a really important set of blood tests we are going to run, and depending on the results, we may need to change your treatment plan. If we need to change your treatment plan, I will have my assistant phone you to schedule a follow-up appointment. If we don't need to change your treatment plan, I will have my assistant call to let you know that. Either way, we should have the results back and have called you within the next five business days. If you have

any additional questions or concerns throughout this process, please do not hesitate to call us. Can you summarize what I have just shared with you to ensure we are on the same page?"

Test Results CAN Go Directly to Patients

The vast majority of test results can be released directly to patients, regardless of whether the provider has reviewed them first. Historically, many provider offices have had a standard practice to not release test results until after the provider had reviewed them. Patients calling for the results were often told, "I'm sorry but we can't release the results to you as the provider has not reviewed them yet."

While it is important that providers review test results and adjust treatment when necessary based on them, legally, a patient (or his representative) has a right to review his medical information regardless of whether the provider has reviewed the results. In addition, the adoption of patient portals driven by "meaningful use" of electronic medical records (EMRs) is increasingly making test results accessible to patients at the same time they become accessible to providers.

In early 2014, the Department of Health & Human Services amended the Clinical Laboratory Improvement Amendments of 1988 (CLIA) regulations to allow labs to give a patient (or a representative designated by the patient) access to his completed test reports upon request. In response, many labs are now sending copies of results directly to patients and/or making them accessible on their patient portals.

Here are some leading practices for handling test results being released to patients prior to providers reviewing them:

- Let your patients know if they may receive their test results before you have reviewed them as their provider.

- Then let your patients know how they will know when you have reviewed the results as their provider. For example, some patient portals have an indicator and notes section when a provider has reviewed the results.

Of course, it is still important for providers to discuss those results with the patient, particularly if the medical condition is complex and requires follow-up care. But if patients don't want to wait for the provider to review their test results, they no longer have to do so. And most importantly, don't have your staff tell patients they can't get their results until after their provider has reviewed them when it's not legally true!

This handout, created by a Studer Group® partner, serves to remind providers and staff about the important points of communicating test results to patients.

MD message at the end of each visit:
"Our nurse (or our team) will always call you with your test results within____days of your visit. We will also review them at your next visit."

"I will always go over your test results at your follow-up visit."

MD or clinic team message to patients:
"If you join myABCMedicine, our patient portal, you can view your test results within____days."

"You will always get a letter from our office with your results within____days."

NEVER SAY, "No news is good news!"
This is not an option. It can lead to potential patient anxiety, possible missed results, and patient perception that the labs must not have been that important for them to know.

Signage DOES NOT replace language.
Signage about lab results expectations can be used but do not replace verbal instruction and dialogue. Quite often, patients become numb to signage.

Figure 12.2 Sample Test Results Communication Card

A Few Additional Tips

Here we've outlined a few more tips that have been used by organizations coached by Studer Group with great success.

- **Personally follow up with patients.** In today's clinical world, patients may receive lab or x-ray results through many different communication channels. In some cases, they may get their results before their ordering provider has had a chance to review them. Even if patients do get results directly from the lab or radiology, it is important to communicate with them in order to place the results in the proper context.

Patients expect that when a provider orders a lab or x-ray, they are going to review the results. Even if the results show everything is normal and no treatment is needed, it is important to always close this communication loop. This tells patients that you took the time to respond directly to them.

Here's an example of how this is done. The primary care provider may send the patient a copy of her lab results—dated, initialed, and sent through the mail or a secure email—with a brief note that reads, "Based on these test results, no change in your treatment is needed at this time."

- **Don't use medical jargon.** When providers communicate results, it's important that they be placed in the proper context. Many times, patients will not understand the actual lab results values. For example, if the normal range for Total Cholesterol Level is less than 200 mg/dl and a patient's Total Cholesterol Level is 220 mg/dl, you might say, *"Your Total Cholesterol Level is 220 mg/dl and normal is considered less than 200. According to the American Heart Association, your value of 220 places you in a borderline high category. However, given your previous reading of 240 mg/dl, you are showing improvement over the last six months, so I recommend we continue on your current treatment plan. What questions do you have for me about this lab result or my recommendation to continue on your current treatment plan?"*

- **Add notes to electronic medical records too.** Some EMRs allow providers to add a note to a lab result before the value is placed in the record. However, others automatically push the lab result to the portal and make adding a note an optional activity. In addition, many lab vendors have patient portals for patients to directly access their lab results. (This allows them to comply with the April 7, 2014, mandate in CMS-2319-F that all CLIA-covered labs provide a way for patients to get access to their lab values directly from the lab.)

  Regardless of how your patients may access online test results, it is important to remember that simply pushing results and including a note about the test results does not guarantee patient utilization. It also does not meet the obligations that many states have put in place for providers to communicate specific positive lab results, such as for communicable diseases including HIV.

  In addition, if you review and push results out only once a week, you may be introducing delays into the communication process that many web-savvy healthcare patients will find dissatisfying. If your practice uses a patient portal to provide test results, it is imperative that you have a timely process for pushing out the results and a tracking mechanism to ensure that patients are accessing the online information or triggering a follow-up process.

  When using a patient portal through your EMR, let the patients know that their test results will be available in that system within the designated period of time. This may serve as an added benefit as to why a patient may want to sign up for the patient portal. (In some practices, a nurse or medical assistant may access the portal with the patient to demonstrate how to use it.)

- **Addressing non-responsive patients.** How many times do you need to try to contact a patient about their test results before you give up? It depends: First, consider if the test result in question requires you to communicate it with the patient under the law (e.g., reportable communicable diseases). Second, consider attempting to contact them through another form of communication—an alternate phone number, an email address, or a mailing address.

  To maintain patient safety and mitigate litigation risk, as well as to create a positive patient experience, clinical practices need to have a standardized and documented process for communicating test results. As part of this, it is important to track and follow up on non-responses. A leading strategy is a minimum of two documented attempts to reach the individual at their most recent phone number and a follow-up letter to their last known address.

- **Document, document, document.** It is important to document every step of the process. This includes steps taken to communicate test results and actual communication in your medical chart. In addition, modern EMR systems should be able to generate daily reports to identify test results received (or running late) and patient communication completed.

Here is a story that shows what great test results communication looks like:

Bettie was getting ready to go on a month-long trip with her husband to celebrate his retirement when she discovered a lump in her breast. She immediately went to visit her provider, family nurse practitioner Cindy, who referred her for a mammogram. Her mammogram was scheduled three days later and then Bettie started to worry: What if something was wrong? Should she cancel their trip? What if her test results weren't back before they were to leave?

The day of her mammogram arrived, and after completing the test, the technician informed Bettie that the doctor would review the results and that their normal process was to get the results back to her referring provider in five business days. But, the technician added, Cindy had informed her that Bettie needed her results right away. The technician said she would flag them for rapid handling and would get the results to Cindy by the close of business that day. Bettie was pleasantly surprised and thanked the technician.

She then checked out, walked out the door, and got in her car to drive home. As Bettie pulled into her driveway 15 minutes later, her cell phone began to ring. Upon answering, Bettie was surprised to hear her provider, Cindy, on the line.

"Bettie," Cindy said, "I have great news! I just heard from the radiology center, and your results are negative. It's just a fibroadenoma and they are typically benign. We will continue monitoring it just to be safe. But for now, please don't worry about the lump and have a great trip."

Bettie was overjoyed and immediately called her husband at work to tell him. Bettie also logged onto Facebook and told her 200+ contacts what an amazing experience she just had with her provider Cindy!

If you remember only one thing from this chapter, it should be this: Always put yourself in the patient's shoes. If you were the one waiting on lab or x-ray results, how would you like to receive information? If your provider promised to communicate the results as soon as they received them, and in a way that you could understand them, how would you feel if a week later you still hadn't received an update?

In summary: Be thorough and consistent. Avoid medical jargon. Try multiple avenues to reach the patient. And always communicate in a timely manner. Your efforts will make it far more likely to get a favorable response to the "Communicate Patient Test Results" CG CAHPS question. But even more important, you'll put patients' minds at ease and help them enjoy the best possible clinical results.

Tools & Resources

Studer Group® offers a variety of tools and resources that support the tactics discussed in this chapter. To access the up-to-date information, and to download a worksheet that will help you create a plan to improve patient perception of care in the "Test Results and Follow-up" arena, please visit www.studergroup.com/CGCAHPS.

HELPFUL, COURTEOUS, AND RESPECTFUL OFFICE STAFF

O ur patients' experiences are shaped by everyone they encounter during their visit. *Everyone.* That means it's crucial for every person who interacts with patients to demonstrate helpfulness, courtesy, and respect.

In the patient's mind, everyone working in a medical office falls into two groups: providers (physicians, nurse practitioners, and physician assistants) and staff (receptionists, clerks, medical assistants, nurses, etc.). In other words, if you are not the main provider, you are likely viewed by patients as staff. Patients simply don't always understand nuances in professional designations—the way they see it, everyone at the practice is there to help them get well. That's not a bad thing!

Although this composite is about "office staff," we have learned that interaction with *any* clinic staff member—including nurses and, at times, even providers—can have a positive or negative impact on how patients will evaluate their experience with "staff." And the overall feeling that

"I had a bad experience" can easily be attributed to clerks and receptionists when actually they weren't the offenders at all. Therefore, all staff members have potential to impact this composite's results, and all staff members will benefit from implementing the tactics discussed in this section.

Conversely, a patient's impression of how office staff treated him can set the tone for the entire visit. We at Studer Group® like to compare this phenomenon to the way that a hospital patient's perception of his Emergency Department care colors his impression of the entire stay. When a patient has a negative experience in the ED, it sets the stage for a negative experience of the entire visit— and thus impacts HCAHPS results. The good news is that when ED perception of care ratings improve, so do comparable inpatient ratings.

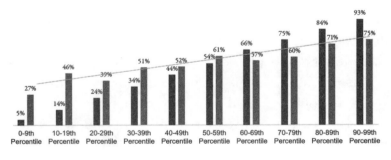

Figure iv.1 Hospital's ED Percentile Ranking Increases,
So Does Its HCAHPS Overall Percentile Ranking

As more evidence is gathered in the years to come, it will be interesting to see if CG CAHPS results follow a similar pattern (in terms of the results in this composite echoing the results in others). We predict that they will. Ultimately, when a patient is treated poorly by office staff, it doesn't matter how great the provider is—the patient experience has already been established as a negative one and it's almost impossible to overcome.

Before we discuss the CG CAHPS "office staff" questions and tactics that can impact them, we'd like to share a story that shows how these tactics affect patients on a personal level—including impacting their clinical outcome:

I was waiting in the reception area of a very large practice when I saw a man walk out of the "back area" where patients are taken to be seen by providers. He looked very agitated and approached the reception desk asking who was in charge. "I've been here since 7:15 this morning and now it's 8:30!" he said. "I've waited and waited in the exam room and nobody has even come to check on me for over an hour."

"Well, your appointment was at 7:45 so you got here too early," the receptionist replied.

Growing visibly more irritated, the patient said, "But it's 8:30 right now, so that's not a valid excuse! Where is Dr. Carlton and when is she going to be able to see me?"

"Oh, Dr. Carlton no longer works at this facility," said the receptionist, examining her nails so she wouldn't have to look this angry patient in the eye. "You'll be seeing Patrice Callaway, our nurse practitioner. She got here a few minutes ago and will be ready to see you soon."

By now, the patient was furious. "Your practice has made me wait like this before!" he shouted. "Now I'm going to be late meeting my client for breakfast—this was supposed to take five minutes."

"I can't wait to post this lovely experience on Facebook," he muttered as he stormed out of the office.

Unfortunately, this is a classic "what not to do" story. Making the patient wait for so long with no word of explanation was the staff's first mistake. But, of course, mistakes do happen. That's why, when they do, it's important to implement service recovery tactics immediately.

In other words, had the receptionist apologized, explained what happened and why it happened, and discussed the next steps the practice would take to make it right, the patient wouldn't have been nearly as upset. In fact, it's possible his loyalty to the practice could have been strengthened (see Chapter 2 for more information on service recovery)…such is the power of a sincere apology.

The Survey Questions

This aspect of the CG CAHPS survey asks patients about the helpfulness, courtesy, and respect of office staff members. Answers are given in frequency scale: *never, sometimes, usually,* or *always*. The percent of patients who responded *always* is publicly reported on a growing number of state and private payer websites as well as www.medicare.gov/physiciancompare.

1. **How often were clerks and receptionists at this provider's office as helpful as you thought they should be?**

2. **How often did clerks and receptionists at this provider's office treat you with courtesy and respect?**

This chapter does not cover all possible tactics. Rather, it conveys a few carefully targeted actions that you can take to immediately impact patient perception of how well your office staff treat patients and respond to their needs.

The following self-test is designed to assist you in determining how you are doing on the basics. We recommend you ask all your office staff members and practice leaders to participate in this self-test and compare your results to determine where to focus first. You may also find it valuable to repeat this self-test a year from now to evaluate your improvement in these areas.

Note: We have adopted the four-response standard of CG CAHPS for the self-test. Using this standard is a great way to build your own competency and experience in what it takes to consistently achieve an "always" response.

Question	Never	Sometimes	Usually	Always
1. How often are we selective in our hiring process and hire only staff with excellent service skills in courtesy?				
2. How often does everyone on our team consistently introduce themselves to our patients and their families?				
3. How often do we consistently acknowledge our patients and families? (eye contact, smile, "good morning")				
4. How often do we manage up one another in the office?				
5. How often do we have a system in place to ask our patients what is most important to them for their appointment each visit?				
6. How often do we use standardized key words in our clinic that we use to communicate with our patients and their families?				
7. How often do we regularly round on our patients in the reception area?				
8. How often do we make our patients feel like we are happy they are at our clinic?				
9. How often do we walk to the patient when calling their name in the reception area?				
10. How often do we round on patients in the exam room every 15 minutes until they have been seen by the provider?				

Figure iv.2 Courtesy and Helpfulness of Office Staff Self-Test

Courtesy and Helpfulness of Office Staff Self-Test Scoring

If you are like 99.9 percent of medical practices, you have likely identified a couple of areas in which you can improve. Don't try to implement all of the tactics in this section at once. Select the one or two most important to improving your practice and start by hardwiring them first.

This section is a little different as each statement provides insight into your performance on both CG CAHPS questions; to focus on a specific area of the self-test, please refer to this chart, which aligns tactics to statements.

Self-Test Question	Key Tactics
1. How often are we selective in our hiring process and hire only staff with excellent service skills in courtesy?	• Fundamental Tactic: Employee Selection
2. How often does everyone on our team consistently introduce themselves to our patients and their families?	• Fundamental Tactic: AIDET®
3. How often do we consistently acknowledge our patients and families? (eye contact, smile, "good morning")	• Fundamental Tactic: AIDET®
4. How often do we manage up one another in the office?	• Fundamental Tactic: Manage Up
5. How often do we have a system in place to ask our patients what is most important to them for their appointment each visit?	• Patient Reception Card • IPC • Patient Visit Guide
6. How often do we use standardized key words in our clinic that we use to communicate with our patients and their families?	• Fundamental Tactic: Key Words at Key Times
7. How often do we regularly round on our patients in the reception area?	• Rounding in the Reception Area[SM] • Fundamental Tactic: Key Words at Key Times
8. How often do we make our patients feel like we are happy they are at our clinic?	• Patient Reception Card • IPC • Patient Visit Guide • Fundamental Tactic: Key Words at Key Times
9. How often do we walk to the patient when calling their name in the reception area?	• Closing the Gap • Fundamental Tactic: AIDET®
10. How often do we round on patients in the exam room every 15 minutes until they have been seen by the provider?	• Room and Round[SM] • Fundamental Tactic: Key Words at Key Times

Figure iv.3 Courtesy and Helpfulness of Office Staff Self-Test Questions and Tactics Guide

This section of the book includes one chapter that covers the two questions of the CG CAHPS "Courteous and Helpful Office Staff" composite. We structured it this way because the two questions are strongly related, and if your organization can hardwire the tactics detailed, you will see improved results for both questions. These tactics, along with one additional tip, will positively impact the likelihood that patients will answer *always*.

CHAPTER THIRTEEN:

PATIENT-CENTERED CARE: FOCUS ON HELPFUL, COURTEOUS, AND RESPECTFUL OFFICE STAFF

"You never have a second chance to make a first impression."
—C. David Carpenter

THE CG CAHPS QUESTIONS:

- **How often were clerks and receptionists at this provider's office as helpful as you thought they should be?**

- **How often did clerks and receptionists at this provider's office treat you with courtesy and respect?**

...And the Tactics That Make "Always" Responses More Likely

Anyone who has ever been treated rudely or dismissively by a clerk in a store or any employee in any place of business knows the truth: A single bad encounter can ruin the entire customer experience. No matter how great the rest of the visit goes, it's forever marred by the unpleasant remark or the unsatisfying exchange. The frustration, irritation, or anger the customer feels lingers on in his memory—and possibly prevents him from ever returning.

The same is true in healthcare. When office staff behave in discourteous ways, or don't do enough to help patients, they notice. Patients begin forming opinions and perceptions of the practice based on the courtesy and respect of the office or scheduling staff who help them make an appointment. This initial encounter, even if on the phone, can set the tone for the entire visit. And of course, how clerks and receptionists behave when the patient arrives for his appointment also has a profound impact on his experience.

A focus group study conducted by Greater Washington Research at Brookings asked the participants for feedback about their experiences in healthcare settings, including community health centers, emergency rooms, private physician offices, and hospitals. Two of the key barriers to quality healthcare determined by the focus group were "frustration with how services were delivered" and "quality of communication with providers and staff." Participants spoke about the frustrations of not "being heard" during visits, encountering rude office staff who appeared too busy to help them, and the sense that they were just "another face or number" moving through the system.[1]

Office staff can start creating that all-important first impression when the patient calls to make an appointment. They can provide details, explain important information, and even manage up the providers during this call. Or if the patient's provider isn't available for several weeks, it is a perfect time to manage up the other caregivers who might have availability sooner.

Regardless of the entry point, standardizing warm greetings and responses can set the tone for a pleasant visit. Patients appreciate it when office staff make them feel welcomed and important, and are grateful when they demonstrate a helpful attitude and anticipate needs. Studer Group® has identified the following tactics to achieve a better patient experience and improve results in the Courteous and Helpful domain.

Tactic 1: Implement AIDET®/Key Words at Key Times

Have you ever arrived for a clinic appointment and stood in front of a closed (and often frosted) window at the reception desk? Typically, the encounter goes something like this: You notice a sign on the window that directs you to "sign in" on the clipboard. You can hear staff conversing and laughing behind the closed window. You know they know you are there, as the door chimed when you entered the office. Several minutes later, the window opens, a staff member grabs the clipboard, scratches out

Cut out the Window

Think about the types of businesses that place a window between the person behind the desk and the public: banks, casinos, gas stations. They're usually places that *need* that separation for security's sake. In general, a medical practice is not one of those places. A window at the reception desk means that the patient's experience begins with a barrier between him and the staff, which is not the impression you should make. Sometimes HIPAA regulations are used as a reason to keep a window separation. However, this decision is based on an inaccurate interpretation of HIPAA privacy rules. Consider removing your windows. Along with other tactics that create good flow and open communication, it will let patients know that they are encouraged to speak to the reception staff.

your name, and calls you up to the window and says, "Insurance card."

Or maybe the clinic you visit doesn't have the infamous closed window, but when you arrive at the reception desk, the staff member working there refuses to make eye contact. In fact, she redirects her body and keeps chatting on the phone. Rather than glancing up with a reassuring smile or even giving you the universal "just a minute" index finger gesture, she simply ignores you. Eventually—finally—she hangs up the phone, looks coolly at you, and says, "Name?"

Either way—closed window or delayed (and impersonal) greeting—you didn't feel welcome, did you? This type of reception does not convey a feeling of courtesy or respect to the patient. In fact, it starts the visit off on a negative note.

Instead, when a patient arrives for their appointment, staff can use AIDET® and Key Words at Key Times to start the visit in a positive way.

- **Acknowledge the patient.** Staff at the reception desk should stop what they are doing, *acknowledge* the patient (the "A" in AIDET), make eye contact, smile, and welcome the patient to the practice. Use warm greetings and responses such as:
    - *"Good morning"* or *"Good afternoon"*
    - *"Certainly"*
    - *"My pleasure"*
    - *"I'm happy to help you with that"*

  This simple act of acknowledgment can set the tone for the rest of the visit.

- **Introduce yourself and your role to the patient.** Telling the patient your name and your role is a common courtesy. Your name badge should be visible. The introduction (the "I" in AIDET) can be as easy as saying, *"Good morning, my name is Danielle. I am the receptionist who will be checking you in for your visit today."* In subsequent visits, we find that patients like to greet office staff by name, creating a friendly bond.

  The introduction is a good time to "manage up"— to position yourself, other staff, the provider, or the practice in a positive way. Managing up reduces patient anxiety and instills confidence and trust. When you do it, patients are more receptive to hear and adhere to what you say. Some examples:

- *"Good morning, my name is Danielle. I am the receptionist who will be checking you in for your visit today. I see that Dr. Hall is your physician. He is a wonderful cardiologist—he takes time to listen to his patients and answer their questions."*

- *"Good afternoon, Mr. Jones. My name is Joseph. I am Dr. Hall's medical assistant. We've worked together for five years."*

- *"We are a great team! I promise we will take excellent care of you."*

- **Manage wait times.** Check-in is also when office staff should inform patients if there is any delay in their appointment time or the provider's schedule. Patients may be frustrated that they arrived on time for their appointment, only to find out that the provider is running behind schedule and it will actually be 45 minutes later than they expected to be seen. Instead of stating, *"Dr. Wells is running behind schedule today,"* office staff should instead explain why the provider may be late in seeing the patient and offer options.

  For instance, *"Dr. Wells has been expecting you. He wanted me to let you know when you checked in today that he's with another patient and it's taking longer than anticipated. He thinks it should be about 30 minutes before you're taken to an exam room. We are sorry for this delay in your visit.*

Please let me know if there is anything I can get for you during your wait." This manages expectations about why the patient may have to wait and reduces their anxiety about why they haven't been called back yet (both the "D" for Duration and "E" for Explanation in AIDET).

What this conveys to the patient is that their time is valuable. It also allows them to state whether they have the time to wait, or if they need to reschedule due to limited time that day. (Chapter 5 addresses tactics for managing wait times in more detail.)

- **Have office staff create their own Key Words at Key Times.** Simply telling staff what to say is not as effective as asking them to create it themselves. This immediately generates buy-in. Remember, key words should feel more like a natural conversation than a memorized script. When office staff put themselves in the patient's shoes, they can tailor the conversation to what *they* would want to hear if they were the ones waiting to see the provider. For example, the key word "help" can be incorporated into conversations as follows:

  ○ *"Mr. Jones, let me* help *you with that."*

  ○ *"I am happy to* help *you."*

  ○ *"Let me* help *you to the chair."*

  ○ *"Is there anything I can* help *you with right now?"*

Incidentally, the act of helpfulness can also be demonstrated in very practical and logistical ways. For example, staff might help a patient with a walker to enter or exit a door, hold a paper still while the patient signs it, or assist a patient in taking her coat off. Telling the patient what you are doing reinforces the behavior and enhances their recognition of the staff member's helpfulness.

- **Validate and directly observe behaviors.** Leaders in the practice should validate and observe office staff using AIDET and key words. Start by listening to staff and noting how well they incorporate AIDET and key words in their conversations. Leaders can ask staff, "How do you introduce yourself to patients when they're arriving at a clinic?" "When you're escorting a patient down the hall, how do you make sure you're introducing yourself and managing up the practice and/or the provider?" and "How do you explain a wait time of longer than 15 minutes to a patient?"

  Leaders can also ask patients, "Who registered you today?" and "Were you kept informed about delays?"

Date:_____ Name:_____ Role:_____

STRENGTHS IDENTIFIED/RATING	ESSENTIAL SKILLS (EACH SECTION EQUALS 10 POINTS FOR A TOTAL OF 90 POINTS)	NEED TO FOCUS ON IMPROVEMENT
	ACKNOWLEDGE	
	Acknowledged while greeting in reception or when entering the exam room (smile, eye contact, hello, etc.)	
	Acknowledged using patient/customer/family name as appropriate	
	INTRODUCE	
	Introduced self and role	
	Managed up team/clinical provider/organization/personal experience/training/skill set, etc.	
	DURATION	
	Gave time expectation, how long expected to wait, next steps in treatment	
	Verbalized next step in care	
	EXPLANATION	
	Explained what will take place, what you are doing, what will happen, and what they should expect, etc.	
	Used language that the patient and/or family understands	
	THANK YOU	
	Thanked the patient and family and showed appreciation (i.e., thank you for trust, for letting me serve you, ask if there's anything you can do before leaving, provide business card if applicable, etc.)	

STRENGTHS IDENTIFIED/RATING	OTHER (EACH ITEM EQUALS 1 POINT FOR A TOTAL OF 10 POINTS)		NEED TO FOCUS ON IMPROVEMENT
(1 pt)	ENGAGEMENT ATTRIBUTES	Active listening	
(1 pt)		Non-multi-tasking	
(1 pt)		Eye contact	
(1 pt)		Tone of voice	
(1 pt)		Appropriate speed of speech	
(1 pt)		Appropriate use of touch	
(1 pt)		Appropriate use of humor/emotion	
(1 pt)		Physical positioning – mirror customer's position, sit without table or desk between if possible	
(1 pt)		Energy mirrors the needs of the patient	
(1 pt)		Washed hands as entering room and as leaving the room	

>90 PTS = COMPETENT EVALUATION SUMMARY: TOTAL: (100 PTS)		
☐ Expert at AIDET® ☐ Would be a good mentor to others	EVALUATOR COMMENTS:	☐ Repeat skills assessment

Evaluator:_____ Date:_____

13.1 AIDET® Validation Tool

Tactic 2: Use the Patient Reception Card

One of the newer leading practices that we've seen early success with is the development of a Patient Reception Card. This is a small card or note given to the patient upon arrival. It is filled out by the office staff upon checking in the patient for her appointment and includes:

- Patient name
- Name of office staff who checked in the patient
- Provider name
- Appointment time
- Arrival time
- A note at the bottom of the card that states, "We're committed to providing you with an excellent experience as a team. If you haven't been seen within 15 minutes of your scheduled appointment time, please check with us for an update."

The Patient Reception Card helps to manage wait times and also to set expectations. For example, it lets the patient know that if he arrives 30 minutes before the scheduled appointment time (which is noted on the card), he may not be able to be seen early. It also includes one staff person's name so the patient knows whom to approach with any questions he may have while he is waiting.

The Patient Reception Card can be coupled with an Individualized Patient Care (IPC) card or the Patient Visit Guide. The Patient Reception Card information can be printed on the front of the card, and IPC or Patient Visit Guide can be printed on the back. (For more information on IPC, see Chapter 10. For more information on the Patient Visit Guide, see Chapter 6.)

Following is an example of a Patient Reception Card.

Your service representative today is:

_____

Your Provider Today: _____

Arrival Time: _____ Appointment Time: _____

If you have not been seen by _____

please ask your service representative for an update.

Questions/Comments: _____

_____

_____

Your thoughts and opinions about your experience are important to us. To help us recognize our staff and improve your experience, please be sure to complete the post-visit survey you will receive by telephone. Thank you!

We are committed to providing an excellent patient care experience. As a team, we work for you and your family in a courteous manner. We know your time is valuable and we will work to limit delays and wait times.

Figure 13.2 Patient Reception Card Sample

Following are some tips for successfully implementing Patient Reception Cards:

- **Provide staff with an example of what "right" looks like.** For instance: *"Good morning. My name is Kim and I'm going to write it down for you on your Patient Reception Card. If you have any questions throughout your appointment, please ask for me. Your appointment today was scheduled for 4:00 p.m. I'm going to write the time you arrived, which is 3:50 p.m. If you haven't been seen by 4:15 p.m. today, we want you to check back with us so we can provide you an update on when we anticipate you'll be seeing the provider."*

- **Get buy-in from providers and staff.** Just as we involved staff in developing their own AIDET and Key Words at Key Times, it's important to include them in the development of the Patient Reception Cards.

Tactic 3: Implement Rounding in the Reception Area[SM]

When focusing on office staff courtesy and helpfulness, periodically rounding on patients in the reception area (a.k.a. waiting room) allows staff to show caring and concern and to reduce patient anxiety about their visit. Staff can use this opportunity to meet patient needs, offer any help, and keep them informed of any delays.

After the patient checks in, record her arrival in the Rounding in the Reception Area[SM] Log. Make a note of her name, appointment time, check-in time, and either where she chooses to sit or a distinguishing feature to help identify her by sight (which also helps when escorting the patient back to the clinical area—see Tactic 4 in this chapter, "Close the Gap").

While reception staff own the process, anyone can round in the reception area; it's a team sport! Receptionists, registration clerks, greeters, medical assistants, nurses, leaders, flow coordinators, and even (on occasion) providers practice rounding. Here's how:

- **First, check to make sure the patient does not have any questions while completing her Patient Visit Guide.** See Chapter 6 for more details on this guide.

- **Round on patients every 15-30 minutes.** While time frames vary in each practice, most begin rounding on a patient 15 minutes or so after her appointment time has come and gone. Then, they round every 15 to 30 minutes thereafter.

- **Use Key Words at Key Times/AIDET.** During the first rounding session, you'll want to say some variation of the key words indicated in the following chart:

A	Hi, Mr. Jones. (Approach individual patient; do not shout or call out to patient across the room.)
I	I'm Danielle and I checked you in today.
D	I wanted to let you know that Dr. Hall is running about 45 min. late; he knows you are here. I know you have been waiting and it is past your appointment time.
E	In the meantime, I want to be sure you are as comfortable as possible. Is there anything I can help you with right now? I also understand your time is very important, so if you feel you need to reschedule your visit, I am prepared to do so and am happy to help with that. TIP: Manage up the provider and offer comfort or distraction measures. If wait is extended, ask if they would like to wait elsewhere and leave their cell phone number so you can call them to return when they can be seen.
T	Thank you for your patience.

Figure 13.3 Sample AIDET® When Rounding

After the first round, you'll condense the AIDET guidelines and provide more of an update or "check in" to let the patient know if anything has changed.

"Remember, I am Bekki. Dr. DeHart is currently finishing up with a patient and the nurse should be out for you within the next 10 minutes. I wanted to update you with this and see if you are still doing okay?"

- **Use a Rounding in the Reception Area**^{SM}

- **Use a Rounding in the Reception Area**[SM] **Log.** Those who round in the reception area should use a log to document the rounds. The log should have pre-printed times and a place for staff to initial and write comments. The manager can then review the log for trends and compliance.

Name: _____   Date: _____

	NAME	APPT. TIME	CHECK-IN TIME	LOCATION IN RECEPTION AREA	DISTINGUISHING FEATURES	TIMES OF ROUNDING		
1								
2								
3								
4								
5								
6								
7								
8								
9								
10								
11								
12								
13								
14								
15								
16								
17								
18								
19								
20								
21								
22								
23								
24								
25								
26								
27								
28								
29								
30								
31								
32								
33								
34								
35								

Figure 13.4 Rounding in the Reception Area[SM] Rounding Log Sample

Tactic 4: Close the Gap

We often speak about closing the metaphorical gap between providers and patients. One simple action that can help do that is closing the literal, physical space in the reception area between staff and patient.

Here is what "open gap" behavior in the reception area looks like: A staff member or nurse opens the door from the clinic area, and with hand on the doorknob calls out the patient name: "Joe Smith. Hi. Right this way." The patient trails behind her and follows her into the exam room. The patient senses the gap (literal and metaphorical) between himself and the staff member or nurse and wonders, *Will I get the personalized care and attention I need?* Others in the reception room will notice and feel the distance as well as the lack of personal attention.

(Remember, even though it's likely to be a medical assistant or a nurse who takes the patient back to the exam room, the patient may well perceive her as a "clerk or receptionist" and may think of her when answering these CG CAHPS questions.)

At Studer Group, we coach our partner organizations to literally close the gap—having staff members and nurses take the extra step into the reception area to greet the patient instead of standing in the doorway. The staff member or nurse then walks *with* the patient back to the clinical area, confirming the patient's name and date of birth for safety. This allows her to begin building a relationship immediately, as it allows her a few seconds to ask the patient how he is feeling or make small talk.

It also allows her to assist patients who have walking difficulties, are managing small children, or otherwise need a little help.

Of course, if the staff member escorting the patient back to the clinical area does not know who the patient is and where he is sitting in the reception area, he can always check with the front desk/reception staff. Some practices take pictures of their patients for the paper chart or EMR and this helps with identification.

In busy practices, if you are a staff member or nurse, you can accomplish several things while stepping into the reception area. For example:

- Thank everyone for their patience. Let them know that someone will be out for the next person shortly.

- Greet and welcome your patient. As you walk to the exam room, explain that to ensure privacy, you will explain next steps in the exam room.

- If a physician is running late, announce the delay to the others in the reception area: *"Dr. Jones is currently running late, and Carra will be out within 10 minutes with an update or to escort you back."*

- If your office utilizes provider wait time boards, make a general announcement to the patients in the reception area as to when the board will be updated. (Or, you could even stop and update the board yourself on the way out the door.)

All of these tips will keep others who are waiting well informed. Even when you are not speaking directly to them, they will feel the personal connection. This builds confidence about the service and care.

Closing the physical gap between staff and patients may seem like a small task, but it can go a long way in developing a rapport with patients that will make them feel that you care. This helps to create a positive patient experience and sets the tone for the rest of the visit.

One More Tip

Here is another tip to consider as you are hardwiring the previous tactics.

Remember the Employee/Provider Selection Fundamental Tactic

In Chapter 2, we discussed the importance of hiring the right people for your practice. This is especially important for this composite. New hires must fit in with your clinic's culture, so if you're looking to create one based on friendliness and courtesy toward patients, you must keep that in mind during the interview process.

The behavioral-based questions are a great place to learn whether a candidate has the qualities your practice wants. Listen for stories that indicate that the person is committed to treating patients with kindness as well as clinical skill.

Is It Time for a Name Change?

Don't call the front area of your practice facility "the waiting room." It's the place where your staff receives patients. By changing its name to the "reception area," you remove the negative connotations of the term "*waiting room.*" (Most people don't like to wait, but they don't mind being received.)

Additionally, "reception area" serves to remind staff of their responsibility to make patients feel welcome and comfortable.

Names really do have meaning. Choose and use them thoughtfully.

Our patients need our help. It's why they come to our practice and it's what they expect. We owe it to them to provide that help in terms of medical care (providers) and a helpful attitude (providers *and* all staff members). They also expect—and deserve—our courtesy and respect.

The great news is that it *doesn't* take a lot of medical training or special skills to provide helpfulness, courtesy, and respect. While we may need to learn certain tactics, such as the ones outlined in this chapter, what we really need is the sincere desire to make people's lives better and easier. That desire—and the vast majority of healthcare workers already have it—is one of the most valuable keys to a consistently excellent patient experience.

Tools & Resources

Studer Group® offers a variety of tools and resources that support the tactics discussed in this chapter. To access the up-to-date information, please visit www.studer-group.com/CGCAHPS.

OVERALL PROVIDER RATING AND PRACTICES TO CREATE AN "ALWAYS" CULTURE

D oes your practice provide a level of care that you would be proud of your mother receiving (without any special accommodations, that is)? If your friend or neighbor was going to be seen in your clinic, would your standard patient delivery model be good enough, or would you alert your team to treat them differently? If your own child was sick, would your standard processes for getting an appointment and receiving care in your clinic be acceptable?

These are the kinds of questions all healthcare organizations need to be able to answer with a resounding yes—or, in CG CAHPS parlance, a resounding *always*.

When we at Studer Group® talk about "always" we often reference "high-reliability" organizations like airlines and nuclear power plants—organizations that do high-stakes work where a single mistake can have life-or-death consequences. Like those who work in air traffic control towers and inside nuclear reactors, healthcare professionals have an obligation to put safety ahead of everything else.

While most people think of safety in terms of medical procedures and drug protocols, it also hinges on making sure all clinical information is up to date. Patient history is a huge part of this. And that means we must take concrete steps to ensure a positive experience with every patient, every time—no exceptions. When patients perceive that we are too busy or we don't care, they'll hold back vital information.

A recent article in the *New York Times*, titled "Doctor, Shut Up and Listen" and written by Nirmal Joshi, chief medical officer for Pinnacle Health System, tells the story of a woman who had been to five physicians claiming symptoms of "rapid heartbeat" and "feeling stressed." Eventually, she was diagnosed with an anxiety disorder and referred for psychological counseling.[1]

When the patient finally came to see Pinnacle's Dr. Martin (physician number six in the patient's journey), he took a careful history and found that she was taking an over-the-counter weight loss product containing epinephrine. When she stopped, so did her symptoms. It seems none of the previous five providers had ever really talked to her in depth—and thus she'd never mentioned that she was taking a potentially harmful substance.

Of course, really talking to the patient—and, of course, really *listening* to what she has to say—is just a fragment of the impression that leads to an "always" culture and favorable results on the overall ratings composite.

Remember, in the patients' eyes, it takes only a single misstep—a 30-minute wait in the reception area, a brusque comment from an office staff member, a physician failing to respectfully listen—to drop the overall rating from a perfect 10 to something lower (perhaps considerably lower). In healthcare, as in any other arena, perfection is incredibly tough to achieve...but that doesn't mean we shouldn't aim for it.

The Survey Question

This aspect of the CG CAHPS survey asks patients to provide an overall rating for their clinical provider. Answers are given on an 11-point scale of 0-10, as opposed to the frequency scale used for the other questions in the survey. The percent of patients who give answers of 9 or 10 is publicly reported on a growing number of state and private payer websites and is starting to appear at www. medicare.gov/physiciancompare.

Using any number from 0 to 10, where 0 is the worst provider possible and 10 is the best provider possible, what number would you use to rate this provider?

The following self-test is designed to assist you in determining how you are doing with your overall performance. We recommend you ask a broad cross-section of your team to participate in this self-test and compare your results to determine where to focus first. You may also find it valuable to repeat this self-test a year from now to evaluate your improvement in these areas.

Note: Although patients use a 0-10 rating scale to respond to the "overall" question, we have adopted the four-response standard of CG CAHPS for the self-test. This allows you to look at the specific actions and behaviors that affect patients' responses to the "overall" question. Using this standard is a great way to build your own competency and experience in what it takes to consistently achieve a "10" rating.

Question	Never	Sometimes	Usually	Always
1. How often do we provide care that you would be proud of your mother receiving, without any special accommodations?				
2. How often is every member of the team held accountable for creating a positive patient experience?				
3. When someone proposes a better way to do something, how often do we readily adopt it regardless of who proposes it?				
4. If your child was sick, how often would our standard processes for getting an appointment and receiving care in our clinic be acceptable?				
5. How often do we hold our physicians and staff to the same standards of behavior?				
6. How often do we respect our patients and fellow team members in this practice?				
7. If your elderly neighbor was going to be seen in our clinic, how often would our standard patient delivery model be good enough? (i.e., you wouldn't alert your team to treat them differently)				
8. How often are you proud to be a member of this practice?				
9. If anyone intentionally violates standard procedures or safety rules, how often are they swiftly corrected?				
10. How often do we do things consistently in this practice, regardless of the shift or physician who is in the office?				

Figure v.1 Overall Provider Rating Self-Test

Overall Provider Rating Self-Test Scoring

If you are like 99.9 percent of medical practices, you have likely identified a couple areas you can improve. Because a patient's overall experience affects the way they rate the provider overall, we recommend that for the statements you evaluated with the lowest rating, you ask yourself "why" and revisit that section or chapter.

In this section, we will review some fundamental tactics that contribute to a positive patient experience and make it more likely that patients will provide a high rating.

Keep in mind that this chapter does not cover every possible tactic. Rather, it focuses on certain carefully targeted specific actions you can take right now—actions that will yield some "quick wins" in how patients perceive your practice.

CHAPTER FOURTEEN:

PATIENT RATING
OF PROVIDER

"We are not here merely to make a living. We are here to enrich the world, and we impoverish ourselves if we forget this errand."
—*Woodrow Wilson*

P atients are just like us. They want (and want their family members and friends) to have the best possible care. For a patient to be willing to return to our practice or recommend our practice to a friend or family member, we need to provide the kind of care that we'd want our own parent, partner, or child to receive. It's important to work hard to deliver quality care that is worthy of that honor— regardless of the patient's ultimate outcome.

And as the following story illustrates, an overall posi- tive experience can happen even in the face of uncer- tainty and continued worry. Rick's wife, Donna, had just undergone a CT scan and a full body PET scan, during which was discovered a lesion on her liver and a spot on one of her ribs. He immediately posts this update on Facebook to share with his friends and colleagues:

The doctor called us on his way home last night on his cell phone. He conferred for over 30 minutes with the chief of radiology who personally went over all of her films with him. What an outstanding person he is. He feels very strongly that the liver mass is benign and he also feels that the bone mass is also benign. However, they want her to have an ultrasound of her liver to ensure that the mass is benign and she will also probably need an MRI of the rib.

He personally called us to let us know because he knew that the report was very scary and he wanted to reassure us. He cannot say for sure 100 percent that everything is benign, but he feels very strongly that it will end up being so. We are exhausted and grateful.

I actually got her scheduled for her MRI on Saturday, tomorrow. Her doctor is so great—he is going to call us with the results ASAP. Hopefully we will know a lot more tomorrow evening. I feel pretty confident that the news will be good. But until it is 100 percent we are still a little concerned. Love you guys.

This is how we all want our patients to feel about their experience with us (and not just because, as in Rick's example, they're likely to immediately communicate it via some form of social media). Of course, Rick's clearly "positive" overall impression would not have been so positive if it had been preceded by a misdiagnosis, or if the physician had displayed a nonchalant or uncaring attitude, or if it had been frustrating or difficult to get an appointment in the first place. Everything works together.

That's why the CG CAHPS question we focus on in this chapter is so incredibly important. The rating it asks for represents the culmination of every interaction a patient has had with your practice, from scheduling their appointment and receiving care through settling their bills:

- It represents the sum of the entire patient experience, encompassing every other CG CAHPS question and more.[1,2,3,4]

- It is a measure of how patient-centered your facility is. Patient-centered care is one of the critical factors in high-quality healthcare[5] and at the core of creating a "Patient-Centered" Medical Home (PCMH).

- It is linked to the quality of care you provide.[6]

- It is the "final grade" you receive in the school of public (patient) opinion. It represents if your patients are loyal to your practice, or would send their family and friends somewhere else.[7,8,9]

- Use of physician rating sites is on the rise, so one negative patient experience may be communicated to many people outside the patient's personal circle.[10]

Your overall rating is based on more than just the other CG CAHPS patient experience questions, but make no mistake, it is highly correlated with those questions. Our analysis shows that the CG CAHPS composite most highly correlated with your overall rating is provider communication—specifically the questions dealing with respect and listening.

But what most powerfully drives favorable results on this question is your culture. That's what patient responses really measure—your quality and your efficiency and effectiveness at delivering Individualized Patient Care. They answer the implied question: *Is everyone working together to always provide this level of care to the patient?*

A Note about Scoring the Overall Rating Question

This question is different from all the other core questions in how it is scored: Instead of the *never, rarely, sometimes, always* scale, it is based on an 11-point response scale from 0 to 10. The Top Box for this question is calculated as the percent of respondents who answered with a 9 or 10 divided by the total respondents. The recommendation for sharing results of this question with the public is to report the data with the label "Patient's Rating of the Provider."

Rating Selected	Number of Responses
Missing/No Response	1
Worst Provider Possible (0)	0
1	1
2	0
3	0
4	1
5	0
6	0
7	2
8	4
9	8
Best Provider Possible (10)	13
Total	30

Figure 14.1 Sample Overall Rating Results

For example, a provider may have 30 CG CAHPS survey responses across different CG CAHPS survey instruments for the time period to be reported. When tabulating the data across the 30 surveys, we might find results such as those presented in the following table. The Top Box score for these results would be 70 percent (21 responses of 9 or 10, divided by the 30 total responses). It is also important to note that many public reporting initiatives *include the non-responses* in the denominator, and therefore it is important to include them in your calculation.

The CG CAHPS question asks the patient to rate the provider, but the overall patient experience is about much more than their experience with any one individual. It's about everything from the initial phone call to get an appointment to their entrance into the reception area to the exam to the discharge and follow-up. As you can see, most of these elements do not involve the provider herself, but other practice staff members. This is why improving results for this question must be a team effort.

All members of the team must feel a sense of ownership over each patient's experience. Each person has a chance to make a patient's encounter better or worse as the appointment progresses.

What this really means is that consistency reigns supreme. If we take our cue from high-reliability organizations like airlines and nuclear power plants (as mentioned earlier), we clearly see that the tactics in this book (in particular the four key powerhouse practices addressed in Tactic 2 in this chapter) need to be hardwired into your organization. Each provider and staff member should know and deploy them as needed so that every patient has an *always* experience.

The other two tactics we explore in the following pages—pre- and post-visit calls—can help you proactively "manage" the patient's experience before and after you actually see him.

Tactic 1: Make Pre-Visit Patient Phone Calls

By now, you've probably noticed that results for many of the composites can be strongly impacted by communication. You can get patients' experience off on the right foot with early and effective communication in the form of a pre-visit phone call.

All patients should receive a pre-visit call to confirm their appointment and to share vital information about the appointment. For new patients this call will also serve as an opportunity to reinforce that they've made a good choice and to provide logistical information (such as where your practice is and where to park). It is also a time to determine the best method to reach them for future communications—for instance, a follow-up on the current appointment, to report lab results, and to confirm future appointments.

Communication with a patient prior to her appointment reminds her that we are expecting her and that we're ready to provide excellent care. It can also help uncover any issues that make a patient visit take longer than planned.

Pre-visit calls are proven to reduce no-shows, cancellations, and tardiness; increase patient experiences and perception of care; and help care to be delivered more efficiently.

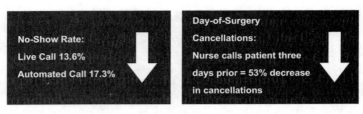

Figure 14.2 Pre-Visit Phone Calls Effect on No-Shows and Cancellations

Calling patients prior to their appointments is an especially effective technique for outpatient areas. One Studer Group® partner realized a $750,000 savings as a result of dramatic reductions in their no-show and late arrival rates. It just makes sense: When patients arrive as scheduled, the practice flows more efficiently, physicians save time, and patients are happier.

Many practices use an automated system to make pre-visit calls. While this is adequate (and sometimes necessary for practices with a large patient volume), an in-person call gives the patient an opportunity to ask questions or change the appointment if needed. Additionally, the caller can give reminders that are specific to that patient's reason for visiting.

In-person pre-visit calls are typically conducted by the flow coordinator or "air traffic controller." They can also be made by a medical assistant or a member of the clinical team, such as an LPN or RN. Calls are typically made 24-48 hours in advance of the appointment.

These calls save time for the patient and for the front desk staff by getting questions answered in advance.

Those practices that have implemented EMRs and have newer technology, such as patient portals, can also offer patients the ability to go onto the portal and complete the clinical intake information that is then reviewed by the clinical team. A section for questions or comments can be added here as well.

Pre-visit calls are also the perfect opportunity to use key words to express gratitude to the patient for scheduling an appointment with this office, ask if the patient needs directions or parking information, and manage up both the clinic and provider. For example:

"Good morning, Mrs. Clark. This is Patricia from Dr. Smith's office, and I am calling to remind you about your appointment Thursday at 10 a.m. Is this appointment confirmed on your calendar?"

"We look forward to seeing you then! Please arrive 10 minutes early to ensure that we can check you in and answer any questions you may have. Do you need directions to the office or parking information?"

"Dr. Smith is an excellent doctor and is looking forward to seeing you on Thursday."

"Do you have any questions for me?"

"Thank you, see you [day or date and time], and have a nice day!"

For existing patients, pre-visit contact can utilize a variety of message delivery options. At checkout, ask patients how they would like to be contacted to confirm their next appointment. Contact delivery options include calls, mailed letter or post card, text messages, and emails.

A message sent through a text-driven option (text message or email) should still convey warmth and gratitude to the patient. For instance:

We look forward to seeing you for your appointment with Dr. Smith on [day, date, time]. Should you have any questions prior to your appointment, please contact us at [insert clinic phone number].

The contact rate for pre-visit calls should be discussed during daily huddles, brief meetings with the care team and staff to plan the day. For instance, let's say you have 24 patients on the schedule and you were able to confirm 22 through pre-visit phone calls. This lets all staff know there is potential for two no-show appointments. They can then proactively have plans to use this time should the appointments not show.

Tactic 2: Teach Providers and Staff the Four Powerhouse Practices—and Connect Back to the "Why"

There are four fundamental tactics that powerfully impact overall provider rating. They are discussed in Chapter 2 of this book, and we invite you to review them carefully. In a nutshell, the four powerhouse practices are:

- **Key Words at Key Times.** These are carefully chosen words healthcare professionals use to "connect the dots" with patients, families, and visitors. They help the patient understand his care better, they reduce anxiety and build trust, and they align the behavior of the staff to the needs of the patient.

- **AIDET®.** This is an acronym that stands for **A**cknowledge, **I**ntroduce, **D**uration, **E**xplanation, and **T**hank You. It's a communication framework that, when used by each provider and staff member during each new patient interaction, alleviates patient anxiety, improves clinical outcomes, and builds loyalty.

- **Service Recovery/CARE℠.** Because things do go wrong from time to time, it's critically important that we know the actions to take to "make it right" with patients. Effective service recovery cannot only restore loyalty; it can actually increase it—meaning that "recovered" patients may become even more loyal than they were before they had the bad experience.

- **Employee/Provider Selection.** Hiring well is a critical step to providing higher quality care at lower costs. When we follow certain proven steps to selecting talent, we make it far more likely that we hire people who are a "good match" for the organization—and keep them.

Notice that, in every tactic listed previously, we provided a brief mention of *why* it's important (more detail on the *why* can be found in Chapter 2). That's because we strongly believe that when healthcare professionals understand the *why* behind the tactics we're asking them to implement, they will work hard to always do them. Their values won't allow them not to.

In the end, the goal of improving the overall rating and other CG CAHPS results is *not* to chase those numbers and win some sort of metrics competition. The goal is to improve the patient experience, and thus the care the patient receives. It is important that all providers and staff members get this.

The *why* behind all of the tactics in this book is to provide better care to achieve better outcomes. CG CAHPS is simply how we measure them. As leaders, we need to state this not once but over and over as we work to improve the patient experience.

We can connect back to the *why* when we train people on how to do the tactics, when we validate and/or remind them, during daily huddles, during staff meetings, and after there has been a mistake or patient complaint. And don't forget to remind providers and staff members about the *why* when we report CG CAHPS results.

Tactic 3: Make Post-Visit Patient Phone Calls

Communicating with patients after the visit allows you to ensure that the communication during the visit was adequate (and to make up for it if it wasn't). Evidence consistently proves that when a patient receives a call post-discharge, providers are able to confirm that the patient is complying with his or her treatment plan, and overall clinical outcomes improve.

Moreover, patients will know that we care about their health when we contact them to ensure they are recovering safely. We encourage offices to make post-visit calls, as they increase adherence to discharge plans and increase patient loyalty and perception of the provider.

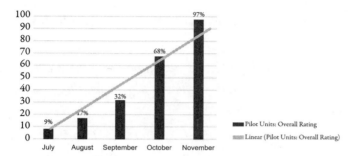

Figure 14.3 Post-Visit Calls Impact on Overall Positive Patient Experience

Benefits of post-visit calls include:

- Improved clinical efficacy
- Reconfirmed home care and follow-up instructions
- Clarified medication instructions
- Reduced patient anxiety
- Reduced complaints and claims
- Increased perception as a byproduct of high quality
- Improved processes
- Increased revenue
- Harvested positive feedback of physician and staff for retention and recognition

- Opportunity for service recovery if a patient did not have a positive experience (see Chapter 2 for more on this)

Here's an example of a post-visit call with a new patient.

"Ms. Davis? Hello. This is Cathy from Dr. Baker's office. Dr. Baker wanted me to call and see how you're doing after your office visit yesterday. Is this a good time?"

"We like to contact our patients after their visits to make certain that we were able to answer all of their questions." (Customize questions based on patient's appointment/diagnosis.)

- *"Do you have any questions regarding your medications or any possible side effects? Have you filled your prescription yet?"*

- *"Do you have any questions on your other care instructions?"*

- *"We want to make sure we do excellent clinical follow-up to ensure your best possible outcome. Do you know what symptoms or health problems to look out for? What will you do if these symptoms occur?"*

- *"Have you scheduled your follow-up appointment?"*

"Ms. Davis, we like to recognize our employees when they've earned it. Who did an excellent job for you while you were in the office? What specific actions did they complete that made you feel this way?"

"We're always working to get better. What suggestions do you have about how we could improve?" (May choose to add specific questions regarding quality indicators such as hand washing, explanation of medications and side effects, etc.)

"We appreciate your taking the time this afternoon to speak with us about your follow-up care. Is there anything else I can do for you?"

Post-visit calls can also be made by providers to their patient one or two days after being seen. Similar to the impact of calls placed by nurses, they can have a dramatic impact on perception of care and clinical quality. However, when placed by providers, they have the added benefit of raising loyalty and improving their reputation.

Here is an example of a post-visit phone call placed by a provider.

"Miles? Hello. This is Dr. Rogers. I wanted to call and see how you were doing today."

(Customize questions based on patient's appointment/diagnosis.)

- *"Miles, did you get your medications filled?"*
- *"Are your symptoms better or worse than when I saw you at the office?"*
- *"Do you have any more questions about your diagnosis?"*
- *"How is the new diet going for you?"*

"My team and I are always working to get better. What suggestions do you have about how we could improve?" (May choose to add specific questions regarding quality indicators such as hand washing, ease of getting an appointment, etc.)

"I appreciate your taking the time to come in for your check-up. I'd like to see you back in six months."

Phone calls are an important point of contact for patients and take up a significant amount of staff time and energy. By using these tactics, you can make sure that the time and energy is spent wisely, and that patients are able to quickly and easily get the information or service that they need.

Provider practices, like all healthcare organizations, exist to serve humanity. The people drawn to this field are driven by a fierce desire to help others. When we can create an organization that patients are willing to sincerely rate as "the best provider possible"—the kind they trust enough to recommend to the people they love the most—we can say we've succeeded in meeting that goal.

Great CG CAHPS results (on this question and on all others in this book) have benefits unto themselves, of course: improved practice reputation and market share, reduced liability risk, and increased reimbursement. But these metrics simply show that we are implementing behaviors that achieve the most important goals: better clinical outcomes and greater professional fulfillment.

That's why it's so important to remind staff of the *why* behind all that we do—to constantly connect them back to purpose, worthwhile work, and making a difference. Everything we do is about building the patient's trust and providing excellent care. The improved results are a bonus.

Tools & Resources

Studer Group® offers a variety of tools and resources that support the tactics discussed in this chapter.

To access the up-to-date information, please visit www.studergroup.com/CGCAHPS.

CHAPTER FIFTEEN:

HARDWIRING BEHAVIORS FOR AN "ALWAYS" CULTURE: ALIGNMENT, CONSISTENCY, AND ACCOUNTABILITY

"We are what we repeatedly do. Excellence, therefore, is not an act but a habit."

—Aristotle

hree frogs were sitting on a lily pad and one decided to jump off. How many frogs were left on the lily pad? The answer is three. If you think you're missing something, pay close attention to the wording. There is a big difference between *deciding* to do something and actually *doing* it. Here's the point for healthcare organizations wishing to make a change: It's easy to *decide* to improve, but to execute consistently on that vision is another story.

If we're not careful, it's all too easy to be one of those "deciding frogs." We intend to hardwire the tactics presented in this book and forever change the way patients experience the care our practice provides, but intentions don't always translate into reality. And the reason why we struggle so much comes down to culture. In short, the culture that's evolved over the years just may not be conducive to getting patients to respond *always* to every CG CAHPS question.

The good news is that a culture can be overhauled— even a deeply dysfunctional one. Before we discuss how to do that, let's explore what the culture we're striving for should look like. In terms of CG CAHPS, an *always* culture means that everyone in the clinic is *always* doing everything possible to make sure patients are so well served that they answer "always" to every survey question and rate your practice a 10 overall.

In larger, more holistic terms, it means that everyone—from the practice administrator to the providers to the nurses to the front office and support service people— lives the clinic's mission to create the best place for patients to receive care...*always*. Everyone in the entire organization *always* holds him or herself accountable to the standards of behavior that create the best environment and outcomes for the patient.

Creating an *always* culture is about taking our focus on providing excellent care from the exam room and applying it to the entire organization. It's about hardwiring excellence into every aspect of our operations. Hardwiring is a measure of frequency and effectiveness. When we've hardwired a new practice or behavior into every function, every process, and the mind of every staff member, then we get "always."

When someone is willing to recommend an organization, that's about more than their clinical experience. It's about every person getting it right every time.

An *always* culture has three major elements:

Alignment. This means all levels of the organization must have the same sense of urgency to enhance the patient experience and, in particular, its links to quality outcomes—not just practice owners but all leaders, providers, and staff.

We recommend that leaders at all levels regularly share the importance of patient experience with the people they lead. They should connect the dots so that every staff member understands *why* these issues are important. Every employee needs to understand that executing the tactics that lead to great clinical quality (and, not incidentally, to high CG CAHPS results) is critical to the clinic's or practice's future.

Consistency. An *always* culture is synonymous with consistency. Every patient must have a consistently good experience, no matter which office they visit or which provider they see, whether it's Monday morning in a primary care office or Saturday night at urgent care, and no matter which providers and staff members are working that day.

Of course, this is not an easy task to accomplish. It requires that proven leading practices (many of which are included in this book) be hardwired into the organization. That begins with leadership. All leaders must speak in the same voice, follow the same processes and procedures, and work toward the same results. And all leaders and staff members need to understand what they're being asked to do and why—and to be held accountable for doing it.

Cross-organizational consistency leads to great clinical outcomes. It ensures that all patients and families have the best possible experience. It allows the hiring of the right employees and creates loyalty. It creates your organization's recognizable brand. And of course, it's good for your CG CAHPS results.

Accountability. It's not enough to set performance goals. Clinical groups must make sure people are actually achieving them. That may mean embracing new systems and processes that hold people at all levels accountable for executing well.

We have found that it's not unusual for healthcare organizations to overstate the performance of team members. This may be due to poor evaluation tools. It's important that your evaluation tools are based on objective, measurable goals and that they allow you to give certain areas more weight than others for specific employees (to take into account the goals of different departments or clinical focuses).

Another common problem is an organization-wide failure to deal with low performers. We've found that 40-60 percent of employees identified by their managers as "not meeting expectations" are not in any performance counseling. Leaders must have a system for bringing low performers up or moving them out, improving the performance of middle performers, and re-recruiting high performers.

So how do you achieve this level of alignment, consistency, and accountability...*always*? Simply, you make sure the right foundation is in place.

It All Comes Back to Evidence-Based Leadership^{SM} (EBL)

The one overarching approach that drives *always* is Evidence-Based Leadership^{SM} (EBL). It is your framework to get to *always* and stay there. You might recall back in the Introduction that we mentioned Studer Group's Evidence-Based Leadership framework as a good foundation for moving CG CAHPS results.

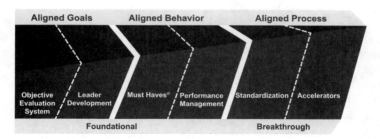

Figure 15.1 Evidence-Based Leadership^{SM} Framework

If you have the EBL framework in place, you are well situated to create an *always* culture. That's because all major components of your organization are aligned and work together in a cohesive, systematic way. And your processes are standardized and consistent, which allows people to execute effectively and opens the door to acceleration—

the phase in which your outcomes start getting better and better.

When EBL is used systematically, the alignment creates an environment that drives consistently excellent care to the patient—no matter where he is in the practice and no matter which staff members he is interacting with.

How Consistent Is Your Care?

Consistency is often where practices have the greatest opportunity for improvement. Some people may do certain things right all the time and some people may get it right some of the time but not all of the time. But "sometimes" is not good enough.

An inconsistent culture hurts you in many ways. It hinders your relationship with colleagues and referral sources, for instance. At Studer Group®, we hear about it all the time—providers saying, "I want my patients to be seen by this specialist, not that one," or, "Don't send my patients to that provider." Inconsistency also hurts your relationship with other staff members. For example, great nurses don't want to work with not-so-great nurses or providers who don't seem to care.

Organizational cultures in which this kind of inconsistency is allowed to exist can't provide the kind of care that leads to favorable CG CAHPS responses.

Here's the bottom line: If we expect staff to get to *always*, we need to expect *everyone* to get to *always*. Providers can provide excellent care, but one negative interaction with someone else can cause a patient to have an overall negative experience with us and to not rank our practice well; similarly, if the staff provides excellent service but the patient's experience with the provider isn't a positive one, the patient is unlikely to rate the practice highly.

We have found that when organizations we coach do well across the board, it's not only because they've adopted the right tactics. It's also because they've moved from an *optional* culture to an *always* culture.

Lasting Culture Change Begins with the "Why"

In working with hundreds of healthcare organizations, Studer Group has developed and refined the Healthcare Flywheel®. The Healthcare Flywheel is pictured on the cover of the books *Hardwiring Excellence* and *A Culture of High Performance* and remains central to our work.

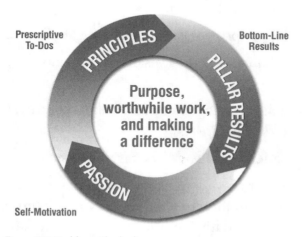

Figure 15.2 Healthcare Flywheel®

The center of the flywheel is the hub upon which everything revolves. It represents the values and ethics that tie into doing work that has purpose, is worthwhile, and makes a difference. It's easy to see how healthcare meets those criteria: When we ask healthcare professionals, "Why did you get into healthcare in the first place?" the typical answer is "to make a difference" or "to help people." (Although we can forget it from time to time when work gets hectic, these really are the reasons most of us are drawn to this calling.)

In other words, we don't get up in the morning and say to ourselves, *I get to go to work today and improve our CG CAHPS results!* Rather, we think, *I get to go to work and help people! Today, I want to make a difference.* So it doesn't make sense to tell our team that their job is to improve the patient experience (as reflected in CG CAHPS results) without first telling them *why* this is important.

So why should practices work on improving CG CAHPS? Well, because it helps us:

- Measure and improve *how patient-centered we are*
- Understand quality in the eyes of our patients *so we can improve*
- Improve patient engagement and adherence, *which improves our clinical outcomes*
- Improve patient loyalty, *which leads to increased volume*

Starting with *why* may seem like a no-brainer, but the truth is that it's easy to forget. After all, how many times do we announce an initiative to improve our finances or attract more patients without telling our teams *why* this is important? Not the lower *why* (to make more money), but the higher *why* (so that we can stay in business and make a difference in the lives of more patients). Probably more often than we care to admit. We need to make it a point not to forget when it's time to hardwire CG CAHPS tactics.

A big part of communicating the *why* is helping people reconnect with the good feelings that come from caring for and making a difference in patients' lives. This does not always happen naturally and it's easy to understand why. Our professional work is focused on diagnosing and fixing things that have gone wrong for our patients, and sometimes we carry this over to our practices—we hear about things that have gone wrong that we need to fix far more often than what is going right.

Unfortunately, accentuating the negative drains our emotional bank accounts to focus on our shortcomings and can leave us feeling burned out and exhausted. We can lose touch with the passion that engaged us in the first place and the difference we really do make. We become victims of "compassion fatigue," and both we and our patients suffer because of that.

One remedy is storytelling. Most of us have stories about why we got into healthcare in the first place. We need to take time to rekindle these stories and add to them. By sharing our stories, we can constantly reconnect providers and staff to the fact that what they do has purpose, is worthwhile, and makes a difference.

"I Can Still Remember..." (A Doctor's Story of Passion and Purpose)

"Without passion, man is a mere latent force and possibility, like the flint which awaits the shock of the iron before it can give forth its spark."

—*Henri Frederic Amiel*

I can still remember the white and green municipal hospital walls in my isolation room at Johannesburg Children's Hospital in South Africa. I was not quite six years old and I was confined there, with my younger sister, after we had contracted poliomyelitis in the early part of 1954.

Annual polio epidemics throughout the world were increasingly devastating, with many victims, mostly children, dying or being left with mild to disabling paralysis. The vaccine that was being developed and tested by Dr. Jonas Salk in his Pittsburgh laboratory was not yet on the market.

Notwithstanding the barriers imposed by being isolated from all things familiar for three weeks and the daily prodding, poking, and repeated lumbar punctures and blood tests, I always recall the warmth and caring of the staff who cared for my sister, my family, and me. This was not "a job" for them; it was "a calling"—they went about their work with a sense of love and compassion, doing whatever they could to make this rather frightening experience a little less ominous for all.

Even at that age, I was aware of the impact that they were having on their little patients, of which I was only one. I was struck by their ability to make a kid who was crying in pain, or upset and missing Mom and Dad, feel better.

To me, it was almost a magical power. As I grew older, I realized that it was more than that—it was magical, indeed, but it was the power of "caring" and the power of "empathy." And I began to realize that it was not just a gift that was foisted upon certain people but an opportunity and a privilege that each of us has within us, to share in our own way. It is therefore a choice—and we can embrace it or let the spark fizzle.

Well before I contracted polio, I had been fascinated by our family physician, who came to our home not only with his doctor's bag that contained all sorts of potions that could heal us, but also with a heart and a sense of humor that calmed our fears. I thought that this was something that I would like to do when I was a "grown-up," but, in the meantime, I would play at feeding mud-and-water concoctions to my sister's dolls to make them feel better. After my hospitalization with polio, I "knew" that this was something that I wanted to do, and my determination never wavered.

Through years of internship, residency training, and working in "clinics" amongst the poor in South Africa, followed by additional residencies and training in Israel and in Canada, that feeling and those memories stayed with me. It was not always fun or immediately rewarding—sometimes, when I was physically exhausted from working more than 36 straight hours or emotionally drained after sitting up all night with a dying patient, I might start to question what I had gotten myself into and why. However, even on the rare occasion that this occurred, it was always short-lived—I was soon reminded by a grateful patient, a grieving family, or a mother who had just experienced the miracle of a new life that what I did had purpose, was worthwhile, and "made a difference."

And today, as a physician, an acupuncturist, and a Studer Group coach, that positive energy still fuels my flywheel.

—*Jeff Morris, MD, MBA, FACS*

To learn more about the Healthcare Flywheel, we recommend reading *A Culture of High Performance* by Quint Studer.

Of course, none of this is easy. Building an *always* culture requires hard work from everyone, and results (whether they're in the form of higher CG CAHPS performance or other quality metrics) won't come overnight. The good news is that as you're striving to transform your culture, there are certain things you can do to "jump-start" your CG CAHPS improvement. We call these Momentum Makers.

Momentum Makers: Tactics That Make a Big Difference

In this book, we've given you plenty of tactics that you can start implementing right away to improve your CG CAHPS results in specific composites. And as we've discussed, they all work together with your culture to impact the question this chapter focuses on.

But perhaps you're looking for one or two changes you can make right now to accelerate your culture change and immediately impact the likelihood of patients giving you overall ratings of 9 or 10. Some quick changes with positive results can energize your staff and providers and give them the momentum they need to implement the other tactics and make wide-ranging improvements throughout the practice.

Tactic 1: Focus on Provider Communication

Remember, the Provider Communication composite is most highly correlated with your overall rating. Specifically, the questions dealing with respect and listening have the highest correlations. That's why it often makes sense to focus on these first. For immediate impact, focus on the following two tactics:

- **Teach Back Method:** The Teach Back Method of explaining diagnosis and treatment information allows providers to not only reiterate and express to patients the importance of their care plan, but also to engage patients in their own care. (See Chapters 6 and 8 for more information on the Teach Back Method.)

- **Key Words at Key Times (particularly when they demonstrate empathy):** Key Words at Key Times, such as "I understand that you're concerned about..." and "I'm going to do everything I can to help you with your pain..." help show patients that you care about their well-being and want to provide the best possible care. (See Chapters 2, 7, 9, and 11 to learn more about Key Words at Key Times.)

As you begin to coach and set goals, focus on those providers who offer the greatest opportunity for impact. For instance, start with providers who see the highest number of patients on their panel.

Next, focus on those providers who are performing at the mid-ranking (overall rank of 6, 7, or 8). Why? It is easier to move a current 8 to a 9-10 level than a 5 to the same level. By focusing on the mid-ranking performers, you can more quickly improve your performance and gain quick wins. Those quick wins in turn will help get your flywheel spinning to work with those providers with larger improvement gaps.

Tactic 2: Leader Rounding On Patients

The purpose of rounding on patients is to demonstrate to the patients and families the organization's commitment to provide quality care and to validate that this level of care is occurring with every patient, every time. Typically the rounding sessions are done by a manager, and frequency varies from practice to practice.

Rounding can take place in a variety of settings within a practice; a leader might choose to round on a patient in the reception area or after her appointment in an exam room. Providers often find it convenient to round on a patient at the conclusion of the clinical portion of an appointment.

By interacting with patients and families, leaders are able to manage their expectations, learn about the effectiveness of their staff and providers, and identify members of the care team for reward and recognition. When done consistently, leaders can manage patient expectations and experiences in real time as opposed to finding out later through complaint letters, poor patient outcomes, or poor patient experience (and thus poor CG CAHPS results).

Another key purpose of rounding on patients is to verify that employees/members of the care team have hardwired specific tools and tactics critical to providing excellent care. For example, if your practice is working to hardwire the tactic of Rounding in the Reception Area^{SM} (see Chapter 13), then the leader who rounds on the patient would ask a targeted question about whether or not they had been given a "wait time update" before being called back to the exam room.

Following are some key words to use when rounding on a patient.

Key Words, Clinic Manager/Leader Rounding: (Please note that the following questions do not have to be asked in totality, but the rounding questions should be tailored to fit specific organizational outcomes and asked to verify hardwiring of specific tactics.)

- *"Here at <organization name>, we want to provide you with exceptional quality care."*

- *"May I ask you a few questions to make sure that we are providing you with care consistent to our mission?"*

- *"When you called to make your appointment for today, were you able to schedule an appointment when you wanted to or needed to?"*

- *"Did you experience a wait today?"* If yes, *"Thank you for your patience; we know your time is valuable. Did our staff keep you informed during your wait?"* If no, *"Excellent. It is always our goal to run on time and be respectful of yours."*

- *"Did someone check in on you while you waited in the exam room to be seen?"*

- *"I see that you are a patient of <provider's name>."* (Manage up—*"S/he is excellent!"*) *"Did <provider's name> answer the questions that you had today during your appointment?"* or... *"Can you tell me about any medication changes that were made today?"*

- *"Were any tests ordered for you today?"* If yes, *"Can you tell me when you will receive the results of these tests?"*

- *"Tell me about a member of our care team I can be sure to thank for you. Please tell me what they did that you exceptionally liked."*

End the round by telling the patient that you wish to ensure that she and her family are very satisfied (without exception) with her care, and if at any time she does not feel she is very satisfied to please let you know. Provide your business card with your contact info.

After completing a round with a patient, it is important to ask yourself the following questions and perform the associated actions (such as coaching a staff member, service recovery, or reward and recognition):

- What did I (we) learn about the care of the patient based on the rounding?

- What must I (we) do with this information?

Tactic 3: Integrated Office-Based Skills Labs

Studer Group coaches recommend that organizations we work with conduct an Integrated Office-Based Skills Lab, which involves all members of the office— including front desk, clinical support staff, and clinical providers. The program uses "mock patients" and preorganized scenarios to practice skills, and the whole group participates together. Just a few hours can make a big difference in hardwiring the behaviors you wish to see in your practice.

First, appoint a planning team to spearhead the skills lab. Then, ask everyone in the practice to submit mock scenarios. Ask them to focus on the types of problems you frequently see: patients arriving 10 minutes late, patients arriving without co-pay, missing information from referring physicians, etc. The planning team will select the best ones or integrate similar ones.

Communicate with invited participants ahead of time and explain the purpose of the skills lab. Emphasize that this exercise (which will take about an hour and a half) is not about diagnostic or therapeutic skills but is about sharing positive behaviors and best practices that already exist and identifying opportunities for improvement, as well as learning from each other in a safe, fun, and collegial environment.

Designate "mock patients." If possible, get administration/office personnel/clinical providers to be the patients. Register the mock patients in the system.

Also, designate reception/front desk staff to handle the mock patients on arrival, as would be typical in your office. Assign medical assistants or other support staff to room the mock patients and prep them (take vitals, etc.) before seen by the clinical provider. Also, designate clinical providers to attend to the mock patients.

Have other staff members or providers serve as "visitors" (one to accompany each mock patient) to serve as "visible" observers. If others are available, have them be "invisible observers" (one to accompany each patient) to provide a slightly more objective perspective.

Finally, ensure that mock patients and observers (visible and invisible) are briefed about the patient's "medical problem" and are somewhat familiar with investigation and treatment options.

Now, it's time for the skills lab to begin. Let's say that the goal here is to learn how to use AIDET® and Key Words at Key Times properly in a variety of situations—and to practice until the tactics feel "natural." The first order of business is to review the *why*. Explain that AIDET and Key Words at Key Times help us communicate clearly, effectively, and in positive ways—all of which reassure the patient, reduce anxiety, help her better understand her care, and ultimately improve the patient experience.

Conduct brief, concurrent role-plays centering on patient reception/front desk interaction; rooming and preparation of the patient; clinical provider interaction/ encounter; and closure of encounter/discharge. The idea is to create typical situations that are as close as possible to real life so that providers and staff can a) see what it's like to walk in the patient's shoes, b) coach and support one another in mastering these powerful tactics, and c) convey a real sense of how important these behaviors truly are to your organization.

One of the designated observers (visible or invisible) facilitates the lab, keeping it on track, refocusing participants if wording becomes too clinical, or some other issue arises. He documents his assessments of each interaction on evaluation forms, especially related to communication, body language, logistics/flow etc. For example, he might notice that a provider had her arms crossed and/ or interrupted the patient.

Afterward, conduct a group debrief with collegial feedback describing strengths and best practices, while identifying opportunities for improvement. At a later time, hold an organizers-only debrief on what went well and what could be done better next time, provide written feedback summaries to participants, and conduct validation as needed (repeat lab, rounding, shadowing, etc.).

Despite the natural anxieties that might develop ahead of this exercise, it is usually a very positive and productive experience that helps to move the office culture and the office-based patient experience to the next level. Studer Group coaches can help your practice plan a skills lab that will put you on track to an *always* culture.

A Skills Lab Success Story

A major medical clinic in the Midwest conducted 54 integrated skills labs to date over 18 months at 46 of the system's 100+ individual sites. As a result, they've enjoyed a jump of 50 percent or greater in five of the six CG CAHPS domains. Integrated skills labs move performance improvement quickly.

"For the most part, participants are curious or a bit nervous at the outset, but 99 percent will express how much they learned by the end of the skills lab," notes Dr. B, a practicing physician and medical director of service excellence at this clinic. "The team concept is key in an ambulatory setting because of the false walls that exist between front office staff, nurses, and providers. Skills labs allow everyone to see the environment and individual encounters from the patient's perspective. Also, they remove the excuse that the scores are poor due to the performance of a particular individual, certain patients, or the vendor survey. The team understands our score depends on everyone working together."

At this particular clinic, the skills labs typically include up to 20 individuals (including four to six providers) and last approximately 90 minutes. Individuals at all skill levels—from physicians and advance practice clinician providers to radiology technicians and front office receptionists—are expected to attend.

Organizers set up a scenario where a mock patient is entered into the electronic health record teaching model. Two observers follow the mock patient through all touch points during the visit, noting written observations on an evaluation form and then sharing both opportunities for improvement and recognition for what went well during a facilitated group debrief.

Then, the organizers summarize data and share with the clinic manager, who follows up with information on tools or articles that can address OFIs. Feedback to improve future skills labs is encouraged.

"Providers can be humble, so we frequently need to connect the dots for them between the importance of narrating their patient care and managing up their expertise with reducing patient anxiety and ensuring better clinical outcomes," adds Dr. B.

Tactic 4: Mystery Shop Your Own Practice

Another valuable validation tactic is to have mystery shoppers (i.e., patients) utilize the services of your practice from start to finish. (This can be done by contracting with a professional mystery shopping service or by having people from other areas of an organization pose as patients.)

Develop a simple form on which to capture feedback on a variety of key indicators. These will center on key tactics your organization is choosing to implement or hardwire/validate at the time.

An easy way to start mystery shopping is to call your offices and request a new patient appointment. For example, the executive director of operations and community health for one organization Studer Group coaches has made it a regular practice to call one or two of her clinics during each of her monthly staff meetings. These calls are done via speaker phone so the entire leadership team can listen in, using a number with a blocked caller ID so the responder does not know who is calling.

By gathering real-world data points on how calls are answered, how long they are placed on hold, the number of transfers, and how many days it takes to get a new patient appointment, leaders are continuously validating and improving their practices.

Another organization coached by Studer Group leverages volunteers, students, and interns as mystery shoppers. They meet with the mystery shoppers ahead of time to review their checklists and prep them on the clinical purpose for their visit. The mystery shoppers are then set up with appointments in the system and proceed to receive care consistent with other patients. (It's important to note that provider leaders carefully pre-select the clinical issues to ensure that the mystery shoppers will not be subjected to undue harm.)

Following each visit, the mystery shopper then completes the checklist, which allows the organization to consistently evaluate each practice on the same objective criteria.

Studer Group's founder, Quint Studer, often offers an alternate definition of the word "culture." He says it's "what people do when no one is watching." Employing mystery shoppers will help you solicit voice of the customer when no one from leadership is directly "watching."

The Time Is Now

Focusing on patient experience is important now more than ever. For a reminder of all the reasons why, please revisit Chapter 1. Here are just a few of the highlights:

- CMS is driving forward under healthcare reform to measure, publicly report, and ultimately link payments to CG CAHPS.

- In many markets, Medicare Advantage, Medicaid, and private payers are already mandating, reporting, and rewarding (or penalizing) on CG CAHPS results.

- CG CAHPS has also been adopted as the standard for achieving and sustaining NCQA and/or URAC certification as a PCMH.

- The American Board of Medical Specialties (ABMS) has embraced CG CAHPS questions as part of the ABMS Maintenance of Certification® (MOC) process.[1]

And because a clinic's or practice's financial health is inextricably linked to its ability to provide excellent care, constant upward trajectory in CG CAHPS and other quality metrics doesn't just benefit you—it benefits your patients and your entire community. When you use the tools and tactics provided in this chapter (and throughout the entire book), you can make that difference.

Ultimately, healthcare organizations exist to serve humanity. The people drawn to this field are driven by a fierce desire to help others. By creating the kinds of organizations that patients sincerely rate "the best"—the kind that they trust enough to recommend to the people they love—we are helping the men and women who work for us serve their highest sense of purpose. That is a true gift to all the healthcare professionals we work with, to the patients we serve, and to ourselves.

It's times like these that illustrate what drives healthcare professionals. Technology may be enhanced, and payment systems may change—but what never changes is the dedication of these men and women to provide the very best care.

Tools & Resources

Studer Group® offers a variety of tools and resources that support the tactics discussed in this chapter. To access the most up-to-date offerings, please visit www.studergroup.com/CGCAHPS.

CHAPTER SIXTEEN:

SETTING GOALS TO ACHIEVE AN "ALWAYS" CULTURE

"Accountability breeds response-ability."
—*Stephen R. Covey*

V irtually everyone in healthcare wants the best for patients. We have said this over and over throughout the book. In the previous chapter, we talked about how to create the kind of foundation that gets everyone aligned and working toward the overarching goal of creating a great patient experience.

However, when it's time to zero-in on what each individual leader, provider, and staff member should do to translate this vision into action, even having the right culture in place and the right behaviors hardwired is not enough. To achieve consistent high performance throughout the organization, we need hard numbers.

We need goals. And we need a way to make sure people are meeting them.

Over and over, and proven in a research study conducted by Studer Group® through the Alliance for Health Care Research,[1] when leaders are asked, "What is the key to sustaining high results?" the answer is *alignment via an objective evaluation tool.*

Ultimately, when individuals are held accountable for metrics (rather than being given a subjective rating like "meets expectations"), they adopt the behaviors necessary to achieve those outcomes. Let's take a look at why it's crucial to implement this type of evaluation and also why it's important to review the right metrics in order to achieve CG CAHPS results *and* sustain them.

Why Objectivity Is Important

Simply put, opinions about an individual's performance can vary from leader to leader. When an evaluation asks for an opinion, you can often end up with performers at all levels receiving similar ratings. High performers may not be appropriately rewarded, and low performers cannot be managed.

Additionally, non-objective evaluations make it difficult—if not impossible—to align individual leaders' goals with the goals of the practice. For example, all providers likely have every intention of providing the highest level of quality care and patient experience. But good intentions can't be measured. Agreeing on exactly what "the highest level of quality care and patient experience" means for each provider and for the practice allows all to have the same expectations.

Providers Welcome Objectivity

The majority of organizations we work with have had some sort of evaluation tool in place to monitor and track performance. Our experience is that almost 99 percent of providers receive an evaluation that *meets expectations, exceeds expectations,* or *substantially exceeds expectations.* The problem is that these evaluation tools may not be truly objective, so even if the individual is receiving a "meets expectations" rating, his actual performance by the numbers may not truly justify the rating.

Why is objectivity so important? Because great providers know they have been performing at high levels and that, too often, their evaluation rating is about the same as a colleague who may not be achieving comparable results. With an objective, weighted evaluation tool, they will be appropriately recognized for their accomplishments. Meanwhile, lower performers will be identified and can be provided the necessary training to improve.

When we work with practices to put in an objective evaluation system, we often find that high-performing providers—those who have better access and better patient experience results—celebrate the change. Even if they were already receiving the "meets expectations" rating, they like having a fairer system. They appreciate that it allows concrete agreement on what's important and what success looks like. It validates the work they are doing and offers guidance on how to get even better. They like the feedback and the ability to have discussion and tracking throughout the year.

As with any change, there may be a level of uncertainty when you introduce a new system. It takes a courageous and value-oriented practice to install an objective evaluation tool. Why? Because it shines a blinding spotlight on how well the practice is meeting its goals (or not) and living up to its mission (or not). *There is no way to sustain a culture of high performance without having an objective, weighted evaluation system in place.*

How to Develop Objective Goals

A good place to start is with the SMART acronym: Specific, Measurable, Attainable, Relevant, and Time-Oriented.[2] Each goal should have all of the elements of SMART. As each goal is created, check it against each letter. Is the goal specific enough? Is it measureable? Is it attainable? (And so forth.)

S	Specific: Be precise and unambiguous	Improve CG CAHPS results for question "How often did this provider listen carefully to you?" to Top Box (9 or 10) of 90% of respondents
M	Measurable: Use concrete numbers	Increase percent of patients seen by the provider within 15 minutes of their appointment time from 60% to 90% by the end of the year
A	Attainable: Stretch, but be realistic	Improve CG CAHPS results for Test Results composite from 7 to 9 by the end of the 4th quarter
R	Relevant: Address the realities of the current environment	Increase patient volume by 2% by June 1
T	Time-Oriented: Provide a timeframe	Staff a practice flow coordinator by May 30 and have them fully trained by September 30

Figure 16.1 Objective Goals with SMART

Goals also need to be weighted.[3] This is true for big, overarching, system-wide goals; for practice goals; and also for individual leader goals.

Weighting solves a problem that many organizations struggle with: too many priorities. We find that when a leader has, say, eight unweighted goals, she will achieve six of them well and the other two not at all. Weighting remedies this because it lets the leader know how best to spend her time—because she'll know which metrics will most powerfully drive her overall evaluation score (and most likely her compensation).

If one of eight goals is weighted at 30 percent out of 100 percent, and the other seven are weighted at 10 percent each, the leader knows exactly where to direct most of her focus. Here's a rule of thumb: 10 percent = awareness, 20 percent = focus, and 30 percent or more = urgency. Not every leader's evaluation will look the same—nor should it.

As you are building your goals, think carefully about what you select to measure. We at Studer Group find that many of the organizations we work with measure Relative Value Units (RVUs) and wonder why they aren't improving patient experience. By placing the RVUs on the evaluation and linking their providers' variable compensation to them, these organizations are saying, "This is what's important to us." And yet the trend in reimbursement is shifting from "volume" (which RVUs measure) to "value" (which CMS and, increasingly, insurance providers pay for).

RVUs don't have to go away, but patient experience metrics can and should be included as goals alongside them. This allows organizations to recognize where they are now and begin to shift to where they are going in the future. What is measured gets results (as long as the list isn't 200 measures long, that is). And yet, we don't see very many practices taking patient experience metrics into account as they set goals for providers.

Practice managers tend to be more diversified in their goals, yet their evaluations are still RVU-heavy. While the presence of RVUs is likely a good thing, many organizations should begin grading practice managers more heavily on patient experience items like access to care, office staff behavior, and test results communication. These are areas they can impact, and, of course, they also can have goals around cost management.

In other words, as organizations set goals with providers and practice managers, it seems they're focusing on where the puck has been in the past rather than where the puck is going in the future. Even though value-based purchasing, population health, and bundled payments are dramatically changing the reimbursement landscape today, we don't see practice leaders getting in front of these measures, even in a minor way.

These medical practices are increasingly taking on ACO, PCMH, and bundled payment arrangements that require certain metric achievement (including patient experience). Yet, very few of the metrics associated with them are built into organizational goals or cascaded to the leaders who actually effect change and are linked to those payment models.

In terms of CG CAHPS specifically, we see three issues that are increasingly important and that should create a sense of urgency. First, we see insurance plans creating narrow provider networks. These narrow networks often consist of just a couple provider groups per geographic area. The provider groups selected are those that demonstrate high quality, low cost, and excellent patient experience performance (CG CAHPS). In other words, your CG CAHPS results may determine whether you get to be an in-network provider or not.

Second, we're seeing insurance plans start to link compensation to CG CAHPS results. For example, Medicare Advantage payers are sharing some of the rewards that they receive from high scores in the CMS Five-Star Quality Rating System with providers—a rating system based in part on patient experience surveys that include CG CAHPS questions. And in some states, we are seeing private payers, like Blue Cross Blue Shield of Massachusetts, link CG CAHPS scores to value-based payment models. This is very different from the HCAHPS launch where CMS drove urgency. With CG CAHPS, private payers are leading the movement.

Third, many payers are pushing or even requiring practices to become Patient-Centered Medical Homes (PCMHs). And part of becoming a certified PCMH is measuring your patients' experience using CG CAHPS questions.[4] In fact, in over 22 states there are now public and private ACOs that require a practice to become a certified PCMH to participate.

To many providers, all this change feels overwhelming. We at Studer Group are finding success helping the organizations we coach make the appropriate shifts gradually. We help them move to a basket of metrics—typically eight to ten organizational goals for the medical practice and six to eight per leader—and then weight them so that people know even within those goals which are the most important. (As we'll discuss later, there should be no more than ten goals for the organization or for any leader, e.g., 10 percent minimum weight per goal.)

Here's how it works: If you are still a "fee for service" practice, maybe RVUs remain at a 50-60 percent weight next year on providers' evaluations. That is fine, but as time goes by, you need to start blending in other metrics.

In year one, you might blend in the overall CG CAHPS rating, or maybe you use the Provider Communication composite rating. For example, the CG CAHPS rating might be 10 percent with the additional 30 to 40 percent focused in other areas the provider can impact. For the office manager, you might use the Office Staff CG CAHPS composite. The same process can also be applied to improving PQRS quality metrics and meaningful use (EMR) adoption.

CG CAHPS data and national benchmarks will quickly build over the next several years. The current and future data collected by CMS can be accessed at http://www.medicare.gov/physiciancompare/. In the meantime, we advise you to work on improving your organization's numbers as compared to previous time periods. Also, beware of using data points provided by survey vendors, as those can shift dramatically each period depending on their client base. The Agency for Healthcare Research and Quality website (https://cahpsdatabase. ahrq.gov) is another great source of publicly available comparative data today.

How Often to Gather Data

Clinical practices and other healthcare organizations should develop a system to obtain **CG CAHPS** data throughout the year. For example, you might survey 1/12 of your patients every month or 1/4 of them each quarter. By gathering the data over time, you end up with a much stronger feedback system. Some survey vendors recommend site visit data, but Studer Group recommends that organizations use longitudinal surveys because that's where all the payers are going.

How to Set and Cascade Objective Goals in Both System and Individual Practice Settings

Effective goal cascading starts with overarching organizational goals, not individual leader or provider goals. The organization's leadership must ensure that the goals are set at the top level and then cascade them down in a relevant and meaningful way to the leaders and providers in their individual areas. First, the organizational goals are set; they should then become the CEO's goals. The vice president's goals are set. The director's goals are set. Finally, the managers', supervisors', and providers' goals are set.

First, senior leaders need to determine what "right" looks like for their organization. How is it measured as an organization? That is step one: reaching agreement on your overall organizational goals.

Senior leaders create these goals, but they need to reflect both the administrative and clinical sides. If your medical group already includes key members of the medical and leadership team, great: You are ready to get started. If not, it's time to remedy this. You can't set organizational goals until you have both sides at the table. It is easier to get buy-in and create an aligned team when those accountable have input. Imagine setting quality goals for a physician team without a representative leader sharing insight. The provider response to these new quality goals might be less than enthusiastic.

Now that the right people are in the room, the focus is on having the right objective, measurable, achievable goals. These goals typically fall under Growth, Finance, Quality, Service, and People categories. They will be shared again and again so that the organization can assess progress as time goes by. It is these organizational goals that are cascaded to the appropriate leaders of the organization.

Certainly, some goals will be based on the financial health of the practice (i.e., budget, productivity, agency reduction). Other goals may be mandatory, based on system or board requirements. For example, a large system may have certain quality metrics they expect every practice to achieve in order to maintain a consistent patient experience among the entire system. Does this mean every physician manager should carry the same quality goal? No, because there are variations in control and influence of particular measures.

So How Do We Account for CG CAHPS?

Figure 16.2 shows how a sample CG CAHPS goal could cascade through the organization. The CEO's goal represents the organization's goal around CG CAHPS—to achieve, say, 70 percent in three out of five composites. Note that the senior physician leader at the system level also shares this organizational goal.

As we cascade to one of the medical practices, see that the medical practice physician leader has individual goals around the Provider Communication composite and Overall Provider rating. These goals impact the organization goals of the system. The medical practice manager has goals around the Access, Courteous and Helpful Office Staff, and Test Results composites. And so on.

Example of how CG CAHPS goals cascade through the organization:

Title	Scope	Access	Provider Comm.	Courtesy & Helpfulness of Office Staff	Test Results	Provider Rating
CEO	System	Composite Bundle (Achieve X%tile in 3/5 Composites)				
Senior Physician Leader	System	Composite Bundle (Achieve X%tile in 3/5 Composites)				
Medical Practice Physician Leader	Practice	Composite Bundle (Achieve X%tile in 3/5 Composites)				
			X			
Medical Practice Manager	Practice	Composite Bundle (Achieve X%tile in 3/5 Composites)				
		X		X	X	
Provider (PFS)	Practice		X			X
Laboratory	System				X	
Imaging	System				X	

Figure 16.2 Cascade of CG CAHPS Goals

The organizational goals are the key drivers, and from them, subset goals are cascaded down (as in the previous example). We find that while a practice may have eight to ten key metrics, individual leaders and providers should carry between six and eight metrics on their evaluations. This allows for prioritization and focus on the most important areas via weighting, which we will shortly address as one of the single best methods for driving outcomes.

As you look to add CG CAHPS to your organizational goals, consider Figure 16.3. Its numbers are drawn from Studer Group's Leader Evaluation Manager® goal library, which contains the data of 80,000-plus leaders. You'll see some sample CG CAHPS goals that medical practices have built into their organizational goals. These are a combination of all composites.

To achieve Top Box for all five CG CAHPS survey domains at the top national quartile as of the peer group year-end of FY12. 5 = 5 out of 5 4 = 4 out of 5 3 = 3 out of 5 2 = 2 out of 5 1 = 1 or less out of 5	Higher is better 5 is 5 and above 4 is 4 to 4 3 is 3 to 3 2 is 2 to 2 1 is 1 and below
Achieve CG CAHPS weighted average target raw score = 79.4 for 7 domains. Target for each domain is established at the 60th percentile and domains are weighted at 40% for Access to Care and 10% each for all other domains. Measured monthly by FYTD raw score as reported on the Performance Scorecard.	Higher is better 5 is 82.9 and above 4 is 81.7 to 82.8 3 is 79.4 to 81.6 2 is 78.3 to 79.3 1 is 78.2 and below

Source: Studer Group Leader Evaluation Manager® goal library
Figure 16.3 Sample CG CAHPS Goals

In Figure 16.4 you can view examples of various medical practice organization goals that incorporate goals from other focuses such as Growth, Finance, People, and Quality.

PFS Stewardship Metric

STEWARDS HP	Productivity (patient visits per month)	Percentage	100% FTE F.P. = 330/mth 100% FTE I.M. = 280/mth FTE Ped = 350/mth Track WRVUs in parallel for JPS PG	3 is baseline 4 is +5% 5 is +10%	Average	20%

PFS People Metric

PEOPLE	Provider Engagement Alignment	Percentage	Employee Engagement Survey Results	3 is 80% 4 is 90% 5 is 100%	Average	10%

PFS Population Health Metric

POPULATION HEALTH	MyChart Utilization	Percentage	Varies by provider	5 is ≥15% 4 is 11.15% 3 is 10% 2 is 6-9% 1 is ≤5%	Average	Non-Weighted 0%
POPULATION HEALTH	Ambulatory Sensitive Care Admissions	Percentage	Benchmark against starting data from impanelled patients	1 is ≥15% 2 is 11.15% 3 is 10% 4 is 6-9% 5 is ≤5%	Average	0%

Studer Group Provider Feedback System[SM]; goals compiled from metric library to represent a complete medical practice example.

Figure 16.4 Example Goals

Earlier we talked about the first step of creating organizational goals. Now, we look to create individual goals. They should connect back to the organizational goals where appropriate so that everyone knows that his or her individual role in achieving success also benefits the entire organization. He or she needs to clearly understand that it's a "win-win."

What we find works the best in the medical setting is to cascade goals through the dyad that includes physician and administrative leaders. It's important to let them take the organizational goals one at a time and think how the two groups pull together to achieve them. Ultimately, each individual leader will take what the dyad develops to build out their own goals.

We cannot stress enough how important it is to set the right number of goals. Think about it this way: If you are a man who travels for business during the week, and you come home for the weekend and your wife asks you to do three things, there is a high probability that you'll be able to get them done—especially if she tells you why and when and what right looks like. However, if she asks you to do 100 things, you probably won't succeed—odds are she will be very upset at the end of the weekend that you have fallen short on many of the goals.

There is certainly some reconciliation involved. If the organization needs to produce 10,000 RVUs of work, then we need to make sure that when we add up all the clinics, we get to 10,000 RVUs. Every clinic in the system needs to be involved in the reconciliation process—i.e., looking at the goals they come up with and making sure all of the numbers work and add up to the organizational numbers.

As we set goals, we need to keep one eye on the big picture and the other on what makes sense for each individual provider. If our overall organizational goal is to improve diabetic care and population health, provider goals will look different depending on specialty.

Primary care physicians will have one goal, internal medicine physicians another, and diabetes specialists still another.

We will need to realize that the podiatrist has a role to play in helping achieve that goal, but only in doing foot exams, which is a small part of the big picture. So we wouldn't ask podiatrists to carry the overall diabetic compliance rate but we would ask them to carry their piece. Remember, in the CG CAHPS world, if we have a medical group of podiatrists, they are part of the group rating that we will all be held accountable for.

For providers, the ability to share goals and then measure across peer groups is key. Benchmarking against the national data is important, but focusing especially at the peer level is a critical first focus. We want to be able to ask: *Are we holding all of our internists to the same level? Are we holding all of our cardiologists to the same level?* And so forth.

If we don't measure across peer groups, we end up in a situation where there's no good way to assess the performance of individual providers. Let's say we have one cardiologist, three internists, and five primary care physicians in one location. The cardiologist might say, "Well, you can't compare me to a primary care doc." That's true, but in a system with multiple locations there might be 20 cardiologists. If you're measuring across peer groups, you can compare them to the others in the system.

Of course, setting the right goals (and the right number of them) is only the beginning. It is critical to have performance conversations with individual leaders throughout the year. This builds teamwork and creates a joint focus on achieving the goals that matter most. If we are not giving people the regular objective feedback they can act on, how can they ever improve?

PFS and LEM: Tools for Objective Evaluations

Studer Group has two web-based tools designed to help leaders build objective goals for individuals that are aligned with strategic organizational goals, assign weight to and prioritize those goals, develop a plan to achieve them, and evaluate individual performance. The Provider Feedback System[SM] (PFS) was designed to evaluate those who provide care to patients, and the Leadership Evaluation Manager® (LEM) was created to evaluate leaders, including physician leaders.

Both PFS and LEM are designed for use in context with Studer Group's EBL framework. By developing performance measures that are aligned with overall strategic goals and by ensuring accountability for those measures, an organization can improve productivity, enhance patient outcomes, and reduce inefficiencies.

The role of the leader is to help individuals understand why a goal matters and then to help them achieve it. Neither a leader nor a direct report should be surprised by evaluations at the end of the year; the leader should be continuously helping them achieve their goals in order to create the maximum potential outcome possible.

Figure 16.5 is a sample performance summary that shows trending for an individual provider and also has an option to show a peer-to-peer comparison. This is an example of the focus of the feedback conversation: assessing progress, celebrating wins, and creating plans for areas of improvement.

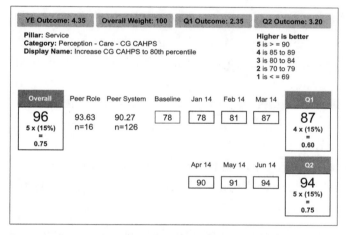

Source: Studer Group Provider Feedback System℠ 5.0
Figure 16.5 Sample Provider Feedback System℠ Performance Summary

We want to create goals that we have to look at throughout the year. A best practice is to look at monthly or quarterly data points and schedule meetings at these times to review. For example, access might be looked at monthly, while patient experience (CG CAHPS) might be looked at quarterly because we need a certain number to make it significant.

Some organizations we coach put parameters in place to keep focus on organizational outcomes. Many call these "circuit breakers" or "organizational cliffs," and they must be hit at the organizational level in order for incentive compensation to open. For example, unless the organizational goal for operating margin and CAHPS are both hit, incentive won't open for any leader in the organization. This helps drive individual accountability, because evaluations are still department result-based; however, it keeps everyone organizationally focused.

As Peter Senge, author of *The Fifth Discipline* and expert on creating learning organizations, writes, the goal needs to be high enough that people know they have to change, which generates the creative tension necessary to make some adjustments. If it's too low, people may think they don't really have to change or they can wait until the last minute to start; on the other hand, if it's too high, then leaders will think it's absolutely impossible to meet it.

We see success when objective measures are created with physicians as a team and are cascaded down so that there are no surprises at rollout. The physician's administrators and staff should know what goals they impact, even if they don't have a formal evaluation in the system. All should be aligned to what they need to accomplish and why. Then as the year unfolds, it's important to keep the progress of these organizational goals in front of all staff so that their behavior and focus can be adjusted for the best outcomes.

Finally, we'd like to reinforce an important point we've made elsewhere. This book goes into a lot of details on the *how* but we won't get anywhere if you don't start with the *why* and connect it back to the mission of the organization. Objective metrics like the ones we're discussing here are the qualifications of the *why*, which is always providing the highest possible quality care to patients. For that reason, we should welcome them—they're the dashboard dials that show us how well we're living up to our mission as an organization and as individual healthcare professionals.

While it does require a lot of upfront thinking and hard work to get everyone aligned and get the goals set and weights assigned, the results are worth the effort. People like clear goals and metrics. The truth is, vagueness and uncertainty create anxiety. Knowing *exactly* what we're going to be held accountable for usually comes as a huge relief—even if the goal we're asking them to achieve is a tough one.

We all want to take the best possible care of patients. This desire to help others is an integral part of our nature as healthcare professionals and is a linchpin of our calling. When we can help the men and women who work for us understand precisely how they can best improve the care they provide—precisely what they can do to contribute to a higher-performing organization—we do them a great service. We empower and energize them. And the patients we care for ultimately reap the benefits.

Tools & Resources

Studer Group® offers a variety of tools and resources that support the strategies and tactics discussed in this chapter. To access the most up-to-date offerings, please visit www.studergroup.com/CGCAHPS.

ACKNOWLEDGMENTS

W e have all heard the expression, "It takes a village." For this particular book, we feel this couldn't be truer. So many different people have helped inspire, shape, and contribute to this book. Without the experience and the insights of countless healthcare professionals, both inside and outside Studer Group®, *The CG CAHPS Handbook* would not be the authoritative and robust resource it is today. To all of them, we offer a collective and heartfelt thank-you.

Specifically, we would like to extend our gratitude to:

The leaders of organizations coached by Studer Group across the nation...

Thank you for your commitment to using Evidence-Based Leadership℠ to create a culture of *always*, so your patients consistently get the best care. By sharing your results and best practices with Studer Group, you've enabled us to build a national Learning Lab of hundreds and hundreds of hospitals and medical groups.

Thanks to this collaboration of some of the top industry minds, we can all learn from each other.

Thank you specifically to the partners below for providing assistance with the material in these pages.

- Alegent Creighton Health, Omaha, NE
- Community Physician Network, Indianapolis, IN
- John Peter Smith Health Network, Ft. Worth, TX
- OU Physicians, Oklahoma City, OK
- Reliant Medical Group, Worcester, MA
- The Ottawa Hospital, Ottawa, ON, Canada
- UAB Medicine, Birmingham, AL
- UW Medicine, Seattle, WA
- Kaiser Permanente, Oakland, CA
- Greenville Health System, Greenville, SC
- PinnacleHealth, Harrisburg, PA

The Studer Group experts who coach these organizations...

Your tireless work on the front lines is making a difference in medical practices everywhere. An extra helping of gratitude goes to those coaches who directly provided their insight and expertise during the writing of *The CG CAHPS Handbook* including:

- Kim Bass
- Nadine Blair
- Dave Brown

- Mike Coppola
- Rachael Johnson
- Jay Kaplan, MD
- Jen Miley
- Mike Nelson, MD
- Julie O'Shaughnessy
- Paul Panico, PhD
- Barbara Roehl, MD
- Richard Rubin, MD
- Dan Smith, MD
- Debbi Watters

...And the other individuals who made it all come together.

Quint Studer—For founding Studer Group and being our Fire Starter. Your vision, leadership, and dedication are the foundation that allows us to work with providers to impact 50 million-plus patients a year.

Dottie DeHart and team—Thanks for your dedication and determination to make this book the best CG CAHPS book out there. All the back and forth to help bring the content in this book to life is no easy task. Your depth of talent is astounding, and it's always a pleasure to partner with you in these adventures.

Bekki Kennedy—Thank you for the amazing job of taking years of extensive research and mounds of evidence and turning it into comprehensive actions that will impact thousands upon thousands of patients. Your drive for excellence brought structure to help the passion behind the writing in this book shine through every page.

Jamie Stewart—Thank you for never wavering in your commitment to completing this book. The management and bringing together of all of the different components, research, and people was an amazing juggling act. You juggled well.

Julie Chyna and Laura Koontz—Thank you for the many hours spent in piecing together the research and musings of the three authors to build the foundation of this book. Your work will help impact healthcare organizations across the nation.

Bill Bielenda, Rachael Johnson, and Penelope Elebash—Thank you for helping our partners implement the Provider Feedback System[SM] for over 10,000 providers. This serves as a rich resource of metrics and data benchmarks for setting and achieving objective provider goals.

Stephanie Striepeck and Lauren Westwood—Thanks for all your time distilling the evidence behind several of the tactics to create the many graphics and tools to help make this book a valuable and useful resource for providers.

Eileen Riggins—Thank you for being the glue that coordinates our physician services work across Studer Group. You are one of the unsung heroes of our success, and without your work "behind the curtain" we would not be the team we are today.

Guy Livingston, Carey King, and Carly Lee—Thanks for collecting and analyzing the data to identify leading practices and measure the impact of our work for our partners.

If we've left anyone out of this list, we offer our sincerest apologies. As we said before, "It takes a village." This book is evidence that human beings can come together and create something greater than the sum of its parts and make the lives of others better for it. Thank you for allowing us to join you in this journey of making a difference.

Appendix: Full Sample of Survey

The following excerpt from the Adult 12-Month Questionnaire 2.0 is taken directly from the Agency for Healthcare Research and Quality (AHRQ) website that hosts all the CG CAHPS surveys. To view or download the complete survey as well as other versions of CG CAHPS, please visit https://cahps.ahrq.gov/index.html.

Your Provider

1. Our records show that you got care from the provider named below in the last 12 months.

   Name of provider label goes here

   Is that right?

   ¹☐ Yes
   ²☐ No → **If No, go to #26 on page 4**

The questions in this survey will refer to the provider named in Question 1 as "this provider." Please think of that person as you answer the survey.

2. Is this the provider you usually see if you need a check-up, want advice about a health problem, or get sick or hurt?

   ¹☐ Yes
   ²☐ No

3. How long have you been going to this provider?

   ¹☐ Less than 6 months
   ²☐ At least 6 months but less than 1 year
   ³☐ At least 1 year but less than 3 years
   ⁴☐ At least 3 years but less than 5 years
   ⁵☐ 5 years or more

Your Care From This Provider in the Last 12 Months

These questions ask about **your own** health care. Do **not** include care you got when you stayed overnight in a hospital. Do **not** include the times you went for dental care visits.

4. In the last 12 months, how many times did you visit this provider to get care for yourself?

   ☐ None → **If None, go to #26 on page 4**
   ☐ 1 time
   ☐ 2
   ☐ 3
   ☐ 4
   ☐ 5 to 9
   ☐ 10 or more times

5. In the last 12 months, did you phone this provider's office to get an appointment for an illness, injury, or condition that **needed care right away**?

   ¹☐ Yes
   ²☐ No → **If No, go to #7**

6. In the last 12 months, when you phoned this provider's office to get an appointment for **care you needed right away**, how often did you get an appointment as soon as you needed?

   ¹☐ Never
   ²☐ Sometimes
   ³☐ Usually
   ⁴☐ Always

7. In the last 12 months, did you make any appointments for a **check-up or routine care** with this provider?

   ¹☐ Yes
   ²☐ No ➔ **If No, go to #9**

8. In the last 12 months, when you made an appointment for a **check-up or routine care** with this provider, how often did you get an appointment as soon as you needed?

   ¹☐ Never
   ²☐ Sometimes
   ³☐ Usually
   ⁴☐ Always

9. In the last 12 months, did you phone this provider's office with a medical question during regular office hours?

   ¹☐ Yes
   ²☐ No ➔ **If No, go to #11**

10. In the last 12 months, when you phoned this provider's office during regular office hours, how often did you get an answer to your medical question that same day?

    ¹☐ Never
    ²☐ Sometimes
    ³☐ Usually
    ⁴☐ Always

11. In the last 12 months, did you phone this provider's office with a medical question **after** regular office hours?

    ¹☐ Yes
    ²☐ No ➔ **If No, go to #13**

12. In the last 12 months, when you phoned this provider's office **after** regular office hours, how often did you get an answer to your medical question as soon as you needed?

    ¹☐ Never
    ²☐ Sometimes
    ³☐ Usually
    ⁴☐ Always

13. Wait time includes time spent in the waiting room and exam room. In the last 12 months, how often did you see this provider **within 15 minutes** of your appointment time?

    ¹☐ Never
    ²☐ Sometimes
    ³☐ Usually
    ⁴☐ Always

14. In the last 12 months, how often did this provider explain things in a way that was easy to understand?

    ¹☐ Never
    ²☐ Sometimes
    ³☐ Usually
    ⁴☐ Always

15. In the last 12 months, how often did this provider listen carefully to you?

    ¹☐ Never
    ²☐ Sometimes
    ³☐ Usually
    ⁴☐ Always

16. In the last 12 months, did you talk with this provider about any health questions or concerns?

- ¹☐ Yes
- ²☐ No → **If No, go to #18**

17. In the last 12 months, how often did this provider give you easy to understand information about these health questions or concerns?

- ¹☐ Never
- ²☐ Sometimes
- ³☐ Usually
- ⁴☐ Always

18. In the last 12 months, how often did this provider seem to know the important information about your medical history?

- ¹☐ Never
- ²☐ Sometimes
- ³☐ Usually
- ⁴☐ Always

19. In the last 12 months, how often did this provider show respect for what you had to say?

- ¹☐ Never
- ²☐ Sometimes
- ³☐ Usually
- ⁴☐ Always

20. In the last 12 months, how often did this provider spend enough time with you?

- ¹☐ Never
- ²☐ Sometimes
- ³☐ Usually
- ⁴☐ Always

21. In the last 12 months, did this provider order a blood test, x-ray, or other test for you?

- ¹☐ Yes
- ²☐ No → **If No, go to #23**

22. In the last 12 months, when this provider ordered a blood test, x-ray, or other test for you, how often did someone from this provider's office follow up to give you those results?

- ¹☐ Never
- ²☐ Sometimes
- ³☐ Usually
- ⁴☐ Always

23. Using any number from 0 to 10, where 0 is the worst provider possible and 10 is the best provider possible, what number would you use to rate this provider?

- ☐ 0 Worst provider possible
- ☐ 1
- ☐ 2
- ☐ 3
- ☐ 4
- ☐ 5
- ☐ 6
- ☐ 7
- ☐ 8
- ☐ 9
- ☐ 10 Best provider possible

Clerks and Receptionists at This Provider's Office

24. In the last 12 months, how often were clerks and receptionists at this provider's office as helpful as you thought they should be?

   $^1\square$ Never
   $^2\square$ Sometimes
   $^3\square$ Usually
   $^4\square$ Always

25. In the last 12 months, how often did clerks and receptionists at this provider's office treat you with courtesy and respect?

   $^1\square$ Never
   $^2\square$ Sometimes
   $^3\square$ Usually
   $^4\square$ Always

About You

26. In general, how would you rate your overall health?

   $^1\square$ Excellent
   $^2\square$ Very good
   $^3\square$ Good
   $^4\square$ Fair
   $^5\square$ Poor

27. In general, how would you rate your overall **mental or emotional** health?

   $^1\square$ Excellent
   $^2\square$ Very good
   $^3\square$ Good
   $^4\square$ Fair
   $^5\square$ Poor

28. What is your age?

   $^1\square$ 18 to 24
   $^2\square$ 25 to 34
   $^3\square$ 35 to 44
   $^4\square$ 45 to 54
   $^5\square$ 55 to 64
   $^6\square$ 65 to 74
   $^7\square$ 75 or older

29. Are you male or female?

   $^1\square$ Male
   $^2\square$ Female

30. What is the highest grade or level of school that you have completed?

  ¹☐ 8th grade or less
  ²☐ Some high school, but did not graduate
  ³☐ High school graduate or GED
  ⁴☐ Some college or 2-year degree
  ⁵☐ 4-year college graduate
  ⁶☐ More than 4-year college degree

31. Are you of Hispanic or Latino origin or descent?

  ¹☐ Yes, Hispanic or Latino
  ²☐ No, not Hispanic or Latino

32. What is your race? Mark one or more.

  ¹☐ White
  ²☐ Black or African American
  ³☐ Asian
  ⁴☐ Native Hawaiian or Other Pacific Islander
  ⁵☐ American Indian or Alaska Native
  ⁶☐ Other

33. Did someone help you complete this survey?

  ¹☐ Yes
  ²☐ No → **Thank you.**
         Please return the completed survey in the postage-paid envelope.

34. How did that person help you? Mark one or more.

  ¹☐ Read the questions to me
  ²☐ Wrote down the answers I gave
  ³☐ Answered the questions for me
  ⁴☐ Translated the questions into my language
  ⁵☐ Helped in some other way

  Please print: _____

  _____

  _____

Thank you.

Please return the completed survey in the postage-paid envelope.

GLOSSARY OF ACRONYMS

ABMS	American Board of Medical Specialties
ACO	Accountable Care Organization
AHRQ	Agency for Healthcare Research and Quality (part of HHS)
AIDET®	Acknowledge, Introduce, Duration, Explanation, Thank You
AMGA	American Medical Group Association
CAHPS	Consumer Assessment of Healthcare Providers and Systems
CARE℠	Connect, Apologize, Repair, Exceed
CG CAHPS	Clinician and Group Consumer Assessment of Healthcare Providers and Systems
CHIP	Children's Health Insurance Program
CMS	Centers for Medicare and Medicaid Services (part of HHS)

CPC	Comprehensive Primary Care initiative
EMR	Electronic Medical Record
EP	Eligible Providers (CMS term for physicians, nurse practitioners, physician assistants, etc.)
FFS	Fee for Service
FQHC	Federally Qualified Health Center
GPRO	Group Practice Reporting Option (component under the CMS PQRS program)
HHS	U.S. Department of Health and Human Services
IOM	U.S. Institute of Medicine
IPC	Individualized Patient Care
KWKT	Key Words at Key Times
MGMA	Medical Group Management Association
MAP	Measure Applications Partnership
MOC	Maintenance of Certification (for physician boards under the ABMS)
MPAPCP	Multi-Payer Advanced Primary Care Practice
MSSP	Medicare Shared Savings Program
NCQA	National Committee for Quality Assurance
NQF	National Quality Forum (a non-profit organization)
P4P	Pay for Performance

PCMH	Patient-Centered Medical Home
PQRS	Physician Quality Reporting System
URAC	Utilization Review Accreditation Commission
VBP	Value-Based Purchasing
VBPM	Value-Based Payment Modifier (the CMS VBP program for providers under Medicare FFS)

REFERENCES

Chapter 1

1   Joshi, N. "Doctor, Shut Up and Listen." *The New York Times* January 4, 2015.

2   Institute of Medicine "Crossing the quality chasm: a new health system for the 21st century." *National Academy Press* (2001).

3   Sequist, T. et al. "Quality monitoring of physicians: linking patients' experience of care to clinical quality & outcomes." *J Gen Intern Med.* 23, no. 11 (2008):1784–1790.

4   DiMatteo, M.R. "Enhancing patient adherence to medical recommendations." *JAMA* 271, no. 1 (1994):79-83.

5   DiMatteo, M.R. et al. "Physicians' characteristics influence patients' adherence to medical treatment." *Health Psychology* 12, no. 2 (1993):93-102.

6   Safran, D.G. et al. "Linking primary care perfor-
    mance to outcomes of care", *Journal Family Practice*.
    47, no. 3 (1998):213-220.

7   Greenfield, S., Kaplan, S., Ware, J.E. Jr. "Expanding
    patient involvement in care. Effects on patient out-
    comes." *Annals of Internal* 102, no. 4 (1985):520-528.

8   Stewart, M.A. "Effective physician-patient communi-
    cation and health outcomes: a review." *CMAJ* 15, no.
    9 (1995):1423-1433.

9   Greenfield. S. et al. "Patients' participation in medi-
    cal care: effects on blood sugar control." *Journal of
    General Internal Medicine* 3, no. 5 (1988):448-457.

10 Fremont, A.M. et al. "Patient-centered processes of
    care and long-term outcomes of acute myocardial in-
    farction." *J Gen Int Med* 16, no.12 (2014):800-808.

11 Totten, A.M. et al. "Closing the quality gap: revisiting
    the state of the science (Vol. 5: public reporting as a
    quality improvement strategy)." *Evid Rep Technol Assess*
    208, no. 5 (2012):1-645.

12 Sequist, T. et al. "Quality monitoring of physicians:
    linking patients' experience of care to clinical quality
    & outcomes." *J Gen Intern Med*. 23, no. 11 (2008):1784–
    1790.

13 Kahn, L. and Carmichael, K. "ABMS National Policy
    Forum Underscores Value of Aligning ABMS MOC
    with National Healthcare Policy Reform Move-
    ment." ABMS press release, April 8, 2009. Business
    Wire website. http://www.businesswire.com/news/

home/20090408005885/en/ABMS-National-Policy-Forum-Underscores-Aligning-ABMS#.VMlgP-GjF-So. Retrieved July 28, 2014.

14 American Board of Medical Specialties. Quality Improvement Reflects Higher Standards http://www.abms.org/who_we_help/physicians/improving_quality.aspx. Retrieved July 28, 2014

15 "Alternative Quality Contract." Retrieved from *Blue Cross Blue Shield of Massachusetts* (2010). http://www.bluecrossma.com/visitor/pdf/alternative-quality-contract.pdf

16 Integrated Healthcare Association. http://www.iha.org/

17 Shortell, S. M. et al. "An empirical assessment of high-performing medical groups: results from a national study." *Medical Care Research and Review* 62, no. 4 (2005):407–34.

18 Baum, N. and Homisakt, L. "Is your glass half full or half empty? Your decision may impact your practice," *J Med Pract Manage* 29, no. 2 (2013):117-120.

19 Safran, D.G. et al. "Switching doctors: predictors of voluntary disenrollment from a primary physician's practice." *Journal of Family Practice* 50, no. 2 (2001):130-136.

20 Hill, M.H. and Doddato, T. "Relationships among patient satisfaction, intent to return, and intent to recommend services provided by an academic nursing center." *J Cult Divers* 9, no. 4 (2002):108-12.

21 Levinson, W. et al. "Physician-patient communication: The relationship with malpractice." *JAMA* 277, no. 7 (1997):553-559.

22 Beckman, H.B. et al. "The doctor-patient relationship and malpractice: lessons from plaintiff depositions." *Archives Internal Medicine* 154, no. 12 (1994): 1365-1370.

23 Hickson, G.B. et al. "Obstetricians' prior malpractice experience and patients' satisfaction with care." *JAMA* 272, no. 20 (1994): 1583-1587.

24 Fullam, F. et al. "The use of patient satisfaction surveys and alternate coding procedures to predict malpractice risk." *Medical Care* 47, no. 5 (2009):553-559.

25 Measure Applications Partnership "Coordination Strategy for Clinician Performance Measurement. Final Report." (2011).

26 Seibert, J.H. et al. "Evaluating the physician office visit: in pursuit of a valid and reliable measure of quality improvement efforts." *J Ambul Care Manage* 19, no. 1 (1996):17-37.

27 Cleary, P.D. et al. "Adapting the CAHPS Survey to Assess Physician Groups: Summary Report of a Pilot Test in Three Markets." *Submission to National Quality Forum* (2006).

28 Hays, R.D. et al. "Patient reports and ratings of individual physicians: An evaluation of the Doctor-Guide and Consumer Assessment of Health Plans Study provider level surveys." *AM J Med Qual* 18, no. 5 (2003):190-196.

29 Levine, R. and Shore, K. "Use of the Critical Incident Technique to Develop Survey Items Measuring Patient Experiences of Ambulatory Care." CAHPS 9th National User Group Meeting, Baltimore, MD.

30 Carman, K.L. et al. "Contextual and Variable Based Analysis of Qualitative Data Using the Critical Incident Technique." Special Panel on Using Mixed Methods in Health Services Research. Academy for Health Services Research Annual Meeting, San Diego, CA.

31 Shore, K. et al. "Perceptions of Specific Clinician Health Behaviors Linked to Health Care Quality." Academy Health Annual Research Meeting, Boston, MA (2005). http://www.academyhealth.org/files/2005/quality.pdf

32 Solomon, L.S. et al. "Psychometric properties of a group-level Consumer Assessment of Health Plans Study (CAHPSTM) instrument." *Med Care* 43, no. 1 (2005):53-60.

33 Safran, D.G. et al. "Measuring patients' experiences with individual primary care physicians: Results of a statewide demonstration project." *J Gen Intern Med* 21, no. 1 (2006):13-21

34 Dyer, N. et al. "Psychometric properties of the Consumer Assessment of Healthcare Providers and Systems (CAHPS®) Clinician and Group Adult Visit Survey." *Med Care* 50 Suppl:S28-34.

35 Kern, L.M. et al. "Patient experience over time in pa-tient-centered medical homes." *Am J Manag Care* 19, no. 5 (2013):403-410.

36 Quigley, D.D. et al. "Evaluating the content of the communication items in the CAHPS(®) clinician and group survey and supplemental items with what high-performing physicians say they do." *Patient* 6, no. 3 (2013):169-177.

37 Drake, K.M. et al. "The Effect of Response Scale, Administration Mode, and Format on Responses to the CAHPS Clinician and Group Survey." *Health Serv Res.* 49, no. 4 (2014):1387-1399.

38 Quigley, D.D. et al. "Specialties differ in which aspects of doctor communication predict overall physician ratings." *J Gen Intern Med* 29, no. 3 (2014):447-454.

39 Schulz, K.A. et al. "Consumer assessment of health-care providers and systems surgical care survey: ben-efits and challenges." *Otolaryngol Head Neck Surg* 147, no. 4 (2012):671-7.

Chapter 2

1 Yang, J. et al. "Positive words or negative words: whose valence strength are we more sensitive to?" *Brain Res* 1533 (2013):91-104.

2 Wang, L. et al. "ERP evidence on the interaction between information structure and emotional sa-lience of words." *Cogn Affect Behav Neurosci* 13, no. 2 (2013):297-310.

3   Baker, S.J. et al. "Key words: a prescriptive approach to reducing patient anxiety and improving safety." *J Emerg Nurs* 37, no. 6 (2001):571-4.

4   Scott, J. "Utilizing AIDET and other tools to increase patient satisfaction scores." *Radiol Manage* 34, no. 3 (2012):29-33; quiz 34-5.

5   Makoul, G., Zick, A., and Green, M. "An evidence-based perspective on greetings in medical encounters." *Arch Intern Med* 167, no. 11 (2007):1172-6.

6   Berry, L. and Leighton, J. "Restoring customer confidence." *Marketing Health Services* 24, no. 1 (2004):14-19.

7   McCollough, Michael A., and Bharadwaj, Sundar G.. "The Recovery Paradox: An Examination of Customer Satisfaction in Relation to Disconfirmation, Service Quality, and Attribution Based Theories." *AMA Winter Educators' Conference Proceedings* no. 3 (1992):119

8   Osteryoung, J. The Jim Moran Institute for Global Entrepreneurship (2010).

9   2012 Physician Retention Survey. *American Medical Group Association* and *Cejka Search* (2012).

10 Waldman, J. et al. "The Shocking Cost of Turnover in Health Care." *HealthCare Management Review* 29, no. 1 (2004):2-7.

11 Rubin, R.A. "Behavioral-Based Physician Interviewing." *Phys Exec J* 38, no. 6 (2012):16-8,20.

12 Rubin, R.A. "Physician Job Interviews That Work." *Studer Group Insights* (2014).

Section One Introduction

1 Merritt Hawkins "Physician Appointment Wait Times and Medicaid and Medicare Acceptance Rates" (2014).

2 Camacho, F. et al. "The relationship between patient's perceived waiting time and office-based practice satisfaction." *N C Med J* 67, no. 6 (2006):409-13.

Chapter 3

1 Lisa Zamosky "What retail clinic growth can teach physicians about patient demand." *Medical Economics* (2014).

2 Stewart Cameron "Adoption of open-access scheduling in an academic family practice." *Can Fam Physician* 56, no. 9 (2010):906-911.

3 Tuli, S.Y. et al. "Improving Quality and Patient Satisfaction in a Pediatric Resident Continuity Clinic Through Advanced Access Scheduling." *J Grad Med Educ* 2, no. 2 (2010): 215–221.

Chapter 5

1 Camacho, F. et al. "The relationship between patient's perceived waiting time and office-based practice satisfaction." *N C Med J* 67, no. 6 (2006):409-13.

Section Two Introduction

1 Doyle, C., Lennox, L., and Bell, D. "A systematic review of evidence on the links between patient experience and clinical safety and effectiveness." *BMJ Open* 3 (2013):e001570. doi:10.1136/bmjopen-2012-001570.

2 Zolnierek, K.B. et al. "Physician communication and patient adherence to treatment: a meta-analysis." *Med Care* 47, no. 8 (2009):826-34.

3 Kelley, J.M. et al. "The Influence of the Patient-Clinician Relationship on Healthcare Outcomes." *Pub Med* 9, no. 4 (2014):e94207. doi: 10.1371/journal.pone.0094207.

4 Levine, R. et al. "Comparing Physician and Patient Perceptions of Quality in Ambulatory Care." *Pub Med* Aug 2012; 24(4):348-56

5 Quigley, D.D. et al. "Evaluating the Content of Communication Items in the CG CAHPS Survey & Supplemental Items with What High-Performing Physicians Say They Do." *Pub Med* 6, no. 3 (2013):169-77.

6   Albert Mehrabian, *Silent Messages 1st edition*. Belmont: Wadsworth Publishing Company (1972).

7   Albert Mehrabian, *Silent Messages – A Wealth of Information About Nonverbal Communication (Body Language)*. Personality & Emotion Tests & Software: Psychological Books & Articles of Popular Interest. Los Angeles: self-published (2009). Retrieved April 6, 2010

8   Smith, D. "Provider dress code and its impact on patient experience." *Studer Group Insights* (2013)

Chapter 6

1   Glauser, T.A. "Communication gaps between physicians and patients with postherpetic neuralgia: results from a national study on practice patterns." *J Pain Res* 4:407-15 (2011). doi: 10.2147/JPR.S27310.

2   Olson, D.P. and Windish, D.M. "Communication Discrepancies Between Physicians and Hospitalized Patients." *Arch Intern Med* 170, no. 15 (2010): 1302-1307.

3   Doak C., Doak L., and Root, J. *Teaching Patients with Low Literacy Skills 2nd edition*. Philadelphia: Lippincott Williams & Wilkins. (1996).

4   Elwyn, G. et al. "Shared decision making: a model for clinical practice." *J Gen Intern Med* 27, no. 10 (2012):1361-7.

5   Kessels, RP. "Patients' memory for medical information." *J R Soc Med* 96, no. 5 (2003):219-22.

6   Anderson, J.L. et al. "Patient information recall in a rheumatology clinic." *Rheumatology* 18, no. 1 (1979):18-22.

7   Negarandeh, R. et al. "Teach back and pictorial image educational strategies on knowledge about diabetes and medication/dietary adherence among low health literate patients with type 2 diabetes." *Prim Care Diabetes* 7, no. 2 (2013):111-8

8   Schillinger, D. et al. "Closing the loop: physician communication with diabetic patients who have low health literacy." *Arch Intern Med* 163, no. 1 (2013):83-90.

9   Wick, J.Y. "Checking for comprehension: mastering teach-back techniques." *Consult Pharm* 28, no. 9 (2013):550-4.

10 Doak C., Doak L., and Root, J. *Teaching Patients with Low Literacy Skills 2nd edition*. Philadelphia: Lippincott Williams & Wilkins. (1996).

Chapter 7

1   McCabe, C. "Nurse-patient communication: an exploration of patients' experiences." *J Clin Nurs* 13, no. 1 (2004): 41-49.

2   Beckman, H.B. and Frankel, R.M. "The effect of physician behavior on the collection of data." *Ann Intern Med* 101, no. 5 (1984):692-6.

3   Rhoades, D.R. et al. "Speaking and interruptions during primary care office visits. *Fam Med* 33, no. 7 (2001):528-32.

4   Swayden, K.J. et al. "Effect of sitting vs. standing on perception of provider time at bedside: a pilot study." *Patient Educ Couns* 86, no. 2 (2012):166-71. doi: 10.1016/j.pec.2011.05.024.

Chapter 8

1   National Institutes of Health. "What is Health Literacy" http://www.nih.gov/clearcommunication/healthliteracy.htm

Chapter 9

1   Coulter, A. "After Bristol: Putting patients at the centre." *Qual Saf Health Care* 11, no. 2 (2002):186–188.

2   Anthony, R. et al. "John M. Eisenberg Patient Safety Awards. The LVHHN patient safety video: patients as partners in safe health care delivery." *Jt Comm J Qual Saf* 29, no. 12 (2003):640–645.

3   Beach, M.C. et al. "Do patients treated with dignity report higher satisfaction, adherence, and receipt of preventive care?" *Ann Fam Med* 3, no. 4 (2005):331–338.

4   Epstein, R.M., Alper, B.S., and Quill, T.E. "Communicating evidence for participatory decision making." *JAMA* 291, no.19 (2004):2359–2366.

5   Kuzel, A.J. et al. "Patient reports of preventable problems and harms in primary health care." *Ann Fam Med* 2, no. 4 (2004):333–340.

6   Coulter, A. "After Bristol: Putting patients at the centre." *Qual Saf Health Care* 11, no. 2 (2002):186–188.

7   American Academy of Family Physicians: Medical errors: Tips to help prevent them. http://familydoctor.org/736.xml (accessed May 23, 2007).

8   Stewart MA. Effective physician-patient communication and health outcomes: a review. *CMAJ*. 1995;15(9):1423-1433.

9   Ibid.

Chapter 10

1   Ogden J., et al. "I want more time with my doctor": a quantitative study of time and the consultation. Family Practice (2004) 21 (5): 479-483.

2   Stewart, M.A. "Effective physician-patient communication and health outcomes: a review. *CMAJ* 15, no. 9 (1995):1423-1433.

Chapter 11

1   Dickert, N.W. and Kass, N.E. "Understanding respect: learning from patients." *Journal of Medical Ethics* 35, no. 7 (2009): 419 – 423.

2   Nelson, M. "Empathy and the impact on clinical outcomes." *Studer Group Insights* (2014).

3   Dolcos, S. et al. "The power of a handshake: neural correlates of evaluative judgments in observed social interactions." *J Cogn Neurosci* 24, no. 12 (2012):2292-305.

4   Quigley, D.D. et al. "Evaluating the content of the communication items in the CAHPS(®) clinician and group survey and supplemental items with what high-performing physicians say they do." *Patient* 6, no. 3 (2013):169-177.

Section Three Introduction

1   Casalino, L.P. et al. "Frequency of failure to inform patients of clinically significant outpatient test results." *Arch Intern Med* 169, no. 17 (2009):1123-9. doi: 10.1001/archinternmed.2009.130.

2   Zimmerman, T. "EMRs do not improve reporting rates of abnormal laboratory results?" *Arch Intern Med* 169, no. 19 (2009):1815-6. doi: 10.1001/archinternmed.2009.368.

3 Christensen, K. and Oldenburg, J. "Giving patients their results online might be the answer." *Arch Intern Med* 169, no. 19 (2009):1816. doi: 10.1001/archinternmed.2009.369.

Chapter 13

1 Patrick, K. and Ross, M. "Putting Patients First: Developing and Maintaining Patient-Centered Medical Practices." *Greater Washington Research at Brookings* (2007).

Section Five Introduction

1 Joshi, N. "Doctor, Shut Up and Listen." *The New York Times* January 4, 2015.

Chapter 14

1 Dyer N. et al. "Psychometric properties of the Consumer Assessment of Healthcare Providers and Systems (CAHPS®) Clinician and Group Adult Visit Survey." *Med Care* 50 Suppl:S28-34.

2 Quigley, D.D. et al. "Evaluating the content of the communication items in the CAHPS(®) clinician and group survey and supplemental items with what high-performing physicians say they do." *Patient* 6, no. 3 (2013):169-177.

3 Bowling, A. et al. "The measurement of patients' expectations for health care: a review and psychometric testing of a measure of patients' expectations." *Health Technol Assess* 16, no 30 (2012):i-xii, 1-509. doi: 10.3310/hta16300.

4 Raleigh, V.S. et al. "Do some trusts deliver a consistently better experience for patients? An analysis of patient experience across acute care surveys in English NHS trusts." *BMJ Qual Saf* (2012) doi:10.1136/bmjqs-2011-000588

5 Institute of Medicine "Crossing the quality chasm: a new health system for the 21st century." *National Academy Press* (2001). Retrieved 2012.

6 Doyle, C., Lennox, L., and Bell, D. "A systematic review of evidence on the links between patient experience and clinical safety and effectiveness." *BMJ Open* 3, no. 1 (2013). doi:10.1136/bmjopen-2012-001570

7 Torres, E., Vasquez-Parraga, A.Z., and Barra, C. "The path of patient loyalty and the role of doctor reputation." *Health Mark Q* 26, no. 3 (2009):183-97.

8 Suki, N.M. "Assessing patient satisfaction, trust, commitment, loyalty and doctors' reputation towards doctor services." *Pak J Med Sci* 27, no. 5 (2011):1207-1210.

9 vom Eigen, K.A., Delbanco, T.L, and Phillips, R.S. "Perceptions of quality of care and the decision to leave a practice." *Am J Med Qual* 13, no. 4 (1998):181-7.

10 Hanauer, D. et al. "Public awareness, perception, and use of online physician rating sites." *JAMA* 311, no. 7 (2014):734-735.

Chapter 15

1 Kahn, L. and Carmichael, K. "ABMS National Policy Forum Underscores Value of Aligning ABMS MOC with National Healthcare Policy Reform Movement." ABMS press release, April 8, 2009. Business Wire website. http://www.businesswire.com/news/home/20090408005885/en/ABMS-National-Policy-Forum-Underscores-Aligning-ABMS#.VMlgP-GjF-So. Retrieved July 28, 2014.

Chapter 16

1 Straight A Assessment. *Studer Group Resources.* Developed with *Alliance for Health Care Research* (2006). https://www.studergroup.com/resources/webinars/current/straight-a-leadership-alignment-action-and-account

2 Doran, G.T. "There's a S.M.A.R.T. way to write management's goals and objectives." *Management Review (AMA Forum)* 70, no. 11 (1981):35-36.

3 Shahin, A. and Mahbod, A.M. "Prioritization of key performance indicators: An integration of analytical hierarchy process and goal setting." *International*

Journal of Productivity and Performance Management 56, no. 3 (2007):226-240.

4 PCMH 2014 Standards and Guidelines. Published by URAC (2013).

ADDITIONAL RESOURCES

About Studer Group®:

Learn more about Studer Group® by scanning the QR code with your mobile device or by visiting www.studergroup.com/about_studergroup/index.dot.

Studer Group's Medical Practice Coaching provides evidence-based tools and tactics that help those in an ambulatory setting achieve and sustain results. Our medical practice experts provide the structure and framework that allows practices to adapt to change quickly. Studer Group's Evidence-Based Leadership^SM framework, paired with onsite coaching and resources specially designed and tested in the outpatient setting, allow practices to truly transform. We are able to tailor our approach and drive results across all pillars to positively impact the pillars and hardwire profitability. Studer Group's unique and proven approach aligns goals, behaviors, and processes to create a sustainable culture of relentless consistency and quality care. This commitment to helping organizations accelerate their ability to execute led to Studer Group's receiving the 2010 Malcolm Baldrige National Quality Award.

To learn more about partnering with Studer Group on your journey to improvement, visit www.studergroup.com or call 850-439-5839.

Studer Group Coaching:

Learn more about Studer Group coaching by scanning the QR code with your mobile device or by visiting www.studergroup.com/coaching.

Healthcare Organization Coaching

As value-based purchasing changes the healthcare landscape forever, organizations need to execute quickly and consistently, achieve better outcomes across the board, and sustain improvements year after year.

Studer Group's team of performance experts has hands-on experience in all aspects of achieving breakthrough results. They provide the strategic thinking, the Evidence-Based Leadership framework, the practical tactics, and the ongoing support to help our partners excel in this high-pressure environment. Our performance experts work with a variety of organizations, from academic medical centers to large healthcare systems to small rural hospitals.

Emergency Department Coaching

With public reporting of data coming in the future, healthcare organizations can no longer accept crowded Emergency Departments and long patient wait times. Our team of ED coach experts will partner with you to implement best practices, proven tools, and tactics using our Evidence-Based Leadership approach to improve results in the Emergency Department that stretch or impact across the entire organization. Key deliverables include improving flow; decreasing staff turnover; increasing employee, physician, and patient satisfaction; decreasing door-to-doctor times; reducing left without being seen rates; increasing upfront cash collections; and increasing patient volumes and revenue.

Physician Integration & Partnership Coaching

Physician integration is critical to an organization's ability to run smoothly and efficiently. Studer Group coaches diagnose how aligned physicians are with your mission and goals, train you on how to effectively provide performance feedback, and help physicians develop the skills they need to prevent burnout. The goal is to help physicians become engaged, enthusiastic partners in the truest sense of the word—which optimizes HCAHPS results and creates a better continuum of high-quality patient care.

Books: categorized by audience

Explore the Fire Starter Publishing website by scanning the QR code with your mobile device or by visiting www.firestarterpublishing.com.

Senior Leaders & Physicians

A Culture of High Performance: Achieving Higher Quality at a Lower Cost—A must-have book for any leader struggling to shore up margins while sustaining an organization that is a great place for employees to work, physicians to practice medicine, and patients to receive care. From best-selling author Quint Studer to help you build a culture that will thrive during change.

Engaging Physicians: A Manual to Physician Partnership—A tactical and passionate road map for physician collaboration to generate organizational high performance, written by Stephen C. Beeson, MD.

Excellence with an Edge: Practicing Medicine in a Competitive Environment—An insightful book that provides practical tools and techniques you need to know to have a solid grasp of the business side of making a living in healthcare, written by Michael T. Harris, MD.

Straight A Leadership: Alignment, Action, Accountability—A guide that will help you identify gaps in Alignment, Action, and Accountability; create a plan to fill them; and become a more resourceful, agile, high-performing organization, written by Quint Studer.

Physicians

Practicing Excellence: A Physician's Manual to Exceptional Health Care— This book, written by Stephen C. Beeson, MD, is a brilliant guide to implementing physician leadership and behaviors that will create a high-performance workplace.

All Leaders

101 Answers to Questions Leaders Ask—By Quint Studer and Studer Group coaches, offers practical, prescriptive solutions to some of the many questions he's received from healthcare leaders around the country.

Eat That Cookie!: Make Workplace Positivity Pay Off...For Individuals, Teams, and Organizations—Written by Liz Jazwiec, RN, this book is funny, inspiring, relatable, and is packed with realistic, down-to-earth tactics to infuse positivity into your culture.

Hardwiring Excellence—A *BusinessWeek* bestseller, this book is a road map to creating and sustaining a "Culture of Service and Operational Excellence" that drives bottom-line results. Written by Quint Studer.

Hey Cupcake! We Are ALL Leaders—Author Liz Jazwiec explains that we'll all eventually be called on to lead someone, whether it's a department, a shift, a project team, or a new employee. In her trademark slightly sarcastic (and hilarious) voice, she provides learned-the-hard-way insights that will benefit leaders in every industry and at every level.

"I'm Sorry to Hear That..." Real-Life Responses to Patients' 101 Most Common Complaints About Health Care—When you respond to a patient's complaint, you are responding to the patient's sense of helplessness and anxiety. The service recovery scripts offered in this book can help you recover a patient's confidence in you and your organization. Authored by Susan Keane Baker and Leslie Bank.

Oh No...Not More of That Fluffy Stuff! The Power of Engagement—Written by Rich Bluni, RN, this funny, heartfelt book explores what it takes to overcome obstacles and tap into the passion that fuels our best work. Its practical exercises help employees at all levels get happier, more excited, and more connected to the meaning in our daily lives.

Over Our Heads: An Analogy on Healthcare, Good Intentions, and Unforeseen Consequences—This book, written by Rulon F. Stacey, PhD, FACHE, uses a grocery store analogy to illustrate how government intervention leads to economic crisis and, eventually, collapse.

Results That Last: Hardwiring Behaviors That Will Take Your Company to the Top—A *Wall Street Journal* bestseller by Quint Studer that teaches leaders in every industry how to apply his tactics and strategies to their own organizations to build a corporate culture that consistently reaches and exceeds its goals.

Service Excellence Is As Easy As PIE (Perception Is Everything)—Realistic, down to earth, and wickedly witty, *PIE* is perfect for everyone in healthcare or any other service industry. It's filled with ideas for creating exceptional customer experiences—ideas that are surprising, simple, and yes, easy as you-know-what. Written by Liz Jazwiec.

The Great Employee Handbook: Making Work and Life Better—This book is a valuable resource for employees at all levels who want to learn how to handle tough workplace situations—skills that normally come only from a lifetime of experience. *Wall Street Journal* best-selling author Quint Studer has pulled together the best insights gained from working with thousands of employees during his career.

The Patient Flow Advantage: How Hardwiring Hospital-Wide Flow Drives Competitive Performance—Build effectiveness, efficiency, and a patient-centric focus into the heart of every process that serves the patient. Efficient patient flow has never been more critical to ensure patient safety, satisfaction, and optimal reimbursement. Authored by Drs. Kirk Jensen and Thom Mayer.

Nurse Leaders and Nurses

Inspired Nurse and *Inspired Journal*—By Rich Bluni, RN, help maintain and recapture the inspiration nurses felt at the start of their journey with action-oriented "spiritual stretches" and stories that illuminate those sacred moments we all experience.

The HCAHPS Handbook 2ⁿᵈ Edition: Tactics to Improve Quality and the Patient Experience— Revised and released in 2015, this book is a valuable resource for organizations seeking to provide the exceptional quality of care their patients expect and deserve. Coauthored by Lyn Ketelsen, RN, MBA; Karen Cook, RN; and Bekki Kennedy.

The Nurse Leader Handbook: The Art and Science of Nurse Leadership—By Studer Group senior nursing and physician leaders from across the country, is filled with knowledge that provides nurse leaders with a solid foundation for success. It also serves as a reference they can revisit again and again when they have questions or need a quick refresher course in a particular area of the job.

Emergency Department Team

Advance Your Emergency Department: Leading in a New Era—As this critical book asserts, world-class Emergency Departments don't follow. They lead. Stephanie J. Baker, RN, CEN, MBA; Regina Shupe, RN, MSN, CEN; and Dan Smith, MD, FACEP, share high-impact strategies and tactics to help your ED get results more efficiently, effectively, and collaboratively. Master them and you'll improve quality, exceed patient expectations, and ultimately help the entire organization maintain and grow its profit margin.

Excellence in the Emergency Department: How to Get Results—A book by Stephanie Baker, RN, CEN, MBA, is filled with proven, easy-to-implement, step-by-step instructions that will help you move your Emergency Department forward.

Hardwiring Flow: Systems and Processes for Seamless Patient Care—Drs. Thom Mayer and Kirk Jensen delve into one of the most critical issues facing healthcare leaders: patient flow.

Studer Conferences:

Studer Conferences are three-day interactive learning events designed to provide healthcare leaders with an authentic, practical learning experience.

Each Studer Conference includes internationally renowned keynote speakers and tracks concentrated on key areas of the healthcare organization. Every track includes breakout sessions and "how-to" workshops that provide you with direct access to experts and conference faculty. The faculty at Studer Conferences go beyond PowerPoint slides and lectures to show you "what right looks like."

Leaders will leave with new tools and skills that get results. Find out more and register for Studer Conferences at www.studergroup.com/conferences.

All Studer Group Conferences offer Continuing Education Credits. For more information on CMEs, visit www.studergroup.com/cmecredits.

JEFF MORRIS, MD, MBA, FACS

Dr. Jeff Morris is a board-certified orthopedic & hand surgeon (Canada), who has lived and practiced in Ohio for the past 24 years. Originally from South Africa, he completed residencies in South Africa, Israel, and Canada. He practiced in Thunder Bay and Burlington, Ontario, before moving to the U.S.A. in 1990. He later gained certification in medical acupuncture and still maintains a part-time practice in non-surgical orthopedics and medical acupuncture.

After completing his MBA at Kent State University in 2000, Jeff served as vice president of medical affairs (VPMA) at two local community hospitals. When these two hospitals engaged Studer Group®, Jeff served as the internal physician champion and helped to elevate the culture of service and enhanced communications to new heights, resulting in a significant improvement in physician and employee engagement, as well as in the patients' perception of the quality of care being delivered.

Jeff joined Studer Group as a coach in May 2010, teaches healthcare marketing in the Kent State University Healthcare Executive MBA Program, serves as an independent medical examiner, and has coauthored a number of other books. As a Studer Group physician coach and national speaker with more than 30 years of experience in clinical practice and 12 years of experience in physician executive leadership, he enjoys sharing his passion for servant leadership and service excellence, as well as "connecting the dots" of enhanced provider communication to a more positive patient experience and superior clinical outcomes. And as a licensed and instrument-rated pilot, he recognizes the many "patient safety" lessons—like checklists and communication skills—that we in healthcare can learn from the world of aviation.

Jeff and his wife and best friend, Cher, reside in Hudson, OH. He is blessed with two of his own children, Amit and Leora; a stepdaughter, Jen; a daughter-in-law, Sandra (Amit); and two toy poodles (Buttons and Cuddles) that have him convinced that they are really humans with four legs!

Barbara Hotko, RN, MPA

 With more than 35 years of experience in the healthcare industry, Barbara has brought her passion, enthusiasm, and *urban edge* to Studer Group,® where she serves as a respected senior leader in the company. Since joining SG in 2001, Barbara has experience as a coach, a mentor, a teacher, a writer, and a national speaker.

Barbara is best known by her partners as a results-driven expert. She has constantly and undeniably raised the bar for healthcare systems, hospitals, medical groups, and emergency departments across the country—a testament to her commitment to doing "simply the right thing to do for patients and healthcare today." Her nursing background, combined with her experience in hospital administration and consulting, provides the expertise necessary to help organizations favorably impact profitability, efficiency, and patient care, all of which pave the way to achieving a culture of high performance.

First and always a registered nurse, Barbara is a graduate of Englewood Hospital School of Nursing in Englewood, NJ, and has a clinical background in critical care and emergency service. Barbara also holds a master's degree in public administration from Fairleigh Dickinson University in Rutherford, NJ.

Barbara and her husband, Daniel, reside in New Jersey. They are blessed with three children, Danielle, Joseph, and Carra—and share the joy of four amazing grandchildren, Colin, Kyle, Sidney, and Sawyer.

MATTHEW BATES, MPH

 Matthew Bates has more than 25 years of experience working in healthcare. As a member of Studer Group's senior leadership since 2012, he is the general manager of their Physician Services offerings and is a co-creator along with Quint Studer of the Provider Feedback System.^{SM}

Matthew was privileged to begin his professional career working for the Medical Group Management Association (MGMA). He then went on to hold leadership roles at Pinnacol Assurance, Solucient, and Thomson Reuters Healthcare. Immediately prior to joining Studer Group®, Matthew was a global managing director of healthcare for Accenture, where he led strategic health analytic solutions.

In addition to his work with Studer Group, Matthew currently serves on several healthcare and environment-focused nonprofit boards and is also a volunteer with the U.S. Medical Reserve Corps.

Matthew has earned a bachelor of science in health-care management from the Metropolitan State University of Denver and a master of public health (MPH) from the University of Denver. He has also held licensure/certification as a certified nursing assistant (CNA), an emergency medical technician (EMT), a FEMA-certified emergency manager, and as a certified professional in healthcare quality (CPHQ).

Matthew resides in Colorado with his wife, Cindy, and their twin children, Zachary and Sophia. They enjoy spending time in the outdoors hiking, camping, snowshoeing, and skiing. And when Matthew finds time to slip away, he can be found standing in small mountain streams fly fishing for trout.